NOTHING Lost FOREVER

the films of
Tom Schiller

NOTHING *Lost* FOREVER

the films of
Tom Schiller

-by-

Michael
Streeter

BearManor Media
2006

Nothing Lost Forever: The Films of Tom Schiller
Saturday Night Live's Visionary Filmmaker

www.nothinglostforever.com

For information, address:

BearManor Media
P. O. Box 750
Boalsburg, PA 16827

bearmanormedia.com

Cover design by Darren McClanahan

Typesetting and layout by John Teehan

Published in the USA by BearManor Media

ISBN—1-59393-032-1

For those who stood by me.

Contents

Tom Schiller directs Bill Murray in *Perchance to Dream*; photos by Christopher Zuk.

Acknowledgements

I would not have been able to write this book without the help of dozens of individuals. I would like to thank everybody who assisted me in writing this book—whether it was locating rare materials, providing photographs and other illustrations, helping me track down certain individuals, reading my manuscript and giving honest feedback, helping me piece together the puzzle, or providing moral support. This includes Christopher Bligh, Dirk Bremer, Tanner Colby, Kathy Corley, Hugh Deloni, Jimmy Fallon, Marc Edward Heuck, Anjelica Huston, Ling Ingerick, Louis and Jamie Klein, Rob Lammle, Marc Liepis, Sarah Livingstone, Neal Marshad, Nancy Martino, Paul Mazursky, Darren McClanahan, Matías Nicieza, Ben Ohmart, Darya Papazian, Jake Perlin, Mark Jennings Reese II, Shade Rupe, Stephen Saban, Jacque Lynn Schiller, Joe Schuster, Andrew D. Schwartz, Chris Sewell, Robert Smigel, James Stephens, Wim Streeter, Petra and Bill Streeter, Matt Underwood, Janet Vasquez and Jan de Waal.

Writing a book about a filmmaker and a film about which very little has been written was a tough process, requiring me to rely almost exclusively on the recollections of those who have worked with Tom Schiller. I am very grateful to everybody who took time out of their busy schedules to talk to me: Dan Aykroyd, Peter Aykroyd, Judith Belushi Pisano, Boaty Boatwright, Bernie Brillstein, Chevy Chase, Tom Davis, Pierre-Henri Deleau, Zach Galligan, Teri Garr, John Hartmann, John Head, Ed Helms, Victoria Jackson, Sheila Kehoe, Leslie McCutcheon, Lorne Michaels, Bill Murray, Mike Myers, Laila Nabulsi, Jackie Schmidt, T. Sean Shannon, John Starke, Lauren Tom, and of course Tom Schiller.

I am particularly grateful to those who did more than they needed to: Laila Nabulsi, for her consistent encouragement and for helping me get in touch with a number of hard-to-reach individuals; Zach Galligan, for his photographic memory and his willingness to share his memories; and Tom Schiller, for his continued support and for allowing me to write about him in the first place.

Foreword
by Tom Davis

Writing a book about Tom Schiller is a great idea. Most people when you mention *Saturday Night Live* still think John Belushi, Gilda Radner, Lorne Michaels—which is fine. The books about the show (of which I'm aware) was firstly *Saturday Night Live*. Published by Avon Books in 1977, it was created by the show itself—a delightful collage of pictures, memos, letters, doodles, etc. Then there was *Rolling Stone Visits Saturday Night Live*, a Rolling Stone book collecting its interviews and stories from Rolling Stone magazine, which, except for a photo, does not mention Franken and Davis—an oversight, in my opinion. Next, in 1986, Doug Hill and Jeff Weingrad wrote the thoughtful *Saturday Night: A Backstage History* with a chronology peppered with pictures and interviews (we all hung ourselves, except Lorne). In 1998, Dennis Perrin offered the reverent, but honest *Mr. Mike: The Life and Work of Michael O'Donoghue*. More recently Tom Shales and James Miller released *Live From New York: An Uncensored History of Saturday Night Live*, a popular poo-poo platter of revealing interviews with even more rope to hang ourselves (except Lorne, who as you can tell, is very cautious in print). Now we have *Nothing Lost Forever*, which is the most scholarly of this series of books (a necessity for an examination of Tom Schiller). But more than that, Mr. Streeter's story may be the most accurate account of the *SNL* experience and angst.

Tom was there with Lorne beside the Chateau Marmont swimming pool as the cerebral cortex of the show formed in its embryonic stage. He was always the one to remind us it was supposed to be fun. All of Tom's sketches, which made it to air, were brilliant, original, and funny; and his films are appreciated even more as the years pass by.

I rarely see Tom of late, but when I do, we always pick it up from the last moment. The chain of friendship, and the bonds formed in the foxhole atmosphere of *SNL* will never be broken. I love Tom as my brother and I am grateful to Michael Streeter for having the sensitivity, the vision, and the purpose to complete this work of faith…AND…it's funny.

Enjoy.

Tom Davis, March '05

A Word from Tom Schiller

Ever since I saw Federico Fellini's *8 1/2* I wanted to be a foreign film director. Which is strange since I was born in the USA. My first short film *The Door*, made when I was thirteen, wasn't exactly *La Strada* but I was so impressed with my own work, I felt everyone in the neighborhood should see it at least twenty-five times. And I made sure they did.

When Lorne Michaels offered me a job as a writer on a new late night TV show he was producing, I declined at first because I explained I was a *filmmaker* and I didn't 'do' television. I finally caved in because at least New York was closer to Europe than Los Angeles. Instead of Belmondo I had Belushi, for Giulietta I had Gilda, and in place of Mastroianni I had Murray.

Setting out to write and direct my first feature film, I really didn't know what I was doing. I just sort of made it up as I went along. Maybe that's why it wasn't released. In that respect, *Nothing Lasts Forever* is a highly personal film that maybe only a few people can understand. Well, maybe two: the author of this book and my brother.

By some fluke, I was able to have an independent film produced by a major studio. My desire to create a movie that looked like it was doomed to the vaults came true.

While MGM apparently wasn't thrilled with it, I was flattered when Pierre-Henri Deleau of the Cannes Directors Fortnight called it 'a masterpiece.' That alone was worth the entire effort: my dream of being accepted by Europeans—the French.

It was my good fortune that late one night in Holland on Netherlands television, the author of this book saw my film. Michael Streeter is exactly the kind of audience I hoped to reach: A seven-foot tall Dutch film fanatic. He tirelessly pursued and interviewed people who have collaborated on my films—

some of whom I haven't spoken to in the last twenty years (and when you read this, you might understand why). He has uncovered minutiae of my work that even I couldn't remember, and maybe didn't want to. My sincere thanks go to him for writing this excellent first compendium of my magnum opus.

Tom Schiller
New York City

Photo by Andrew D. Schwartz.

Introduction

"Nothing lasts forever. Not even your job."

That's what an MGM executive told the cast and crew of *Nothing Lasts Forever* a few days before shooting was set to begin. They gathered at Trader Vic's Restaurant at New York's Plaza Hotel for the pre-shoot party, and the MGM executive stood up to give a short speech. He started by bringing up some of the rules that were to be adhered to on his set. For example, the exec warned that no profanity was to be used on his set. And definitely no spitting.

Actually, it was not an MGM executive giving the speech. Tom Schiller and production associate Laila Nabulsi hired an actor to address their guests posing as an MGM executive. It so happened to be that the actor was an African American dwarf with a speech impediment. He was terribly inarticulate, and each time he tried to say the word *film*, it came out as *flim*.

The cast and crew were in stitches, but the supposed MGM executive had a point. Their jobs didn't last forever. Just like on any movie, the cast and crew finish the film and move on. After a few months of dedication and hard work, it's over. With *Nothing Lasts Forever*, many of them realized that they had been a part of something special. Each day they reported to the set, they were reminded of it by the illustrious set designs and strange conceits that they would have to work with. They didn't necessarily think the film would be successful, let alone turn out to be anything but a disaster, but they knew they wouldn't work on something like this ever again. Maybe the movie didn't last forever. But their memories of making it did, especially since they were among the few who have had the good fortune of seeing the finished film.

Tom Schiller has a unique sense of humor and an unmatched style evident in most of his works, including his film about Henry Miller, his short films at *Saturday Night Live* and his feature film *Nothing Lasts Forever*. My goal for this book is to give Schiller the scrutiny and printed analysis that his work deserves, with hopes of raising his achievements to a higher level. Of all of Schiller's friends and former colleagues that I have spoken to, many of them agreed that Schiller would have become the type of director who would have made film after film and would have amassed a critically acclaimed body of influential works by now. His feature directing career looked promising, until it was decided that *Nothing Lasts Forever* would remain in the vaults. It is the only feature film that Schiller ever directed. Instead of being a veteran director, Schiller's place in Hollywood is among the *would-be* Woody Allens and *faux* Fellinis. He deserves much better.

Another reason I took it upon myself to write this book is because the story behind *Nothing Lasts Forever* is a classic example of the studio system. How Schiller was handled by the executives at MGM is almost paradigmatic of the wheeling and dealing behind the doors of the major studios. Many films are withheld from release each year, but in most cases, those films are dreadful and the studios are within reason to keep them off the screens. Despite being a film that will not appeal to everyone, with *Nothing Lasts Forever* this clearly was not the case. Even though the film has been seen by few people, the fact that it was called "a masterpiece" (by Pierre-Henri Deleau of the Cannes Film Festival), "brilliantly eccentric" (by Stephen Saban of *Details Magazine*), and that it was invited to the Cannes Film Festival two years in a row proves that this was not what MGM had initially made it out to be.

This is not a biography of Tom Schiller. Stories about his background, child-hood, family, friends and personal life are presented only when contextually rel-evant. There is much more to Tom Schiller, and obviously, some of it does tie into his work. But Schiller is a relative unknown and not a public figure. I tried to convey what kind of a person he is through his work. Schiller can save the rest for his memoirs, should he ever choose to write them. Instead, this book is in part my own analysis of his style and the themes that recur throughout his body of work. The other part is a fun, anecdotal behind-the-scenes account of the making of his films, told from the viewpoints of his friends, colleagues, and Tom Schiller himself.

My appreciation for Tom Schiller began in the early 1990s when I was eleven or twelve years old. I had never heard of Tom Schiller, and even though I was very familiar with the many stars it had spun off, I had no idea what *Satur-day Night Live* was. It did not air in the Netherlands, where I lived at the time.

I remember reading about a black-and-white movie from 1984 with Zach Galligan and Bill Murray that was going to be on around midnight on the RTL4 television network. I was intrigued. How could there be a movie with Bill Murray and the guy from *Gremlins* in black-and-white? Why would such repu-table actors lend their names to such a project? I guess I was more than just intrigued…I was bewildered.

I stayed up late and was blown away. I didn't know what to make of the movie, but it was something I knew I would never forget. Most evident to me from watching *Nothing Lasts Forever* that night was that it was made by someone with an undying love for film, which is perhaps why it appealed to me so much.

A few years later, I had a similar experience watching a condensed re-run of *Saturday Night Live*. After moving to the United States, I had quickly become obsessed with the show and was fascinated by a black-and-white film that looked like it was made fifty years before. Starring John Belushi as an elderly version of himself who visits the graves of his *Saturday Night Live* cast members, *Don't Look Back in Anger* is a brilliant short film on its own, but because of the irony that surrounds it, it can put a lump in just about anyone's throat.

These are but two pieces of Tom Schiller's impressive oeuvre, which spans more than four decades and substantiates that he is an immensely talented director.

Schiller's style and sense of humor stem back to the short films he made as a teenager in Los Angeles and continue through his most recent commercials.

1. The most obvious characteristic of a Schiller film is that it looks like it was made in a different time period. Schiller is a master at recreating the look of a genre or a decade—even a specific film. A prime example of this is *Java Junkie*, a typical 40s or 50s *film noir* modeled in part after Billy Wilder's *The Lost Weekend*. *Dieter's Dream* pokes fun at German pseudo-realism combined with a reference to the opening sequence of Fellini's *8 ½* as Mike Myers' Dieter leaps into the sky and is chased by a leather-clad S&M mistress reminiscent of *Ilsa, She Wolf of the SS*. And Schiller's four-part *Broadway Story* is a dead-on replica of the *Broadway Melody* and *Gold Diggers* movie franchises of the 1930s, with Jan Hooks, Phil Hartman and Jon Lovitz effectively mimicking the early talkie acting style.

2. Schiller likes to manipulate time in general. Take one of his most endearing works: *Don't Look Back in Anger* is set in the future, when John Belushi, playing himself at age ninety, visits the graves of his *Saturday Night Live* cast members. The film was made in 1977, when Belushi was twenty-nine years of age. This means that the setting of the film is supposed to be 2038. Instead, the film looks like it was made in the 1930s or 40s. Everything from the music and Belushi's clothing to the scratches on the banged-up film print indicate that the film was produced before Schiller and Belushi were even born, making the film a patchwork of past, present and future. He applies this to many of his films. Schiller's feature film *Nothing Lasts Forever* includes a scene that takes place in a 1980s new age espresso bar, references to the So-Ho art scene of the early 80s, and in the second half, a trip to the moon. Yet the set and costume design, in addition to the cinematography modeled after a film from 1939, indicates that the film takes place between 1930 and 1950. Like many of Schiller's works, *Nothing Lasts Forever* is an amalgamation of various different time periods.

3.   Schiller also frequently edits stock footage into his films. *Nothing Lasts Forever* has transition shots that were taken from silent films. Schiller was unable to shoot exterior street scenes in New York with people walking around and going about their business like they did a half a century before because 1982 New York didn't look like the old New York that he wanted to present in his film. Since his film was in black-and-white anyway, he fused his own footage with old public domain documentary or newsreel footage from decades before, in effect creating a montage that furthers the storyline. Schiller uses stock footage in most of his films and is a master at blending old and new into a pastiche of different eras.

4.   Schiller's sense of humor is ingenuous and inoffensive—but never bland or cornball—and sophisticated and erudite—but not exaggeratedly highbrow. Schiller sketches and films are rarely serious, as they tend to deal with light subject matters. On the rare occasion of a weighty topic, such as death in *Life After Death* or cloning in *Clones Exist Now*, the subjects are still approached with a light sense of humor.
Schiller is able to seamlessly merge the sophisticated and the unsophisticated. Traces of a childlike sense of humor can be found in films dealing with cultured topics. An example is the sophomoric concept of chimpanzees dressed in human clothing. Schiller makes extensive use of elegantly-clothed primates in a short film about the historically accurate and well-documented correspondence between Vincent and Theo Van Gogh.
On the other hand, Schiller rarely falls into the frowned-upon pit of bathroom humor, the key exception literally being his very first film *The Door*. Schiller's humor is consistently clean and inoffensive. While it is arguable that Schiller was daring and took risks, his works have never been dangerous. From Schiller one can expect mischief, not mayhem.
It is no surprise that Schiller himself has a childlike innocence to him. He is well-cultured, well-traveled and knows a lot about the worlds of film, art and philosophy. But he is also the eternal child. His chin is always up and he is rarely seen without a smile on his face—an enthusiasm not often found in adults. It is evident from the retrospective nature of his work that he yearns for the simpler days of his childhood. This might explain the aforementioned manipulation of time, as well as nostalgia, another common theme in Schiller's works.

5.   Nostalgia is particularly prevalent in Schiller's later short films at *Saturday Night Live*. Produced between 1988 and 1994, these films are more referential to classic films than the *Schiller's Reel* films he produced between 1977 and 1980. *Love is a Dream, Falling in Love, The Violin* and *Laura*, to name just a few, all capture the bittersweet feeling of nostalgia. More specifically,

they capture a longing for the way movies used to be made; the movies Schiller grew up watching on television.

But most nostalgic of all are the two *SchillerVision Theatre* mini-specials that he made for the show during that time. *Schillervision Theatre* was a take-off on the television variety specials of the 1950s, complete with inappropriate corporate sponsors, an odious host (played by Schiller himself) and a variety of special guests. By condensing these specials, which would ordinarily run one or two hours long when they aired in the 1950s, into just three minutes, Schiller made them even more obnoxious than they already were.

6. Like the films of Woody Allen or (albeit alluding mostly to obscure popular culture) Quentin Tarantino, Schiller's works also incorporate many references and in-jokes, often relating to his substantial knowledge of art, philosophy and film history. There are jokes or comments about artistic, literary and philosophical movements that are hysterical to those who are in the know, but will fly right over the heads of the majority. For example, *Art Is Ficial* and *Nothing Lasts Forever* have jokes concerning Dadaism. The jokes are guaranteed to amuse those who are familiar with that art movement, but will leave anyone else left in the dark.

7. The acting in Schiller's films is noteworthy. Schiller rarely goes for realism, so the performances in his works are no exception. They are exaggerated and melodramatic, just like in the classic films that Schiller often aims to recreate. The acting is very old-fashioned, although the performances never appear antiquated or stoop to scenery-chewing. The most notable example of this is Zach Galligan in *Nothing Lasts Forever*. Galligan plays the part with the same charm of Andy Hardy. It is outdated by today's standards, but works because Galligan is accurately channeling a different time period with his old-fashioned charisma and naiveté.

8. Finally, another characteristic of a Schiller film is its music. Few of his films have modern or popular music. There is plenty of classical music (preferably from a scratchy record player) and old crooner music like Eddie Fisher's 'Oh! My Pa-Pa' in *Nothing Lasts Forever*. The short films *Love is a Dream* and *Falling in Love* were completely built around classic songs. Schiller was able to immerse himself into the time periods he was trying to recreate, carefully selecting his music from a vast collection.

Evident from his ability to recreate dead genres, his time capsule humor, his obscure references, the old-fashioned performances he is able to get out of his actors, and his use of music, Schiller can be considered an auteur filmmaker. His distinct style and humor weave throughout his entire body of work.

Chapter 1
The Door To Directing

Tom Schiller's unique style and sense of humor are apparent in his very first film, *The Door*, made in 1962. Schiller made the film with his best friend Jeff Benjamin when they were teenagers. Using the family 16mm camera, the five-minute film follows Benjamin, dressed completely in white, running around UCLA and Westwood Village in Los Angeles and frenetically trying to open various doors.

The Door is enjoyable and thrilling, a remarkable feat considering the fact that Schiller was just thirteen years old when he made it. It could easily double as an early-effort student film. While the lighting is inconsistent at times and there are some problems with the exposure, it is clear that Schiller knew what he was doing.

The action is set to Henry Mancini's theme song from the television series *Peter Gunn*, which later became somewhat of an anthem for The Blues Brothers. Schiller later replaced that music with Elmer Bernstein's much faster, frantic music from the Frank Sinatra classic *The Man with the Golden Arm*, which gave the film a more frenzied pace.

The film opens with a wide shot of a young man running through the street. It is quickly followed by a shot of a wall upon which the title of the film is painted, accompanied by a scream (one of only two sound effects in the film). Then the camera follows Schiller's friend as he runs from building to building and door to door. The camera is fixed on the young man's feet, alternating with shots of him running in the distance and close-ups on his hands trying to open doors. His face is never seen as he runs down flights of stairs, through hallways, alongside the busy Los Angeles traffic and maneuvers his way over benches, through heaps and piles of rubble, and so on.

The boy tries each door, but none of them will open. Finally, he

©Schillervision

7

finds a doorknob that will turn. The music pauses for a moment and the boy opens the door and walks in. The pause in the music has a comedic effect because the music stops so suddenly—perhaps unintentional, as it might have been necessary to accommodate the inserted sound effect of a doorknob being turned. After the door closes behind him, the camera pans up on the door to reveal the sign on the door: Men.

©Schillervision

Schiller's end-of-film punch line approach is common in his short films. In this regard, the film is very much like his later film *Mask of Fear*. It, too, begins as a straight thriller, and the joke isn't revealed until the last moments of the film.

After finishing *The Door*, Schiller put up a metal plaque in an alley near Westwood Boulevard, where the film was shot. The plaque reads: 'On this spot in 1962, Tom Schiller and his best friend Jeff Benjamin made their first movie, *The Door*.' The plaque is still there today, although the last time Schiller checked, it was behind a dumpster.

It's possible that Tom Schiller inherited comedy from his parents. Both of his parents were incredibly funny, although only his father made a living at it. Tom Schiller sees himself as a continuation of his father's comedy legacy, but their humor is in no way similar.

Bob Schiller wrote for the highly popular radio shows of Jimmy Durante, Abbott and Costello and Ozzie and Harriet, to name a few, before moving to the exciting new medium of television. With his long-time writing partner Bob Weiskopf, Bob Schiller began working at Desilu Studios in the early 1950s. After writing for *Make Room for Daddy* and *Our Miss Brooks*, they were brought in to write for *I Love Lucy* in its fifth and sixth seasons. The immensely popular comedy show began airing in 1951, and Schiller and Weiskopf, along with regulars Madelyn Pugh Martin, Bob Carroll Jr. and Jess Oppenheimer, wrote for the show between 1955 and 1957.

I Love Lucy ended its run in 1957, but Lucille Ball and Desi Arnaz immediately continued their popular characters Lucy and Ricky Ricardo in *The Lucy-Desi Comedy Hour* the next Fall. These hour-long specials aired sporadically over the next three years.

Schiller and Weiskopf's association with Desilu continued with Lucille Ball's third show, this time without Desi, called *The Lucy Show*. Schiller and his partner stayed with the show for its first two seasons, from 1962 to 1964. Throughout the many years that Bob Schiller worked at Desilu, his son Tom vividly remembers the many visits to the studio.

The comedy duo of Bob Schiller and Bob Weiskopf continued writing for many other successful television series and specials, including *The Flip Wilson Show*, *The Carol Burnett Show*, *The Beautiful Phyllis Diller Show* (along with a young Lorne Michaels, who later became Tom Schiller's close friend and boss) and many others. They also wrote and produced *The Good Guys*, a sitcom with Bob Denver and Herb Edelman that began its two-season run in 1968. They then wrote for *All in the Family* throughout its entire run, from 1971 to 1979— winning an Emmy in 1978—as well as its follow-up series *Archie Bunker's Place* from 1979 until 1983. Plus, they were writers and producers on the equally successful *All in the Family* spin-off *Maude* (1972-1978). In short, Bob Schiller is nothing short of a comedy legend in the world of television.

Tom Schiller learned comedy by being around his father, but never directly. "My father didn't really sit down and teach me about how to write comedy, ever," he says. "I kind of got it through osmosis and by going to the set and watching him and watching the shows being rehearsed."

On a few occasions, Bob tried to instill his wisdom into his son. For example, the elder Schiller told him that there has to be a joke point after a few lines. Tom Schiller never wrote for a sitcom, so he didn't get to apply that wisdom. His father also said that comedy is in the eyes. Lucille Ball certainly utilized that rule on *I Love Lucy*, albeit in an exaggerated manner typical of vintage television comedy.

"But what about *The Blues Brothers*?" Tom asked his father years later. "They wore dark glasses through the whole thing." To that, Bob Schiller had no answer.

It is tough to see a direct link between the works of Bob and Tom Schiller. If anything, it's more of an emotional link. They have the same sensibilities and Tom Schiller learned to look at things differently thanks to his father. Maybe what Tom inherited from his father is best described in simpler terms: the ability to make people laugh.

"He is mostly a state-of-the-art situation comedy writer. He's a master at that," says Tom Schiller about his father. "While I respect that, I like to try a lot of different kinds of humor."

While the connection between the humor and writing might be tough to pinpoint, there is one important component that Tom Schiller first learned from his parents during his childhood: making films. Whenever the Schillers went on a holiday, they brought along their Bell & Howell 16mm camera and a one hundred foot load of film. Instead of making ordinary home movies, they made short films complete with characters and a plot. All of the families that went on the trips would appear in the film—parents and children—and the Schillers made take-offs on the motion pictures that were popular at the time. They had a lot of fun making them, and this served as an inspiration for Tom Schiller to make his own short films.

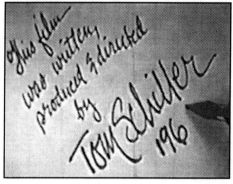

©Schillervision

Schiller's mother in particular often encouraged him to pick up the camera and go make films. She even made an animated film herself once, after taking an extension course at UCLA Film School.

Schiller's first animated film was *Dos Chodos Ray*, made in 1966, although it is better described as a collage with some animation. His friend John Whitney Jr. made him an animation stand on which he could place his camera. The title was fabricated by Schiller—it has no meaning or significance, but it sounds daring and exotic. Etchings, illustrations from books, pictures from magazines, kaleidoscopes and all types of interesting images are edited together with African percussion music playing in the background. The result is an interesting collage of a variety of themes and ideas. The film is clearly experimental. It's just Schiller having fun with the film camera.

The film begins with illustrations of strange animals and other creatures. There are illustrations of strange fish-like creatures, but also of humanlike mutants that are hauntingly drawn in biblical fashion. They are in fact images from *The Seven Deadly Sins, Big Fish Eat Little Fish* and other sixteenth century etchings by Pieter Bruegel the Elder. The camera pans across the photographs and illustrations, sometimes zooming in. The rate at which these pictures appear slowly increases until they appear so fast that it is barely possible to make out what is on the screen. But then it slows down again. After that, pictures of women—presumably from magazine advertisements—are animated: their eyes become green, and Schiller draws on the pictures in stop-motion animation.

The process of drawing is also animated, such as the creation of a spiral which is later scratched out. Some images are juxtaposed, such as a skull and the American flag, presenting an interesting contrast—timely, considering the film was made while the country was at war in Vietnam, and Schiller was decidedly anti-war.

Schiller utilizes color but with little consistency from shot to shot. The film closes with Schiller writing his name several times in different ways—first by hand, then via animation, being stamped, and finally in a book that closes itself.

"I just doodled around, put up weird pictures and collages, and made things move over them," says Schiller. "I put in colors that I liked, and drawings that appeared magically and disappeared into nowhere."

It is evident from *Dos Chodos Ray* that Schiller was influenced by the works of designers/filmmakers Charles and Ray Eames, for whom he worked as a projectionist when he was a teenager. The husband-and-wife team behind such films as *Toccata for Toy Trains* (1957) and later *Powers of Ten* (1977) produced numerous abstract films, and their impact on Schiller shows. Even though Charles and Ray Eames are more famous for their other contributions to the American post-war culture—most notably, the Eames chair—they managed to produce over seventy-five films during their long careers.

The Eameses made films that highlighted everything from modern art to science. They mostly produced short films and documentaries, many of which were funded or commissioned by companies like IBM. Many of the shorts that the Eameses produced were educational (such as *Atlas* and *Powers of Ten*), but they also managed to make abstract pieces (like *Blacktop* and *Kaleidoscope Jazz Chair*) and children's films (*Toccata for Toy Trains*, a colorful stop-motion animation film involving toy trains). The couple also designed museum exhibits and for their touring Franklin and Jefferson exhibit in the 1970s directed the documentary *The Worlds of Franklin and Jefferson*. For many of their films, the Eameses collaborated with renowned composer Elmer Bernstein.

After *Dos Chodos Ray*, Schiller made a similar experimental film entitled *Supra-Market*. Made with his friend John Whitney Jr. in 1966, *Supra-Market* is a montage of products at the supermarket. The shots move very fast, at times giving the film a chaotic feel. It begins with close-ups of words on signs, jars and cans. "Salad of the Month," "Tasty," "Bottoms," "Balls," "Good for breakfast," "Cheese," "Blood Sausage," and so on. The words are random, but when put together provide an avenue for free association. The camera moves through the aisles and shows all the neatly stacked cans and fresh produce. There are shots of a broken jar, a hanging scale filled with bananas, a statue of the Jolly Green Giant, and even a brief glimpse of the boys themselves

© Tom Schiller and John Whitney

when Schiller points the camera directly at a mirror. Arguably, some of the images are suggestive, such as the numerous shots of sausages being squeezed, followed by various Gerber baby products, a bag of pfeffernuts excitedly being wrung, and a container of Vaseline.

Supra-Market is an improvement over *Dos Chodos Ray* in that it is more focused. With *Dos Chodos Ray*, Schiller filmed all kinds of pictures and objects, while with *Supra-Market* he restricted himself to a specific location and a specific theme. The images connect more easily because they are all presented within the same context.

Supra-Market can easily be construed as commentary on commercialism and consumerism—which is quite an accomplishment coming from teenagers. The film recreates the calm, spacious and highly organized feel of a supermarket, complete with "clean-up in Aisle Six" announcements and soothing Muzak to present grocery shopping as something that has come down to a scientific process. Its statement, if there is any, is not as blatant as it is in George Romero's 1978 film *Dawn of the Dead*—a piece of social commentary disguised as a horror film, it likens shoppers to zombies—but it is obvious that it is a concept that resonates with Schiller. He unabashedly revisits consumerism in his feature film *Nothing Lasts Forever*.

Schiller's close friend John Whitney Jr., who had helped him make *Supra-Market* and was a son of the noted abstract filmmaker John Whitney, was running sound for Academy Award-winning documentary filmmaker Robert Snyder. It was through him that Schiller eventually met Snyder. Upon meeting Snyder, he asked if he could become his apprentice. Snyder agreed, and Schiller was hired. Schiller was still in high school and took the job as part of a high school work program. He would attend classes in the morning and go to work for Snyder in the afternoon. Off-and-on for the next seven years, Schiller helped Snyder make his documentaries, learning every aspect of editing, sound and camerawork. This was Schiller's film school.

Robert Snyder had already been a seasoned filmmaker for many years. He studied under pioneer filmmaker Roberty J. Flaherty, widely considered the father of the documentary film, and the man behind the legendary Inuit documentary *Nanook of the North*. Snyder won the Academy Award in 1951 for producing the documentary feature *The Titan: The Story of Michelangelo*, and was nominated again in 1958 for *The Hidden World*, a documentary about insects narrated by Gregory Peck. Snyder was best known for his biographies and could effectively get into the time and mind of his subjects in order to present how they brought their legendary works to the world.

Snyder slaved tirelessly over his films. He always had several projects running concurrently and took months, often even years to finish them. Schiller would come from school and sit behind the editing equipment set up in the garage at Snyder's house in Pacific Palisades and put films together. For some of his subjects, Snyder ended up producing more than one version of the documentary, adapting it for European television markets.

Schiller worked for Snyder on a number of different documentary features with such luminary subjects as novelist and diarist Anaïs Nin (*Anaïs Nin Observed*, 1973) and abstract expressionist painter Willem De Kooning (*A Glimpse of De Kooning*, 1968). The young apprentice learned a lot from Snyder's subjects, and because the films took so long to make, Schiller sometimes got to know them fairly well.

Such was the case when he worked on *Buckminster Fuller on Spaceship Earth* (1967) and *The World of Buckminster Fuller* (1970), about celebrated architect, engineer and philosopher R. Buckminster Fuller—who also happened to be Snyder's father-in-law. To Schiller, the experience of meeting Bucky Fuller, as he was called, was like meeting Pythagoras or Euclid. "He could talk to you and just fire you up about architecture and about how the resources of the world should be used," recounts Schiller. "And about using more with less, and building structures for humanity." Doing the documentaries on Fuller also took Schiller to Maine to visit Fuller's house on Bear Island, and to Chicago to visit some of the geodesic domes that Fuller had designed.

The documentary subject who made the biggest impression was Henry Miller (1891-1980). Snyder made three documentaries about the notorious novelist: *The Henry Miller Odyssey*, *The Life and Times of Henry Miller* (both 1969), and *L'Odyssey d'Henry Miller*, all versions of the same project. *L'Odyssey* was produced for French television and *Life and Times* for British television. In addition, Snyder also wrote the biography *This is Henry, Henry Miller From Brooklyn*.

Miller is well-known for testing the limits of the obscenity laws in the United States. He lived in France between 1930 and 1939, at times homeless and begging for food and money. There he wrote the autobiographical *Tropic of Cancer*, a guttural, episodic account of his expatriate exploits in Paris. His first and most famous work, it was published in France in 1934 but was banned in the United States, where his work was considered profane and obscene due to its explicit language and detailed descriptions of sexual acts. Nevertheless, *Tropic of Cancer* and Miller's other books of that period were illegally imported into the country and brought him an underground popularity. It wasn't until the 1960s that the Supreme Court finally ruled that *Tropic of Cancer* could legally be imported or published. The decision became a landmark victory for freedom of expression in the United States. Miller left France at the outbreak of the Second World War and returned to the United States in 1940, ultimately settling in California in 1944 where he spent many more years writing and painting.

On meeting Schiller, Miller quickly took him under his wing. "I was running sound on the documentary," Schiller recalls. "And he said to me, 'Hey, you remind me of myself when I was your age. Come over anytime, wake me up, I want to talk to you.' So, I visited Henry all the time for the next seven years."

Despite the age difference of more than sixty years, Miller and Schiller got along famously. Talking to a literary legend like Henry Miller was inspirational

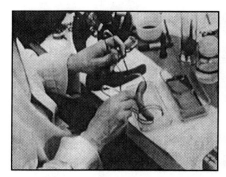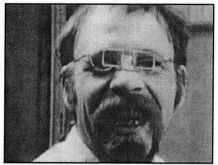

The Enigma of Dr. Schiller, ©Schillervision

to an aspiring artist such as Tom Schiller. Miller essentially became his teacher, his mentor, educating him in literature and recounting great tales of living in Europe. The two became very close, their friendship lasting until Miller's death in 1980. "He was highly enthusiastic, and you'd go away glowing after having a dinner conversation," Schiller recalls. "You'd just be bursting with wanting to be creative, and write, and make films. He was wonderful."

Schiller was never crazy about school, so instead of going to college after high school, working as an apprentice to Robert Snyder became his primary job. He worked off-and-on for Snyder over a seven-year period. Sometimes he was working for him full-time and sometimes part-time. But he also took an extended period off to travel. Schiller went to Europe, where he bought a car and drove around, hanging around in different places. He ended up in Copenhagen, where he stayed for close to a year. He took a lot of time to write, draw, and make experimental films. One such film was *The Enigma of Dr. Schiller*, a stylish black-and-white short about a scientist who spends years working on a groundbreaking invention, which finally, in the climactic conclusion, is revealed to be the hot dog.

Later, Schiller moved to London for a year, where he spent much of his time hanging out at a bookstore frequented by all kinds of writers. Schiller befriended several of them and would make short documentaries about them.

Schiller eventually returned to California, wiser, worldly, and ready to make his first real film.

Chapter 2
Schiller and Miller

Schiller worked with Robert Snyder on 1969's *The Henry Miller Odyssey*, the ninety-minute documentary in which Henry Miller returns to his old stomping grounds in Brooklyn and Paris, talks with contemporaries like Lawrence Durrell and Anaïs Nin, reads, relaxes, reveals his attitudes on a variety of subjects, and reflects on his own life and work. However, this was not entirely the Henry Miller that Schiller came to know so well over the years.

Undoubtedly, *The Henry Miller Odyssey* is a very personal documentary that does an excellent job of giving its viewers a look inside the life and mind of Miller. But there was a different side that Schiller wanted to try to reveal. "I felt that there was a Henry Miller I knew that could be captured in a more concise and shorter way," he says, "by keeping him in his bathroom, talking about the pictures on his wall."

Miller liked the idea, so in 1973 Schiller wrote and directed the thirty-five-minute documentary *Henry Miller Asleep & Awake*. Spontaneous and mostly unrehearsed, Schiller shot the film over the course of four or five day sessions. The film is set entirely in the two most private rooms of any home: the bedroom and the bathroom.

The documentary starts by panning through Miller's bedroom in his Pacific Palisades home. Miller himself is asleep and in the stages of waking up, rolling around underneath his bed sheets and making exaggerated groaning and yawning sounds as he climbs out of bed and stretches. Miller was already in his eighties when he made this film, and it is obvious—not just from his wrinkles—that he is in the final stages of his life. He is an old, wise man about to pass his knowledge on to a new generation.

After he wakes, he takes Schiller and the camera into his bathroom, a spacious shrine covered wall-to-wall with photographs, paintings, quotes and clippings. The floor creaks as Miller walks through the hallway. At the bathroom mirror, Miller examines himself and tries to shape his face so that he looks younger. He then turns around to face the camera and begins talking about his bathroom. "As you sit here and you're relaxed," Miller says, "why, you're free to

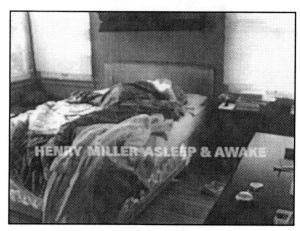

make free associations." And that was his intention for this room. He says that every now and then, he would look at all the pictures and think about what they mean to him and why he put them up there. As such, he spends a lot of time in the bathroom. He also jokingly mentions that visitors often spend a lot of time there, leading him to believe that they might be lost or constipated.

In his bathrobe, Miller points out many of the items hanging on the wall and enthusiastically discusses them. Although Miller was eighty-one when *Asleep & Awake* was shot, the film shows him as a terrific conversationalist, enthusiastically telling the stories behind everything from "the Buddhists to the whores" he has plastered over his bathroom walls. He describes his bathroom as a voyage of ideas. It's a microcosm, he says, that anyone can explore.

Schiller had hung out at Miller's home many times and was captivated by the gallery of memories that Miller had turned his bathroom into—quite the opposite of the inoffensive paintings and birthday calendars found in most residential restrooms.

One of Miller's longest monologues in the film concerns Junichirô Tanizaki. An enlarged cover of his book *Diary of a Mad Old Man* hangs on the wall. In addition to his fascination with the author and his novel *Kagi* (*the Key*, which he spends several minutes summarizing), Miller also talks about how he was a judge at the 1960 Cannes film festival. He explains that he was the only one who stuck up for the film *Kagi*, while everyone else favored Fellini's *La Dolce Vita*.[1]

Miller also points out two artworks featuring Hoki, his fifth and last wife whom he met at the Imperial Gardens restaurant. This leads to a story about the Japanese writer/actor Taiji Tonoyama, seen in a nearby picture with Miller at the same restaurant, who asked Miller how many women he thinks he has slept with in his lifetime. Tonoyama estimated that he himself had slept with about 250, but suspected that Miller, with his reputation, had slept with at least a thousand. Miller was a little embarrassed by the situation, especially because his wife was sitting nearby. Nevertheless, Miller modestly answered: forty or fifty.

At one point, Schiller stubbornly speaks from behind the camera, pointing at a picture of Blaise Cendrars, and asks: "Who is that over there, Bing Crosby?"

"Bing Crosby? Farthest from the world," Miller replies. Miller goes on to explain that French poet and novelist Blaise Cendrars is his idol and the one writer that he respects most. "If today I could imitate Blaise Cendrars, I would do it with a whole full heart." Miller then tells about Cendrars' tough life, and how much he venerates his works—many of which Cendrars wrote with just one hand. According to Schiller, Miller specifically instructed him to ask about Bing Crosby. Cendrars has a much tougher, weathered face than Crosby, and there is hardly any resemblance between the two.

Miller tells all kinds of interesting stories throughout the film. He explains that he is hard of hearing, except when he travels by airplane. When he is up in the sky, not only can he hear perfectly, but he can also hear celestial music. He claims that he has asked pilots about it, and they hear the same sounds as well.

He also points out a corner of his bathroom hidden behind foldout blinds that holds his obscene pictures. Unclad men and women are pictured in various profane poses. Miller explains that his bathroom has a reputation and says that he put up these pictures for people who come in having already heard a lot about the room and expect to be shocked. Being the author of such sexually charged fare as *Tropic of Cancer* means that he has a reputation to live up to. The pictures behind the blinds prove satisfactory. As Miller puts it, they're dirty pictures.

In his longest and most sincere discourse, Miller recounts a Zen Buddhist story about Roshi Bobo, a young monk who finds himself unable to reach enlightenment after many years of waiting and trying. After fifteen years, at the age of thirty, he leaves his monastery and tries to experience civilian life. He soon ends up in the red light district where he experiences the act of sexual

©Schillervision

intercourse for the first time. The experience is a revelation and he finally experiences Satori, the goal of Zen Buddhism. Miller explains that Bobo went to the very end of doubt and despair. He had to go to the end of the tunnel before finally seeing the light. Miller argues that this is what psychoanalysis fails to achieve. Satori cannot be reached by visiting a therapist. Miller further equates this to William Blake's idea of reaching heaven through hell, that there is no one way to reach paradise. "One should accept his doubts completely," Miller warns. "Accept despair and anguish and frustration and see it through. Don't go to a doctor. Don't go to an analyst, above all."

After pointing out a picture of Hermann Hesse, the German-born author of *Siddhartha* (which Tom Schiller cites as a big influence), and discussing Hesse's ideology, Miller explains that writers rarely look good. They are often alone with their thoughts and always living in an abstract realm of ideas, and as a result they are often hunched over and thin-blooded.

Miller also shows a picture from the set of the 1970 *Tropic of Cancer* film adaptation. In the photo, Miller is seen alongside the female stars of the film. Miller says that the best part of the film is that a good view of frontal nudity is shown. The photo is from a German newspaper, and the caption underneath reads 'Ohne Eros sind wir alle Nullen,' which Miller translates as 'Without love, we're nothing.' Miller cleverly remarks that his book *Tropic of Cancer* is not very much about love.

To discuss Gurdjieff, Miller leans against the sink. The enigmatic Gurdjieff is the most interesting of all the masters that Miller has read about. For twenty-one years, Gurdjieff wanted to be looked down upon rather than venerated, which Miller finds fascinating. Sadly, Miller doesn't really expound on Gurdjieff, but he does tell an amusing story of when a gendarme saved Gurdjieff's life and Gurdjieff waited three years before thanking him.

When Miller crosses the shower, he finds a nude woman bathing herself.

©Schillervision

Miller dries her off and she laughingly leaves the room. The woman was a dental hygienist friend of Miller's wife Hoki. Schiller and Miller came up with the idea to find a way to break up all the dialogue. It's a silly and unexpected moment in a documentary, though not completely surprising coming from Henry Miller.

There are also several prints of Paul Gauguin paintings on the wall. Miller points out one of Gauguin's early works, as well as another painting with the words "Where do we come from, what are we, and where are we going?" inscribed in the top left corner (it is also the title of the painting, an oil-on-canvas from 1897). It is the eternal, unanswerable question of identity, a thought which Miller says he visits regularly. He tells about being in Brooklyn as a young man and buying a pack of chewing gum out of a slot machine. Above the machine was a little mirror in which upon looking into, Miller saw someone else's face instead of his own. It was a scary, haunting feeling. He claims this also happens to him regularly in his dreams. It gives him the feeling that he does not know who he is—a loss of identity—which is troubling. Miller continues talking about his recurring dreams, until he discusses the process of waking up.

Suddenly, as if he has just awakened himself, Miller is standing outside in New York, the city where he was born. The street is completely empty. He is still in his robe, but he says that he suddenly remembers who he is. He takes off his bathrobe to reveal that he is wearing a suit underneath. As he walks through the street with his cane, he talks about how horrible, ugly and full of misery the city is, and that he has a hard time understanding how he survived living there as a child. He grumbles his way through a list of words to describe how he felt when he lived in New York: starvation, humiliation, frustration, despair. He blames this for his recurring nightmares. "I don't know now whether I'm really awake or dreaming. The whole past seems like one long dream punctured with nightmares," he exclaims and walks down the street as the end credits roll.

©Schillervision

Henry Miller Asleep & Awake is obviously a documentary, but on numerous occasions it breaks the rules that a documentary ordinarily obeys—such as by finding the woman in the shower and Miller's sudden appearance on a street in New York. Nonetheless, it gives a good overview of who Henry Miller is aside from knowing him personally. It serves as a great companion piece to his written works.

The closing scene that takes place in New York City was not filmed on location. It was shot on the 20th Century Fox studio lot, where there was a short street of buildings designed to look like old New York. This explains why the street is so old-fashioned and empty.

The appearance of the nude woman in the shower was obviously rehearsed, and the opening and closing scenes were also clearly staged. Also, Miller had put up a couple pictures that weren't normally on view in the bathroom so he could talk about them. Aside from that, *Asleep & Awake* was not scripted or rehearsed in any way.

Miller appears very personable, and his dialogue is very inviting. It was a great idea of Schiller to put Miller in his bathroom. As a result, the viewer gets to know the author presumably well by witnessing a personal tour of his bathroom—traditionally a private area.

Schiller enjoyed making the film and took about a month or two to edit it. "I would show it to Henry and we'd talk about it," he remembers. "Take things out, or move things around." *Henry Miller Asleep & Awake* played in theaters in London and was broadcast on PBS. It also aired in Germany and Italy.

©Schillervision

Chapter 3
Saturday Night

When Lorne Michaels started putting together ideas for a weekly variety program to replace Johnny Carson reruns on Saturday nights in 1975, Tom Schiller was among the first people on board. Michaels was a television comedy writer who came from Canada to work as a junior writer with Bob Schiller on the short-lived *The Beautiful Phyllis Diller Show* in 1968. "I didn't know anybody in Los Angeles," Michaels recalls. "I just moved out from Canada and Bob was incredibly kind to me, despite the difference in generations. He was a mentor." He moved back to Canada to do his own show, *The Hart & Lorne Terrific Hour* for CBC, but he would return to L.A. occasionally for periodic work, such as *The Dean Martin Summer Show*. "I stayed at Bob and Sabrina's house. And Tom I knew a little bit, and then got to know more."

"My dad kept saying I should meet this guy," Tom Schiller recalls. "He's from Canada, and he knew all the best restaurants in Los Angeles. And I said: 'I don't care about the best restaurants in Los Angeles.' But one day he came over and we started to hang out and we became friends. Then I went over to the Chateau Marmont (where Michaels frequently stayed) and he always kept talking about this new TV show he was planning."

In June of 1975, Schiller accompanied Michaels on a trip to Joshua Tree National Park. They spent much of their time talking and Michaels put together the format of the show. Nobody was expecting Lorne Michaels' show to become the cultural phenomenon that it became, so when Michaels asked Schiller to be his assistant, Schiller needed some time to think about it. Anyone hired at the show would have been happy if it lasted three or four seasons, let alone one. It was a big risk, and it meant holding off on his filmmaking plans. He kept thinking to himself, "I don't do television, I do films."

On the other hand, there was the possibility of eventually making short films for the show. Michaels hinted that he could do films on the show…just not immediately. Schiller's friend Henry Miller strongly cautioned him to stay away from the superficial world of television, but he decided to go anyway and moved to New York. Schiller was among the first to be brought on-board by Lorne Michaels. He helped Michaels in holding auditions and finding the cast, finding writers, and general preparations for *NBC's Saturday Night*.

The original cast of Not Ready for Primetime Players consisted of Dan Aykroyd, John Belushi, Chevy Chase, George Coe, Jane Curtin, Garrett Morris, Laraine Newman, Michael O'Donoghue and Gilda Radner. The writing team consisted of Chase, O'Donoghue, Michaels, the team of Al Franken and Tom Davis, Anne Beatts, Herb Sargent, Rosie Shuster, Alan Zweibel and Schiller.

"Tom Schiller was sitting by the pool at the Chateau Marmont reading scripts and went to Lorne and said 'Hey, Lorne, you've got to read these guys. They're a comedy team,'" recalls Tom Davis, then an unemployed stand-up comic and one half of the comedy team of Franken and Davis. "We were hired last out of all the writers, and Tom Schiller was the reason that we got hired."

A Writers Guild ruling stated that Al Franken and Tom Davis could be hired and paid as one person because they were a team. During the first season, they barely got by on their *Saturday Night* salaries. "I had a six-week contract and was making soup to eat, I was being paid so little," says Davis. "We were given the shittiest desk to sit at—we were just kind of in a hallway. I thought I was going to get fired at any minute. I was not allowed in the big meetings where Michael O'Donoghue and Anne Beatts and Lorne Michaels and Chevy Chase started the initial fission experiments."

After the second season, Franken and Davis got an awful lot of material on the show and were even promoted to featured cast members. "We were up there," says Davis. "That's when we were really hot. I will always be in Tom Schiller's debt for being the guy who got us hired when we needed a break."

Tom Schiller was initially hired by Lorne Michaels to be his assistant, but when the cast and writing team started to come together, it was not certain what his exact position was going to be. Even when he was officially credited as a writer, which was decided before the first show, there was some ambiguity about what he was going to do.

"He was there when I got there," says Chevy Chase, who was head writer together with Michael O'Donoghue. "It was never made clear to me when I got there what his function was, but I could tell immediately that he was a funny guy and had some very unusual perspectives, which I thought were very valuable."

NBC's Saturday Night premiered on October 11, 1975.[2] Stand-up comedian George Carlin served as host and both Billy Preston and Janis Ian were musical guests. With four musical performances, four different stand-up comedy routines from Carlin, a so-called musical performance by Andy Kaufman, a short film by Albert Brooks, the *Weekend Update* news segment and an appearance by the Muppets, the first episode had just ten chances for the cast and writers to show off. The second episode had nine musical performances, hardly allowing the cast to shine at all. But after that, the show quickly became the way it is today, focusing mostly on sketch comedy.

In order to get something on the air during the first episode, not only did Schiller have to compete with the nine other writers, but he also had to compete with the cast. The cast members were also expected to write for the show, but because NBC could only hire a finite number of writers, most of the cast was not credited as such.[3]

Many other sketches were planned for the first episode, but because the dress rehearsal ran hours over, they were not performed on the live show. Still, one of Schiller's ideas made the cut. It was in fact a pre-taped commercial for Triopenin arthritis medication—one of the first bits taped for *NBC's Saturday Night* at Studio 8H.

The commercial is cleverly shot. The camera is fixed on a man's hands while a voice-over describes how the arthritis pills work. Meanwhile, the two hands (belonging to Chevy Chase, who is not seen aside from his arms) keep trying to open the bottle, but the top just won't come off. Chase is a great 'hand actor,' something he had already proven a year earlier in the comedy vignette film *The Groove Tube*, in which he plays out an entire scene using only his fingers.

The announcer continues about the soothing benefits of Triopenin while Chase's hands are still meddling with the bottle and getting more and more frustrated by not being able to open it. Finally, the commercial closes with a picture of a broken Triopenin bottle with the pink pills spilled out and the voice-over reading "Now with the new childproof safety cap."

Schiller was very proud of it and received great response to the bit. Viewers mailed in, writing how much they liked seeing *Saturday Night* make fun of the hard-to-open child-proof medicine bottles. In addition to writing *Triopenin*, in the first show Schiller also was an extra in several sketches and appeared in the pre-taped bit *Show Us Your Guns*.

Schiller quickly became friends with Chevy Chase. "He was like my right-hand man at *Saturday Night* the first year," says Chase. "I would say he was one of the funniest people I ever met. He made me laugh and I made him laugh."

"Chevy and I were friends for thirty weeks," says Schiller. Chase was the first break-out star to come out of *Saturday Night*, and the first to leave for a successful career in Hollywood. Even though he is often associated with the show, he left during the second season, having appeared as a cast member in thirty episodes.

"I think we were both very affectionate toward each other. I didn't personally lay my hands on him but I do thank him for all the fellatio," Chase jokes. In all seriousness, Chase had a tough time adjusting to his sudden stardom, but Schiller was by his side. "Tom was there, sharing with me this rise that happened in that year. He was like a reality check," Chase recalls. "He had his own take and view of what was happening to me as it related to people on the street noticing me and asking for autographs. He always had a funny and down-to earth, real—but skewed to his personality—take on me and this period of my life."

Chase and Schiller would often spend their Sundays together. Sunday was the one free day of the week, and a short one at that, since the entire night before it was spent at the infamous *Saturday Night* after-parties. Chase usually woke up around eleven or twelve on Sunday morning, and the two would spend the day hanging out, having brunch, and recovering from a week of intense work. "Just walking with him," Chase recalls, "and laughing at things we would observe. He would come up with thoughts and just click with me right away."

Schiller wrote the classic sketch *Fooling Death*, a parody of Ingmar Bergman's *The Seventh Seal*, for Chevy Chase and Louise Lasser. For various reasons, the July 24, 1976 episode hosted by Lasser is considered one of the worst in the history of *Saturday Night Live*. One exception that night was *Fooling Death*, a typically sweet Schiller piece about Sven and Inger, a Swedish couple in love. Throughout the entire sketch, Sven and Inger sit on the living room floor, lovingly staring at each other and occasionally touching each other's faces in a sensual manner. Meanwhile, a Swedish voice-over (with English subtitles at the bottom of the screen) explains how Sven and Inger fell in love.

Shortly thereafter, Tom Schiller slowly walks in. He plays Death and is dressed completely in black with his face covered in white make-up—just like Bengt Ekerot in *The Seventh Seal*. It is revealed that Schiller has been narrating the sketch all along. Sven and Inger do not take notice and Schiller continues speaking in Swedish in the background. Lasser is touching Chevy Chase's face and uses her hands to make silly shapes with his lips, causing the audience to crack up.

Schiller explains that he is Death and he has come to take their lives. Sven and Inger finally notice him, and Sven asks Death, in plain English, if he can pick up the pizza he just ordered. Death agrees, and Sven gives him the keys to his Volvo. Sven and Inger look at each other again and continue to play with each other's faces as if nothing happened. The car is heard driving off in the background, and the subtitle at the bottom of the screen reveals the punch line: "So Sven and Inger fooled death. There is no pizza in Sweden."

The sketch is typical of Schiller's worldly humor. Despite its dealing with death, it manages to be very sweet and innocent. No other writer at *Saturday Night Live* would have written a take-off on a Bergman film. Certainly not Michael O'Donoghue.

In that regard, it could be argued that Schiller brought a sense of balance to the show. Another writer and occasional performer at *Saturday Night* was the late Michael O'Donoghue, former editor of the *National Lampoon*. Even though O'Donoghue and Tom Schiller were good friends and appeared to have a lot of respect for each other, they were polar opposites in terms of their brands of comedy. Both were far away from the mainstream, which was exactly where *Saturday Night* strayed as well, but O'Donoghue believed in dangerous comedy. His comedy was often about death and immoral acts, while Schiller's was more about art and culture. One of O'Donoghue's routines was an impression of what talk show

Photo by Judith Belushi Pisano

host Mike Douglas would look and sound like with big steel needles plunged into his eyes. "Michael was caustic, acerbic and hard-edged," cast member Dan Aykroyd remembers. Schiller, on the other hand, had more of an innocent approach to humor, which most likely carried over from his father and the Lucille Ball shows. Schiller could be mischievous as well, but his humor seems to stem from more innocent sensibilities, especially when compared to Michael O'Donoghue. "They were definitely yin-yang, negative-positive," Aykroyd adds.

Of course, that's not to say that Schiller wasn't hip. He fit in perfectly with the *Saturday Night* crowd, but it was also obvious that Schiller had traveled and been exposed to different cultures. "He brought some left-angle thinking that was needed," says Aykroyd, "and some out-of-the-mainstream, certainly European influences. He had an intellectual and absurdist slant on things."

"That was the wonderful thing about Schiller," says Tom Davis. "He was never interested in being mainstream. He had a certain marvelous fault line, like with earthquakes, where wonderful ideas would erupt from, moving the tectonic plate of his skull. It was just a whole world in there, and it was always oozing with wonderful new ideas."

"I'd go in in the early morning and get out at 2 a.m. with Lorne. By and large, we were up there and not seeing much of how the world looks taking our work," says Chevy Chase. "Tom had the right perception of things, from not only his point of view, but maybe from the point of view of the outside world."

Of the entire writing crew, the comedy of Schiller and O'Donoghue was the most out-of-the-mainstream and ahead of its time. If Michael O'Donoghue was *Saturday Night Live*'s counter-cultural master, perhaps Schiller provided the unheard-of voice of, what else, counter-counter-culture.

Schiller also regularly contributed to *Weekend Update*, the mock news portion of the show originally anchored by Chevy Chase. He was known for his 'courtroom drawings,' which were artist renderings that went along with descriptions of major court cases read by Chase. The twist was that the artist renderings were childlike drawings. It was a popular *Weekend Update* bit that recurred quite often.

"I even have one framed that I look at all the time. All the drawings from Patty Hearst locked in the closet," says Chevy Chase, recalling one such courtroom drawing which dealt with the SLA and the kidnapping of Patty Hearst. "They looked like Picassos, and very much had that sort of cubist feel to them. At the same time, they looked like a child's drawing. They were very funny."

Furthermore, Schiller frequently made appearances on the show as an actor. He appeared in almost every episode during the five seasons that he was with the show. In the early days of *Saturday Night Live*, the cast consisted of only seven Not Ready for Primetime Players while in the past decade there have been an average of fifteen per season. As a result, many parts in sketches were given to the writers. "He did a very good Desi Arnaz," Lorne Michaels remembers. "It was one of his secret skills."

When Strother Martin hosted the show on April 19, 1980, Schiller was even an official member of the ensemble. He was pictured in the opening credits as a 'featured' player.

One example of his acting abilities can be seen in the first-season episode hosted by Richard Pryor, in which Schiller appears as a conspiracy theorist. After the Albert Brooks film, Pryor is about to begin a monologue when an audience member (played by Schiller) screams "I have proof!" He then walks up to the stage and starts talking about the John F. Kennedy assassination. He mentions the CIA, Lee Harvey Oswald and the grassy knoll, and tells that they are all interconnected. Pryor pretends to have no idea of what is happening. The audience member continues his conspiracy rants until gunfire is heard and he falls to the ground. Pryor is clueless and nervous, and fearing he might get shot himself for saying the wrong thing, he says that he had nothing to do with it and that he doesn't care who killed who.

From the first year, the 1975-1976 season, Schiller's best-known contribution is *Samurai Hotel*, featuring John Belushi, Chevy Chase and host Richard Pryor. Belushi included his impression of Japanese actor Toshirô Mifune in his audition and just about everybody at the show agreed that it was brilliant.

"John created the Samurai at home, before he was cast for *SNL*," recalls Judith Belushi Pisano, widow of John Belushi. "He was intrigued by a television film festival of Toshirô Mifune and he just began imitating him, sort of unknowingly. John would sit so close to the television that when there was a close-up of Mifune, it appeared as if he was looking in a mirror—John would reflect what he saw." Belushi made deep guttural grunts, much to his wife's amusement. To make the impression perfect, she brought out an elastic band so that he could put his hair up, and he put on a robe that worked for a

Samurai. She then took a pole from the closet—a clothes bar that had not been put up—and that became his first sword.

When it came time to go down for the audition, Belushi wasn't pleased because he felt he did not need to audition in the first place. People that he had hired at the *Lampoon* were now being hired for *Saturday Night*. They didn't have to audition, so why should he? To add to the insult, Belushi had to wait four hours before he could finally come in and do his audition. "He was annoyed and probably nervous," Pisano recalls, "He hadn't gone on many auditions, since he usually got jobs from people seeing him work. I suggested he do the Samurai because it was unique and really funny. So he went in and improvised."

It was a big hit at the audition. "He did a Samurai pool player when he was auditioning for us and it was hilarious," says Chevy Chase. "He looked like Toshirô Mifune somehow. I had known John longer than anybody there and worked with him for a year and a half at the Village Gate Theatre, so I knew his Samurai stuff very well."

But how were they going to incorporate it into the show? Schiller was trying to think of something ever since he witnessed the Samurai character at the auditions. He just came up with it one day while he was walking down the street with Chase. *Samurai Hotelier* popped into his mind. Chase loved it, so the two of them rushed back to the seventeenth floor of Rockefeller Center where Chase worked out the sketch with Schiller, Lorne Michaels and Alan Zweibel, whose desk was next to Schiller's. It aired just two days later. Michaels thought 'hotelier' sounded too sophisticated and might confuse some viewers who don't know what it means, so he changed the title to *Samurai Hotel*.

In the sketch, Chevy Chase plays a traveler who walks into a hotel lobby where the Samurai works behind the counter as the hotelkeeper. The Samurai replies only with grunts and sword-showmanship to the traveler's inquiries: A room overlooking the park, a king-size bed and room service. The traveler then writes down his information in the log, while the Samurai continues to grunt and swings his sword. The traveler then asks for a bellboy to take his bags upstairs. The bellboy, another Samurai played by Richard Pryor, is called up and the two Samurai begin yelling at each other. Chase tries to interrupt their screams and grunts to ask which of the two is going to carry his luggage.

The two Samurai then break out their swords and challenge each other with their moves—taking down a ceiling decoration in the process. Belushi's Samurai then makes the mistake of muttering "yo momma-san!" Pryor goes ballistic, chopping the hotel counter in half. Belushi immediately calms down and replies in English that he'll carry the bags up to the room himself.

The idea was that Belushi's Samurai character would have a different job each time he appeared, so Schiller wrote a list of possible professions for the character, ranging from baker to TV repairman to general practitioner. It was then turned over to another writer. Alan Zweibel, who co-wrote *Samurai Hotel*,

Tom Schiller, Dan Aykroyd and John Belushi. Photo by Judith Belushi Pisano

went on to write most of the thirteen other *Samurai* entries. The character also made appearances during the performances of Frank Zappa in the two episodes where Zappa was a musical guest. Tom Schiller named the character Futaba, after a Japanese restaurant that his family used to take him to in Los Angeles, and aside from his one line in *Samurai Hotel*, Futaba never spoke in English.

A different profession each time proved to be an excellent formula. "John was terrific at communicating non-verbally, and in classic Samurai costume the whole thing was absurdly silly," says Judith Belushi Pisano. "Tom had the right idea to place the character where he seemed totally out of context." Indeed, the sketches that stick to this formula are the best. There were a few Samurai sketches that strayed, such as *Samurai Night Fever* with O.J. Simpson, that were not as amusing as the others.

Frequent host and special guest Buck Henry appeared in many of the sketches. Playing the mild-mannered customer Mr. Dantley, he had to guess what Futaba was saying each time. When Futaba swung his sword, he was uninhibited. Belushi really got into the action, which at one point almost sent Mr. Dantley to Samurai Cemetery. In *Samurai Stockbroker*, Henry got a bit too close and was cut in the forehead by Futaba's sword. After a momentary pause, Henry continued the scene with his hand covering the cut. He hosted the rest of the show with a bandage on his forehead.

The sketches were an enormous success, and Belushi's Samurai character has become somewhat of an icon, and certainly one of *Saturday Night Live*'s greatest characters. Whenever there was a new Samurai sketch, it was usually the first sketch after the monologue—perhaps the most important slot.

A few years later, Belushi went on to work with Toshirô Mifune in Steven Spielberg's *1941*, and Mifune also invited the Belushis for dinner when they were in Japan to promote *The Blues Brothers*.

Nevertheless, *Samurai Hotel* is not a signature Tom Schiller sketch. It's the concept that shows what he brought to the show. It was Schiller's idea, but it was really Chevy Chase and Alan Zweibel who ran with it. "When it comes to writing, it was, for me, a rather thespian kind of sketch. It was loose and easy and simply allowed John to do his Samurai character," says Chase.

Schiller's part-assistant, part-writer position and his sibling-like relationship with Lorne Michaels allowed him the freedom to roam Studio 8H and the *Saturday Night* offices. "If I was alone with Lorne in the office and there were no other people allowed in for the time being, Tom could walk in," says Chase. "It was just accepted. One felt one could trust Tom and that he should be allowed into the room anytime." Other writers wouldn't dare enter, and if they did, they were quickly sent out.

"I think he was part of the Board of Trustees of the university that I call *Saturday Night Live*," says Dan Aykroyd.

"I hate to sound like a cliché, but the guy was most in the moment of anybody in the show," offers Tom Davis.

In general, Schiller's contribution to the show was not like any of the other writers. "Although he was credited as a writer, he never really came up with long sketches—the year that I was there, at least," Chase adds. "He came up with ideas and concepts that were far better than most of the sketches being written, and that can be, in itself, more valuable. He rarely actually sat down at a typewriter and handed in pages of dialogue."

But that's not to say Schiller did not write many sketches—at least in comparison to some of the other writers. As was the case with any writer on the show, not all material was accepted. There were many sketches that were performed in dress rehearsal early Saturday evening, but did not make it to the live show. "You stay up late and you call your family and friends to tune in," Schiller says, "and then you're waiting and waiting and then at a quarter till one you get cut, and you have to phone everybody and it just dies. It's terrible."

Chevy Chase sums up Schiller's first-year contribution to *Saturday Night* best: "He was always around to come up with an idea, a line, or a concept, on any sketch that I might be working on. He would occasionally write things but most of the time he just had very funny, off-centre concepts that we would put together ourselves, the two of us. It's a lot more valuable than saying 'He wrote the Samurai sketch.' That's a very easy sketch to write. He was really much more valuable than that."

Chevy Chase left the show in 1976 to move to California, where he had fallen in love. "I wanted to marry this girl that everybody knew was not right for me," says Chase. "I think Tom knew, too, but he didn't even say it. The marriage lasted about ten minutes. But he was very close and supportive of me. It's hard to find friends when you're in that position.

"I can't say enough about how close we were and what a wonderful relationship it was, and I think the only reason that it faded out is because I moved to LA to get married," Chase adds. "So I missed him, but over a period of time, we just sort of fell out of touch."

Schiller found that he had a lot in common with Chase's eventual replacement, Bill Murray, who worked on the show from 1977 through 1980. "I think we were both weird," says Murray. "We both fueled each other's mischief. He can create fun out of thin air. I was able to do some mischievous things that he would think about doing but might not necessarily do on his own. I sort of supplemented his wickedness."

Murray's favorite sketch that Tom Schiller wrote is a commercial parody called *Ruth Gordon's No Liquid Diet*. At this point, Murray had only been a cast member on the show for a few weeks and he was not yet getting as much airtime as he had hoped. He was happy to be in any sketch.

Ruth Gordon's No Liquid Diet had the famous elderly actress who hosted the episode in which it was set to appear promoting a weight-loss plan that worked by not drinking any liquids. The sketch also had some music to it. According to Schiller, "Ruth Gordon hated it, although Bill and I thought it was the funniest thing going."

"We worked on it together," Murray recalls. "It was fun because I don't know if Ruth particularly liked or got the sketch, under the idea that she had a diet with no liquids." The sketch was performed during dress rehearsal, but did not make it to the final show.

In terms of whom Schiller preferred to collaborate with most, Dan Aykroyd stood at the top of the list. "I liked Aykroyd to write with because he had a sort of crazy mind," Schiller says. Aykroyd was only twenty-three when *Saturday Night* began, but had the wisdom, talent and personality of someone much older. Dan Aykroyd thinks the two of them hit it off so well because of their different backgrounds.

"We came from polar opposites on the planet in upbringing," the actor recalls. "He was the son of one of the great geniuses of television, a kid who'd grown up in Hollywood. I grew up in Quebec, the son of government workers, with not even a hope of blasting out of Ottawa to do a career in show business. And then I guess it was us coming from completely different backgrounds. Him, from the Judaic tradition; me, from the Catholic dogma. We had a lot in common on that level and a lot of differences too, because of the rigidness of the way religion is thought of. And then we sort of relayed that it all means nothing anyway. He's one of the greatest free-spirited existentialists I've ever met."

Of all the pieces that Schiller wrote, Lorne Michaels and Dan Aykroyd most enjoyed the recurring *Bad Theater* sketches. In each one, Aykroyd plays a quaint British character named Leonard Pinth-Garnell, an expert on performing art who

Tom Schiller and Dan Aykroyd. Photo by Judith Belushi Pisano

introduces horrible stage productions. Then the productions are executed on the stage behind him. The intentionally terrible productions are hilarious and full of the clichés and pretentiousness found in many stage productions. The series included such entries as *Bad Playhouse, Bad Opera, Bad Ballet, Bad Cabaret for Children*, and many others. At the end of each sketch, Pinth-Garnell introduces the cast and then reiterates how awful the preceding production was. He usually closes the sketch by tossing the script into a garbage bin. Dan Aykroyd's favorite entry was *Bad Musical*, in which he introduces a musical about the life of Dutch microscopist Antony van Leeuwenhoek, played by John Belushi.

Pinth-Garnell was a great character, and Dan Aykroyd got it right. More than just a British accent, Aykroyd brilliantly varies the speed of his speech. There are some sentences that he's able to spit out in a single breath. Together with Schiller, Aykroyd managed to create a character that encompasses a snobbish art professor, a stage actor who sees himself as a great performer but has never been anywhere near Broadway, and Orson Welles.

In some of the bad productions, Pinth-Garnell even joins the cast, though despite partaking in them, Pinth-Garnell is just as critical. Another recurring character that appeared in most of the sketches is Ronnie Bateman, an ambitious actor played by Bill Murray.

During the fifth season, after Dan Aykroyd had left the show, Laraine Newman took over as Lady Pinth-Garnell. In 2001, Dan Aykroyd reprised his role as Leonard Pinth-Garnell in *Bad Conceptual Theater* during an episode hosted by John Goodman. However, Tom Schiller had absolutely nothing to do with the sketch. Even though former writers are sometimes brought back to the show to contribute a sketch or two, Schiller did not write it and was not even aware of it. "When you write a sketch," Schiller says, "it becomes property of the show and they continue it if they want."

Schiller himself has two favorite sketches: *Bad Musical* and *The Treasures of Morton Kamen*, in which archeologists in the future find the room of an ordinary man named Morton Kamen and his wife Shirley. Laraine Newman plays Tina Gemini, the host of a futuristic television show called *Archeologicus*. She shows pictures and points out relics of the preserved room. When Kamen and his wife Shirley died, the air conditioning was set so high that the two were perfectly preserved. The archeologists came across tuna casseroles, and conclude that they were sacrificial offerings. They found Lacoste shirts with crocodile logos on them, and assume that our civilization revered crocodiles as gods. They also find a "primitive recording device," which turns out to be the Kamens' answering machine. The archeologists conclude that the message and the beep were used to brainwash others into becoming slaves. But the biggest mystery is a pair of rubber S&M underwear hidden in a closet, its tag reading "Sale of this novelty item to minors is forbidden by law"—which really has the archeologists guessing.

The Treasures of Morton Kamen is an example of Schiller's thoughts on how today's society will be looked upon in future. Schiller takes such a common, culturally accepted concept of a shirt with a crocodile on it and tries to perceive it from a completely different angle. Time capsule humor, as it can be called, is one of Schiller's specialties. It's a theme that recurs in many of his other works, such as the short film *The Acid Generation—Where Are They Now?* which looks at hippies from the 1960s and imagines what they will be like when they are eighty years old.

Chapter 4
Saturday Night Shorts

The short film has always played an important part at *Saturday Night Live*. The very first show was a true variety spectacular: comedy sketches, music, the Muppets, the news, fake commercials, stand-up comedy, special appearances by Valri Bromfield and Andy Kaufman, and a short film. The short film definitely added to that sense of variety, but perhaps more importantly, it allowed the show an exception to the limits of live television. While live television is great for spontaneity and a constant sense of excitement, there are certain concepts that cannot be realized within those bounds. As a result, the short film (in addition to the pre-taped fake commercials) provided an opportunity to break away, to not make the show seem confined to the stage. In that regard, it was an important ingredient.

A number of cast and crew members at *Saturday Night* carried a rich background in filmmaking. Cast member George Coe, who was several years older than all the other cast members, had done work for the *National Lampoon Radio Show* and was specifically brought onto *Saturday Night* to play older characters. In 1967, Coe was nominated for a Live Action Short Subject Academy Award for his film *De Düva: The Dove*, a humorous take-off on Ingmar Bergman's *Wild Strawberries*. Coe co-directed and starred in the fifteen-minute film, which so authentically recreated the look and feel of a Bergman film that many people believed that it was actually done by the acclaimed Swedish director himself.[4]

Other crewmembers with a background in film were Gary Weis, who was involved with pre-taped segments early-on and replaced Albert Brooks as the resident filmmaker, and John Head, the *Saturday Night Live* talent scout who also organized a home movie contest for the show. Schiller had known Weis since he was fifteen, and always admired him for the movies he made. In 1973, Weis and Head collaborated with record producer Joe Boyd on the theatrical documentary *Jimi Hendrix*.

Albert Brooks made his name on the stand-up comedy circuits and just finished shooting a supporting part in Martin Scorsese's *Taxi Driver* before the first show in September of 1975. His short films were typical Albert Brooks—

cynical, curmudgeonly, but incredibly funny. Ever the grouch, his films are not misanthropic, but some people might mistake them for it. They revealed his personality in the same way that his later feature films did, by mocking the masses.

His first film, *The Impossible Truth*, is presented in the form of a news magazine in which unusual people are examined. One of the profiles is of a blind New York taxicab driver. The interviewer asks the driver how he became blind and why he still drives. The driver insists that he needs to keep driving—it's his job, and it's better than sitting at home collecting welfare. Another part of *The Impossible Truth* is a press conference for Jerusalem businesses relocating to New Orleans. The end of the film promises future installments, with profiles of a woman who swims twenty-four hours per day and a man who can eat a thousand eggs. *The Impossible Truth* is typical of Albert Brooks' humor, but most of his other *Saturday Night* films were very different. Brooks usually appeared as himself, while in *The Impossible Truth*, Brooks can only be heard as an off-camera interviewer.

For the next week's untitled film, Brooks sits in front of the camera and introduces himself to the audience. He says that the viewers will get to know him through the medium of film, so he wants his viewers to get to know him a little. He tries to show some home movies, but a young girl playing his daughter walks in and bites him. The home movies he finally plays show Brooks as a child growing up in a dysfunctional family. The clips are a good way for the viewers to find out who exactly Albert Brooks is and what his humor is like. Brooks then explains what his viewers can expect from his future films. Essentially, the film is a preview of what's to come in future installments, but Brooks humorously disguises it as a desperate attempt to seek approval from his audience.

Brooks' films were well-received but not everybody at *Saturday Night* was happy with them. He had the out-of-the-mainstream, underground type of humor that appealed to *Saturday Night*'s sophisticated viewers. It was the humor that was typical of the show, and in that regard, his films fit in very well. But the main problem was that Brooks produced his short films in Los Angeles, which did not always mix well with *Saturday Night*'s New York atmosphere.

Another problem with Brooks was that he made one film that was ridiculously long. It aired, upon host Rob Reiner's insistence, as part of *Saturday Night*'s third episode. Aside from The Not Ready for Primetime Players, who were finally given a chance to shine this week, the episode was a disappointment. The show from the week before had a whopping nine musical performances, leaving little room for the cast to prove themselves. This week, there was no musical performance at all. Rob Reiner had an overlong, unfunny monologue that he had written himself, and to add insult to injury, Lorne Michaels had to put on a thirteen-minute short film—about ten minutes too long—to further drag the pacing. Michaels was against it, but Reiner, who in his introduction to the film brings up that Albert Brooks is his best friend, insisted.

That thirteen-minute film, titled *Operation*, had to be split in half with a commercial break. The film itself is very amusing but at this length it obviously did not belong on *Saturday Night*. In the film, Brooks begins by addressing the audience and explaining that he once wanted to become a doctor. He says that to try to reach his boyhood dream, he placed an ad in ten leading newspapers, stating that he would like to perform open-heart surgery. Several weeks later, Brooks' dream becomes reality. Brooks and a team of medical experts perform surgery on an old man who needs the surgery. Brooks says that he did some studying, but he is mostly clueless about what he is supposed to do.

Once surgery starts, Brooks asks where the anesthesiologist is. Since he is the chief surgeon, the other doctors tell him that he was supposed to arrange for it himself. So, they take a break and wait for an anesthesiologist to arrive. With the patient finally under anesthesia, Brooks is ready to begin cutting…but now the surgeons begin arguing. Once that is settled, the surgery starts going along fine, until Brooks brings in the patient's wife and shows her around the surgery room. One of the film's funniest moments occurs when after three hours of surgery, there is an emergency. A dead body is suddenly wheeled out of the room. It is not the patient, but the anesthesiologist who died of a heart attack. Brooks' patient is fine. The surgery was successful, and the film closes with Dr. Albert Brooks thanking the old man for letting him operate on him. *Operation* is a classic Albert Brooks film, but it simply did not belong in the context of a ninety-minute *Saturday Night* show.

In the next film, which has no title, Brooks explains that he is sick and there will be no new short film this week. While Brooks is talking about how sick he is, the doctor calls, recommending him not to do any further films. A delivery boy also drops by, further delaying Brooks' message. The film ends with Brooks coughing away as he is trying to get his message across from his sickbed before his four minutes run out.

After six films, which were spread out over the course of nine shows, Brooks was dropped—an early casualty along with cast member George Coe and Jim Henson's Muppets. Filmmaker Gary Weis, who had already done some film work for the show, supplanted him. Weis' first film aired during the December 20, 1975 show, hosted by Candice Bergen. Meanwhile, Brooks' final short aired during the following live show, on January 10, 1976. Ironically, Brooks' final piece finds him visiting the National Audience Research Institute, where Brooks is examined by researchers to find out what audiences want him to do on television. He opens the film by telling the viewer that this is his last film in the series, but that he may be back with more films. At the end of the film, Brooks is presented with an 822-page report of the research findings, which he promises to read a synopsis of during his vacation. "The next time I see you," he says, "I hope and pray to be more of what *you* want." It was an interesting way to close his short-lived tenure at *Saturday Night*.

Gary Weis' films were more akin to music videos and on-location pre-tapes than short films. Many of them were documentaries about real people. In a way, Weis' films were similar to Albert Brooks' films, but without Brooks' first-person perspective. But not all of Weis' films were documentaries. There were music videos, slow-motion montages and other experiments. Weis' work was avant-garde. It was more stylish and artistic than anything that Brooks produced for the show.

Starting December 20, 1975, there was a new Gary Weis film almost every week. The films were usually untitled. The host would often announce them from the main stage, or a character might announce it at the end of a sketch: "And now, here is this week's film by Gary Weis." It was a regular part of the show, just like *Weekend Update*. What kind of film Weis would make each week was unknown—they were completely different from week to week—but viewers could expect something artful, funny or heartfelt.

Weis' first short film was a touching music video set to Paul Simon's 'Homeward Bound.' Aired shortly before the holidays, it was the last bit of the night and intended as a Christmas wish at the close of the show. The film consists entirely of people on the street and at airports being reunited for the holidays. Weis' next film was not in search of laughs, either. It is a montage of different lounge piano performances, including Ray Charles, performing the same song, 'Play Misty for Me.' All the pianists were recorded at different events and venues, but Weis cleverly edits them together, almost giving the feeling that they were performing together.

In his third film, and his first funny short, Buck Henry takes to the street and tries to find the funniest person in small-town Irvington, New York. The mild-mannered but dependably funny Henry asks random people who the funniest person in town is. Henry then locates the named person, and again asks who he thinks is the funniest person. He goes through a chain of individuals until he ultimately finds the funniest person in town.

In one short, Weis visits the Paramount Novelty Store where the owner, an old lady, dryly explains the workings of the whoopee cushion, black soap, the laugh bag and other popular gags. In another short, Weis visits the apartment of actor/writer Taylor Mead, who talks about his relationship with his cat. Weis made another short with Mead in which the eccentric underground celebrity, again in his messy apartment, discusses television. There were also montages, such as slow motion video footage of sports fanatics set to Ray Charles performing 'New York's My Home.'

The host also regularly played a part in Weis' films. Frequent host Buck Henry appeared in a few films. When Raquel Welch hosted in 1976, Weis made a film of her dancing. That same year, Elliott Gould visited a school where he sings and dances with young children. When acting legend Broderick Crawford hosted, Weis made a film with him in which they revisited the neighborhood where Crawford grew up. Perhaps his most popular short, *The Rutles* starred Eric Idle as a member of a popular British musical group. The film spoofed the early black-and-white television performances of The Beatles, as well as the playful montages in which the Fab Four engaged in all kinds of tomfoolery—running around fields, appearing from behind trees and the like. *The Rutles* short was so popular that it was turned into a television special for NBC, which Lorne Michaels produced and Weis again directed.

Aside from Weis, the most active filmmaker at *Saturday Night Live* was Walter Williams. In its first season, *Saturday Night* had organized a home movie contest administered by John Head, who also was a talent scout for the show. *Saturday Night* invited viewers to send in home movies of approximately two minutes in length on 8mm or 16mm stock. The contest was won by *The Mr. Bill Show*, a film about a yellow-haired Play-Doh doll named Mr. Bill. In the film, a spoof of classic claymation television like *Davey and Goliath*, the high-pitched Mr. Bill is tormented by Mr. Hands—a human hand. Part of the joke is that the film is not animated in any way. Mr. Bill never moves, unless it is by Mr. Hands' action. New Orleans native Williams made the film with his Super8 camera for less than twenty dollars.

The Mr. Bill Show garnered such a positive reaction that it became a recurring bit, running regularly until 1981. The ultra-cheap shorts put Mr. Bill in a variety of perils at the mercy of Mr. Hands, including being catapulted into a wall, squashed by shoes on a sidewalk, going up in flames, and thrown across the Rockefeller Center hallway after spinning in the revolving door. Essentially, the same joke was repeated film after film, adding Mr. Bill's similarly-mutilated best friend Spot the yellow dog and the evil Sluggo to the cast of characters. Each time he or his claynine friend was hurt, Mr. Bill screamed out a high-pitched 'Ohh Nooo!' in pain.

'Ohh Nooo!' became a catchphrase and the Mr. Bill film series spawned a *New York Times* number one bestselling book, numerous video compilations and in 1998 a short-lived children's television program. The Mr. Bill shorts were very juvenile compared to the rest of the show. Williams was wise to turn the character into a children's program in the 1990s. While it might have been considered daring for its suggestive violence at the time—tearing the limbs off a human being is much different from doing that to a claymation character—it is now considered tame and appropriate for all ages.[5]

As part of the home movie contest, *Saturday Night* showcased several other short films. Harry McDevitt's *The Apple Follies*, is an inexpensive stop-motion animated film starring apples. At the end of the film, the director sits down and eats the stars of his film. In Phil Van De Carr's *P-Nut Fever*, stop-motion animated peanuts seek to exact revenge on a peanut-eater. John Brister made another stop-motion peanut flick, *Spanish Peanuts*, which at least looked a bit more professional. Another contest submission was Howard Grunwald's *A Home Movie*, which was literally a home movie. Following a long list of opening credits, all the film consists of is a single shot of a house. The best broadcasted entry in the contest was directed by high school student David Massar. It was the only aired entry that did not rely on a simple gag or bad stop-motion animation. In the untitled film, random strangers enter a public restroom and sing together as they stand in front of the urinals. It was a slick, smart and funny film, and Massar went on to become a television producer and director.

While short films directed by amateurs were being shown, Tom Schiller's filmmaking abilities had to wait by the sidelines. Michaels had originally intimated that Schiller could do short films as well, and he finally delivered at the start of the third season.

"Films were his first love," says Lorne Michaels. "He's enormously creative, obviously, but at the time, Gary Weis was making short films."

"I think I was always angling to do it," Schiller says. "I always kept saying, 'I want to be a filmmaker.'" In 1977, Michaels asked Schiller to make one-minute conceptual films, although only the very first film would have a running time of one minute.

"I just wanted an outlet for Tom," Michaels recalls, not wanting to pressure Schiller into just writing. "When your dad does that, there's a greater burden on it.

"It was just a sort of natural outlet because Gary didn't work with the cast, whereas Tom really knew the cast," Michaels adds. "Gary knew them as well, but Tom had been much more involved in the actual creation of the show every week. So when he was going to work with Gilda, he designed a film for Gilda. When he was going to work with John, he designed a film for John. And the same for Bill Murray." Plus, Weis was beginning to move on. He already directed the summer special *Things We Did Last Summer* (an hour-long special of filmed bits that showed what the *Saturday Night Live* cast did over the summer break) and would soon start work on *The Rutles* with Eric Idle.

Schiller's films were not officially meant to replace those made by Weis, but they eventually did. Schiller was anxious to make films again, and this was the first time he would make them professionally and get paid for it. With a small budget and creative freedom, Schiller made seventeen intentionally rough-looking but stylish short subjects over the next three seasons—each labeled *Schiller's Reel.*

Chapter 5
Schiller's Reel

The *Schiller's Reels* are real short films. As opposed to Gary Weis's shorts, Schiller's films have a genuine cinematic feel to them. It is easier to see the craft that went into making them. "I like to craft my films like miniature movies," Schiller says. "Gary Weis' were more casual."

Sometimes Schiller came up with a great idea in the morning and executed it the very same day. Often it was just him, a cameraman and a sound person. Later, John Belushi's friend Laila Nabulsi was added to the small crew as a production assistant.

"Do you have an assistant?" Belushi asked before he and Schiller started work on *Don't Look Back in Anger*.

"No," Schiller answered. Whenever he went to shoot something, he had a cameraman and sometimes a sound person if he couldn't do it himself. But other than that, he did almost everything himself.

"Well, now you do," Belushi forcefully replied, pushing Laila Nabulsi towards him. From that point on, Nabulsi became Schiller's associate, although she quickly took on the duties of a producer.

Laila Nabulsi, a young aspiring actress, was a close friend of Belushi and his wife. They knew each other since the *National Lampoon* days and Nabulsi began hanging out with the *Saturday Night Live* crowd as well. "She was kind of around on the scene at that time," Schiller recalls. "She was a friendly person— sociable, nice. She was always around the show and around John Belushi."

"Everything I learned, I learned from Tom," says Nabulsi, who years later became a movie producer. "It was like going to film school with Tom as my teacher. Tom was just a natural. He knew what he was doing all the time—it was so great to work with him."

"She was a valuable asset," Schiller recalls. "With her charm on the street she could get people to sign a release form, which was always important. And I'm always grateful to her for her collaboration."

Schiller wrote down all kinds of ideas he had, and would go over them with Nabulsi and as many other people as possible in order to decide which to execute. Schiller kept a big book of ideas and asked almost anybody—ranging from friends to taxi drivers—if they liked his ideas. A *Schiller's Reel* shoot was often just a fun day on the town, and some of them Schiller shot while he was on vacation. He usually shot on 16mm film—sometimes color, sometimes black-and-white—though on a number of the films he used 8mm.

Some of Schiller's shorts were laugh-out-loud funny while others were amusing and cute. He got off to a great start with one of his funniest.

The first *Schiller's Reel* was the one-minute documentary *The Acid Generation- Where are they Now?* In the film, Schiller answers a question that was prob-

Schiller's Reel	Airdate	Host
The Acid Generation – Where Are They Now?	October 8, 1977	Madeline Kahn
Life After Death	November 19, 1977	Buck Henry
Don't Look Back In Anger	March 11, 1978	Art Garfunkel
La Dolce Gilda	April 15, 1978	Michael Sarrazin
Sushi By the Pool	October 8, 1978	The Rolling Stones
Arrivederci Roman	November 18, 1978	Carrie Fisher
Picasso, the New York Years	February 17, 1979	Ricky Nelson
Perchance To Dream	March 10, 1979	Gary Busey
Clones Exist Now!	May 26, 1979	Buck Henry
Java Junkie	December 22, 1979	Ted Knight
Linden Palmer: Hollywood's Forgotten Director	February 9, 1980	Chevy Chase
Mask of Fear	February 23, 1980	Kirk Douglas
Art is Ficial	November 7, 1981	Lauren Hutton

Unaired	Production Year
Saturday Night In London	1977
Bar Mitzvah 5000	1977
Henry Miller On Television	1977
Search For Alaska	1980

All films ©Schillervision

ably on many people's mind during the sixties: What will happen to the acid generation? Is it a phase that they grow out of, or will they go on like this—protesting, tripping, not working—forever? By the seventies, most of them had already conformed to conventional lifestyles. But how will they look back on it? In *The Acid Generation*, Schiller gives his own humorous take on what they will be like when they have grown old. He superimposes two elements to create his own take on it.

While running archive footage of the flower children in the sixties—protests, concerts and peace gatherings—a professional-sounding voice-over reads: "The sixties; a time of change, love-ins, and head trips. The sixties meant peace marches, LSD, Dylan and Woodstock; the hippies who dropped acid—and dropped out. But where are they now, the survivors of the sixties? Where are their heads at, and just how much do they remember today?" The music ends and the first interviewee is introduced– a woman in her seventies or eighties with a strong German accent. "The sixties were beautiful," she says. "I tripped every day. I was high for about three years."

Another former flower child, identified as Captain Acid in the subtitle, adds: "You just can't get good acid these days." All of the people interviewed are senior citizens, and the film includes footage of them sitting and walking around at a rest home and basking in the sun.

"I wrote lines on a piece of cardboard and went to a Senior Citizens area in Venice, California," says Schiller, who made the film during a break. "I gave them twenty-five dollars to read off the cards." The result is very comical, and somewhat foreshadows a theme that Schiller would explore often in his films: Aging and the passage of time.

The Acid Generation marks the first time Schiller plays with time, a concept that Schiller revisits many times in his later short films as well as his feature film *Nothing Lasts Forever*. The film looks like it is set in the 1970s, but many former hippies won't be eighty until around 2020 or 2030.

Additionally, many of his short films start out with a voice-over or text introduction. The openings are often slightly disguised as serious documentaries. In this first *Schiller's Reel*, the punch line comes very quickly, but for other shorts the joke is not revealed until the very end.

Schiller considers *The Acid Generation* to be among his best. Part of the reason that it works well is because it's so short and to-the-point. The film could have easily lasted up to three minutes, but then it would have run the risk of going stale quickly due to the lack of a plot or storyline. *The Acid Generation* is as concise as it can be and packs as many laughs as possible into a little over one minute. The concept is quickly introduced and the punch line is delivered immediately thereafter.

With one of the old men who appears in the film, it is all too obvious that he is reading something from a piece of cardboard in front of him. Whether intentional or unintentionally included in the film, the idea that Schiller reveals how he made the film adds to the humor in the same way that intentional shoddiness added to the humor of Walter Williams' *Mr. Bill* shorts. Sometimes, giving away a bit of the filmmaking process can add an additional layer of comedy.

The film closes with the narrator concluding the film with typical rest home piano music playing in the background and a shot of two seniors holding up their hands and making the 'peace' sign. The narrator explains that even though the acid generation has gotten a little older, "most of them still have their heads in a beautiful, beautiful place."

The idea behind the film is typical of the visionary Schiller. Listening to septuagenarians and octogenarians discuss their drugs habits from when they were in their twenties is hilarious, but maybe it's something we'll actually witness twenty or thirty years from now when that generation really does hit the rest homes.

Similar in its foresight is Schiller's second *Schiller's Reel*. *Life After Death*, subtitled *A Report from the Other Side*, first aired in November of 1977 and was rerun during another live show two years later. Once again a documentary in disguise, the film takes a humorous, straight-forward approach to a question on everyone's mind: What happens when we die? It happens to everybody, yet nobody really knows the answer. Schiller adds to that question by asking more about the process. Do we have

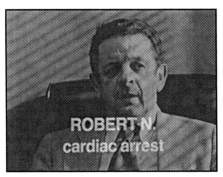

©Schillervision

to wait in line? Do we have to take a number like we have to do at the grocery store? Is there a waiting room?

A drab voice-over reads the opening crawl while Tomaso Albinoni's funeral favorite 'Adagio' plays on an organ in the background. The narrator introduces death as the unanswerable question, the great enigma. He then describes how people who were declared clinically dead have returned with matching stories of what happened to them on 'the other side.' Three survivors tell of their specific experiences.

The two-minute film plays it straight until it's halfway in. The first survivor is Robert N., who talks about what happened to him when he had a heart attack. He describes hearing his doctors proclaim him as dead. He then talks about how wonderful he felt and how he found himself in a big white room where he had to take a number. The punch line was accompanied by a big laugh during the show.

The second piece of witness testimony comes from Mort S., who died of parasitic infestation. He remembers his body rising up like an elevator and being led into an area where he had to take a number and sit down. The third survivor is Suki L., a drowning victim, who also convincingly recounts her journey into the afterlife and having to take a number and sit down.

The idea of having to take a number upon dying is amusing in itself, but when presented as dry as in *Life After Death*, it becomes even funnier. The funniest bit comes at the conclusion, when a big sign saying 'NOW SERVING' is shown, with an old-fashioned counter clicking from the number 32 over to 33.

Life After Death is better executed than *The Acid Generation*. According to the opening narration, death is a great enigma, so the use of black-and-white stock adds to the mysterious mood. *Life After Death* also makes use of better actors. The acting is more convincing and it's clear that the three witnesses were not reading their lines from a piece of cardboard. They even use body language to communicate what happened to them on their journey. The actors in the film had no experience, with the exception of Suki L. Suki was in fact Suki Love, a friend of John Head. Mort S. and Robert N. were acquaintances of Schiller's.

Even though they weren't professional actors, they are very convincing and articulate and much better at saying their lines than the retirement home dwellers of *The Acid Generation.*

Tom Schiller claims that his comedy rarely deals with death, but perhaps in his subconscious, it does figure into his work. *Life After Death* is the first such example, and quite blatantly so. But more importantly, *Life After Death* is an example of Schiller's way of looking at things. Death is something everybody has to deal with, and many people obsess about what happens to us in the afterlife, if there is such a thing. Schiller's way of presenting death is essentially as a human process. It is not something that happens magically, but needs some form of administration. The process has been depicted in films and cartoons many times—heaven as a beautiful floating cloud in the sky with a big golden gate, and hell as the dark underworld with sputtering pools of magma. The descriptions of death in *Life After Death* don't get that far—the witnesses only reach the purgatory that is the waiting room.

Sushi by the Pool stars Desi Arnaz Jr., Carrie Fisher, Hal Holbrook and the late Steven Keats. In the film, a group of young Hollywood stars and managers sit beside a pool in the Hollywood Hills while several earthquakes occur. There are numerous conversations going on at the same time, and a little can be heard from each one

©Schillervision

throughout the film—much like in a Robert Altman movie. It's very tough to follow any of the conversations aside from the main conversation, though occasionally a vague line like 'Don't go into the Jacuzzi, it's not at the right temperature' or 'Aykroyd's name came up' will stand out. The Altman trick is very effective, although Schiller claims that it was unintentional. He blames it on bad soundmixing.

The main conversation is between a young actor who is relatively new to the business, played by Desi Arnaz Jr., and a slightly older man who has been in the business much longer, played by actor Steven Keats (*Death Wish, Hester Street*). Keats gives all kinds of advice and speaks as if he knows everything about the way Hollywood works. He is trying to get Arnaz interested in a script. Arnaz tries to listen but is the only one at the party who seems to be disturbed by the earthquake. With the first tremor, everybody pauses their conversation and look up to see what's going on, but quickly resume their conversations as if nothing has happened. Keats tells Arnaz that it's nothing to worry about.

Sushi by the Pool lampoons the way business is conducted between actors and managers and producers. Arnaz is the innocent outsider—he doesn't even know what sushi is. He is relatively new to the scene with only television guest appearances under his belt. Steven Keats tries to convince him to take the acting job while dropping names like Nicholson and Redford, but Arnaz says that his manager advised him against it. Carrie Fisher, who frequently hung out with the *Saturday Night Live* cast, plays Desi Arnaz Jr.'s opposite. She is a starlet sitting by the pool who appears to be completely under Keats' spell.

Arnaz enthusiastically reads off his track record: "I did a *Love Boat, M*A*S*H, Rockford, Donnie and Marie, Big Event…*" Another tremor begins to rumble, and Arnaz becomes a bit nervous while continuing down his list of credits. "…*Starsky & Hutch,* two *Spider-Man* and *A Woman Called Moses.*" Finally, the biggest earthquake hits and the camera starts shaking while actor Hal Holbrook runs down the hill behind a Hollywood mansion screaming "Earthquake! Run! Get out of here!"

Chaos ensues, champagne glasses tumble over, starlets jump into the pool, but Keats keeps going after Arnaz for the part. "If it's points you want, you've got 'em!" he screams over the loud rumbles. The film then cuts to after the earthquake. It ends on a shot of the pool with a lawn chair sunk to the bottom and at least a dozen *Variety* newspapers floating at the surface.

Chevy Chase was originally supposed to appear in the film and run down the hill, but he flunked out at the last moment. The house belonged to a producer friend of Schiller's, so the producer called his friend Hal Holbrook as a last-minute replacement. Holbrook was more than happy to appear in the film, even though running down the steep hill was very dangerous. After Holbrook ran down the hill, Schiller cautiously asked him to do it again, this time for the close-up. To Schiller's surprise, Holbrook happily obliged. After it was over, he told Schiller that the set had a good vibe.

In reality, Arnaz, then twenty-five, already had a lot of experience in Hollywood at that time. It's true that he'd been on *The Love Boat*, but he had also headlined a number of movies. And, of course, he was raised in Hollywood. His parents were Lucille Ball and Desi Arnaz, and he was a regular on *The Lucy Show* as a teenager.

When the big earthquake starts and Hal Holbrook starts running and screaming down the hill, Arnaz is the only one that seems to take notice. He is playing the clean-cut newcomer who has not yet adapted to all of the conceited customs of Hollywood. The film pokes fun at Hollywood actors, and it wouldn't be the last time that Schiller made light of some form of pretentiousness or snobbishness.

Schiller was obviously a child of Hollywood, so he witnessed many pool parties where all everyone talks about is themselves or the film business, rather than the art of acting or filmmaking. He had known Desi Arnaz Jr. for years, dating back to the fifties and sixties when their parents worked together.

Sushi by the Pool was another film that Schiller shot in one day when they were in Los Angeles, so it was a fun day by the pool where he and Laila Nabulsi invited a number of their friends to be extras—among them singer Libby Titus. "The best thing about *Sushi by the Pool* was that we got Hal Holbrook to run down the mountain screaming that there's an earthquake," says Schiller.

While Tom Schiller's short films were well-received at the show, they weren't nearly as popular as Walter Williams' films. Williams' Mr. Bill was a nationwide sensation. Whenever Schiller met people and told them that he made short films for *Saturday Night Live*, they would repeat the catchphrase 'Ohh Nooo!' in the squeaky Mr. Bill voice, assuming that Schiller made the Mr. Bill shorts. It was an awkward situation and Schiller repeatedly had to explain that that was a different filmmaker. Although they were good friends, Schiller was envious of Mr. Bill's popularity and the two had a friendly competition going.

After Schiller had made a number of short films for the show, Lorne Michaels became fully trusting that Schiller would deliver the goods each time. He no longer required them to be pre-viewed in advance of the dress rehearsal. "Tom would make his films and I would see them," Michaels recalls. "The early ones I saw a lot of, but by the middle of 78-79, I would see them at dress rehearsal. And I was perfectly happy with that relationship. They weren't judged on whether they were popular. They were only judged on whether they were good."

Shot on Super 8 while vacationing in Rome, Schiller's next film *Arrivederci Roman* is a fake home movie taken by an elderly American couple on vacation in Rome. It makes fun of the boring home movies and slide shows back before video cameras were popular. Whenever an Aunt and Uncle returned from vacation, they would run the projector and show everything from their trip. Because

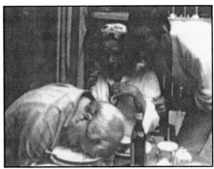

©Schillervision

there was no sound, they narrated everything that was projected onto the screen. Of course, the films were amateurishly made and sometimes they'd film the most boring things, like shopping. *Arrivederci Roman* is such a film, but thankfully, it runs less than two minutes and it's funny.

Schiller was traveling in Rome and met up with a friend who was there as well. He got the idea to do a short film for the show with the Super 8 camera that he brought along almost anywhere, so his friend found two older Americans. They drove around the city and shot everything in one day.

The elderly couple is played by Mary Harding and Eugene Walter, American expatriates who had appeared in numerous Federico Fellini films. Whenever Fellini needed Americans in his films, Harding and Walter were among the ones he frequently called up. Walter also translated hundreds of Italian screenplays into English for directors like Fellini and Franco Zeffirelli. If you watch a Fellini or Zeffirelli film, you're probably reading the subtitles that Eugene Walter wrote.

The film is excitedly narrated by the wife as she shows it to some friends at home. She talks about their visit to the Roman Coliseum and about how her husband Roman could not get the camera to work to take a picture. They meet the sly Tony, an archetypical Latin Lover, who takes a photograph of them and then spends the rest of the vacation with them.

Poor Roman has to carry all the bags of expensive clothes that his wife buys, and has to sit by as Tony can't keep his hands off of her. While eating spaghetti at a restaurant, Roman suddenly passes out and his face falls right into his bowl of angel-hair pasta. His wife almost begins to cry in the narration and explains that this is when Roman had his heart attack. He is rushed to a hospital and dies at 5:45 Roman Time. Subsequently, Roman's wife and Tony run off together and get married. The honeymoon was covered by Roman's insurance. "I'm sure he would have understood," she says to close the film. "Arrivederci Roman, wherever you are! And thanks."

The film also makes fun of the American tourist and their way of looking at other cultures. Harding's obnoxious narration is amusing but the biggest laugh comes when Roman dies during dinner. As with many of Schiller's short films, the punch line again comes at the end. The other similarity to Schiller's other works, most notably his commercials, is that he takes a form of filmmaking—in this case the home movie, and convincingly recreates it in order to make fun of its conventions. In the case of *Arrivederci Roman*, it's the shaky, amateurish camerawork and the obnoxious voice-over.

Schiller then directed and starred in the fake documentary *Picasso—The New York Years*. Schiller plays a reporter who visits some of the trivial locations that Pablo Picasso visited during the nine years (1933-1942) he spent in the Lower East Side of New York City. *Picasso* is yet another example of Tom Schiller puttering with the concept of time. Some of the people he interviewed in this piece were probably not even born in 1942. Moreover, Picasso never lived in New York.

Picasso—The New York Years was a one-day shoot. Tom Schiller and Laila Nabulsi had a cameraperson around and tried to think of something that they could film. Schiller had the *Picasso* concept written down in his list of ideas and decided in the morning that they were going to do it. It was executed that very same day in the Village and the Lower East Side. "We spent like a day just going around places, making it up," Nabulsi recalls.

Schiller hosts the documentary himself and in his opening bit explains that Picasso spent most of his life in France. But what most people don't know, he says, is that Picasso spent nine years living and painting in New York.

©Schillervision

Schiller makes his first stop at Weitzman's Delicatessen, a typical New York Deli which Schiller describes as "a gathering place for artists and writers." An old man behind the counter remembers Picasso's favorite—the triple-decker sandwich special. The next stop is Atlas Barber School where Picasso had attempted to make a career change. Inside, Schiller interviews an old man sitting by the door, who explains why Picasso's ambitions to become a barber didn't work out: He was too artistic. Schiller then asks the old man to point out Picasso in a group picture that hangs on the wall. The man points at a random face in the crowd and says that that was Picasso. Additionally, a bartender at Pat's Bar remembers that Picasso always came in with a couple of women and that his beverage of choice was the Screwdriver. Finally, two butchers explain just how much Picasso loved their veal.

Of course, none of these recollections are real. Schiller told random people to say the lines or to play along, and Laila Nabulsi asked them to sign a release. "You give 'em some money and they sign a release," Schiller says. "People love doing that, especially in New York. They're talkative and they're actors anyway."

Schiller closes the film in front of a large sculpture outside Washington Square Village. He explains that Picasso left the giant sculpture, which he dubbed 'Gotham Gal with Legs,' as a symbol of his love for New York when he left in 1942.

Clones Exist Now! is a short documentary in the vein of *The Acid Generation* and *Picasso—The New York Years*. Combining two trademark Schiller tricks—using generic stock footage and asking random people on the street to read a few lines—it offers the premise that scientists have been able to clone humans since the 1930s, and that now clones can be found all over America.

The film begins with a close-up of a newborn baby, with Schiller providing the voice-over and explaining that this child is a clone. He then makes the claim that clones have existed since the 1930s. In 1932, a Danish scientist named Hans Heiser was able to clone meat cell tissues. Schiller illustrates this by showing black-and-white clips of his early short *The Enigma of Dr. Schiller*, in which a mad scientist is seen doing scientific experiments with a hot dog.

©Schillervision

Schiller next shows an old clip of the so-called Bevelman twins, experimental Swiss clones. But further experiments did not take place because the twins had respiratory problems. Thirty-five years later, an American scientist has figured out how to clone humans and has a number of celebrity clones that are available for sale. A family with a new-born child is interviewed and enthusiastically reveals that their new baby is a clone of the late French composer Maurice Ravel. "We had always wanted a musician in the family," the mother says, "and we thought this was a fine opportunity."

The film then moves to a clone playground where parents take their clones to interact. A number of the parents are interviewed—one mother even says that whenever she travels, she just puts her clone in her luggage. Again, Schiller took his camera out on the streets and gave people some money to read lines, while Laila Nabulsi followed him with the release forms.

Clones Exist Now! is one of several films in which Schiller uses archival footage and pretends that it is something else. Here Schiller takes old footage of two young girls performing synchronized acrobatic tricks next to a swimming pool and claims that they are experimental clones from Switzerland.

The film also makes an obscure reference to Maurice Ravel. Even though Ravel is a well-known French composer, most *Saturday Night Live* viewers are not likely to know of him.

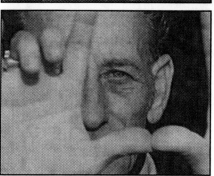

Linda Palmer, Director
Career Highlights
1934 - *A Dime a Dozen*
1936 - *Swingin' Squadron*
1939 - *Let's Make Money!*
1942 - *Spanish Venus*
1949 - *Tic Tac Toes*
1950 - *Whistling Legs*
1951 - *The Big Tango* (unreleased)
1952 - *Senorita Cadillac*
1952 - *Bells of Obscurity*
1957 - *Wiki-Wiki Hi Jinks* (uncredited)

©Schillervision

In terms of its use of a combination of signature Schiller tricks, his next film is similar to *Clones Exist Now!* The three-and-a-half minute documentary *Linden Palmer-Hollywood's Forgotten Director* aired in February of 1980 when Chevy Chase returned to host the show that had made him a superstar. The film catches up with Linden Palmer, a once-successful filmmaker whose legacy has now been almost completely forgotten. Once he was a highly respected, acclaimed director, but now nobody recognizes him anymore. The film includes interviews with Palmer walking through a park while he reflects on his directing career—sometimes using his hands to form a window, as directors sometimes do when they are trying to visualize a shot.

"I was driving around with a camera crew one day after shooting something," Schiller recalls, "and I spotted this guy in a distinctive style of jacket and I thought 'That guy really looks like he used to be a Hollywood director.'" Schiller went up to the man and asked him if he wanted to be in his short film. The old man was flattered, and Schiller had him say a number of lines while he shot him walking around in Battery Park. He was not really a former director—just someone who looked like one. The old man's real name, Linden Palmer, even sounded like that of a director, so Schiller used it. As it turned out, Palmer was a retired Merchant Marine but had also worked as a prop man on films when he was younger.

The film begins with a gentle voice-over bringing up the concept of fame and how the once-famous fall into obscurity and are no longer recognized in public like they were before. The narrator then introduces Linden Palmer, one such man who was once a highly sought-after director but now has faded into obscurity.

Palmer mentions how he misses the many actors he has met and locations he has visited, and the film begins to cover his many so-called successes starting with musicals in the 1930s and early 1940s. Clips from these fictional films, such as *Swingin' Squadron*, *A Dime a Dozen* and *Let's Make Money* are shown. Schiller uses generic stock footage from terrible public domain films that look like low-rent knock-offs of *Gold Diggers* or Busby Berkeley musicals of that period and claims that they were classic films directed by Palmer.

Palmer next discusses working with Marilyn Monroe and Charles Chaplin. The voice-over claims that Palmer directed the young Monroe in her first screen role. Two random film clips are shown, and the narrator points out which characters in the clips are Marilyn. They barely resemble her. Then, Chaplin starred as a flamenco dancer in Palmer's 1951 film *The Big Tango*, but the picture was blacklisted and never released—prophetic, considering Schiller's sole feature film, which he directed three years later, would end up unreleased as well. The actor seen in *The Big Tango* is clearly not Chaplin.

A year later, Palmer adapted Arthur Miller's non-existent play *Bells of Obscurity*—a title that certainly rings true for Linden Palmer. The stock footage used to represent the film seems to be an old advertising film for bonds or insurance policies. A clip from the film, which the voice-over describes as "a sophisticated examination of small-town morals" with "brash language [that] shocked moviegoers in 1952" has some terrible, hackneyed acting—just like most educational, industrial and advertising films of the 1950s.

It wasn't until several years later that Palmer made what could have been his big comeback—a musical comedy for Disney starring Mouseketeers Frankie Avalon and Annette Funicello as teenagers confronting maturity in Hawaii. In a *double entendre* that must have slipped past the NBC censors, the voice-over adds that Palmer was fired by Disney for refusing "to use animals in a certain sequence." The 1957 film, entitled *Wiki-Wiki Hi Jinks*, would be his last.

Palmer then gives some generic, worthless advice to up-and-coming directors: Watch the old directors, make sure your actors know their lines, and that you are ready to shoot when you get up before the camera. The film closes with some clever words from the narrator: "Old directors never die. They just dissolve, and fade out."

Linden Palmer—Hollywood's Forgotten Director is notable for its creative use of stock footage, but it's also an examination of fame and what happens once it passes. It suggests that people who are famous are almost like an elite, higher being. But when their time in the limelight is up, they slip into obscurity. In fact, they become like everybody else who has never experienced fame in the first place. The narration suggests, much like the general consensus on the idea of being famous, that life after fame is a shameful existence. The formerly famous are labeled as *has-beens* or *washed-up*. The closing of the film mockingly treats Palmer as someone who was once great, but no longer is, even though he's still the same person.

The concept behind *Linden Palmer—Hollywood's Forgotten Director* is brilliant, and Schiller communicates it well. Arguably, a weak spot in the film is Linden Palmer's way of communicating. He has the look of an old film director—especially the manner in which he wanders the park—but he simply does not talk like one. His voice seems too insecure and not forceful enough for a Hollywood director. Hollywood directors are generally individuals who know exactly what they want, or at least lead their crews to believe so. Palmer speaks slowly, unsure of what he will say next. He also isn't very articulate, which directors generally need to be in order to effectively communicate their ideas. However, this might be due to the fact that there was no script used in making this film.

Nevertheless, the fact that the film is a joke should not be overlooked. Its intention is not necessarily to convince the viewers that Palmer was a real director. Despite the incredibly bad film clips and faux shots of famous movie stars, the film is reasonably convincing and likely to fly over the heads of some *Saturday Night Live* viewers.

Mask of Fear also ran in February of 1980, during the show hosted by Kirk Douglas.[6] The film accurately recreates a typical 1950s black-and-white crime drama. It is one of Schiller's slickest-looking short films and a prime example of Schiller's ability to emulate classic filmmaking styles.

For *Mask of Fear*, Schiller had the help of cinematographer Frederick Elmes (*Eraserhead, Blue Velvet, The Hulk*), which might explain its aesthetic superiority.[7]

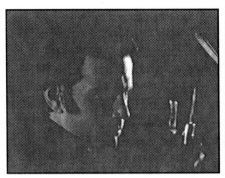

©Schillervision

Mask of Fear was also a much bigger production than most of Schiller's other short films. The film looks a lot like a theatrical motion picture, unlike most of Schiller's other films which tend to have a rough, almost homemade look.

In the film, a middle-aged couple in a suburban neighborhood ready themselves for the night. The wife is played by Joan Hackett and the husband is played by Jack Garner.[8] Unbeknownst to husband-and-wife, a pair of thugs drive up in front of their house to rob them—or so it appears. The thug duo, played by actors John Brent and Chris Rubin, patiently wait in their car, one of them smoking cigarette after cigarette. As they are waiting for the right time to strike, the tension builds and the cigarette smoke makes for quite an atmosphere. At 1:50 am, the thugs put on black ski-masks, take out a knife and leave their car. They force entry through the back door of the house.

The couple wakes up as they hear the thugs' footsteps outside their bedroom door. As Garner opens the door to reveal the ski-masked thugs pointing a gun at them, Hackett screams with fear. They are both pushed against the wall. Up until this moment, the film has been an authentic-looking thriller without a single joke. The total time to build up to this moment is two minutes, a very long time for television comedy.

Finally, one of the thugs bluntly explains why they have come. "You're going...skiing." Stock footage from the 1940s and 50s of people skiing follows, accompanied by a happy melody. The film has taken a sharp turn, building itself up as a straight thriller but ending as a sophomoric gag. "It's just a pure one-joke film," Schiller admits.

The film is another example of Schiller's creative use of stock footage. *Mask of Fear* is unique, however, in that it is one of Schiller's few films that builds up almost to the end and has a single punch line conclusion. Furthermore, the lighting and use of shadows are more effective than in any other *Schiller's Reel*. Of all the *Schiller's Reels* of the classic era, 1975 to 1980, *Mask of Fear* is the most atmospheric and alongside *Java Junkie* the most stylish. Aside from the gag ending, the film is very dark. The fact that it's set at night adds to the overall feel of the film, as does the use of black-and-white film stock. It has the visual qualities of a *film noir*, which would not have translated as well in color.

A few of the short films that Schiller made between 1977 and 1980 did not air—either because Lorne Michaels cut them out of the show before air time or Schiller did not like them himself. *Bar Mitzvah 5000*, which had nothing to do with the year 5000, was "a very corny depiction of a friend's bar mitzvah that was just done as an impromptu thing," according to Schiller. The film went behind the scenes at the Jewish event, looking at all the preparations that had to be made. At that time, NBC and *Saturday Night Live* didn't want to run sketches, commercials or films that could be perceived as derisive towards Jews. The film didn't even make it to the dress rehearsal, but still made a nice gift for the family that appeared in the film.

Henry Miller on Television had Schiller's good friend talking about how much he hates television, with one exception: Jack Paar. Even though it's a funny concept, Schiller doesn't consider this to be one of his better works. It's also not a typical Schiller film—it's more like something Gary Weis would have done. A year earlier, Weis had made a similar short film in which poet/actor Taylor Mead similarly shared his thoughts on television. Sadly, *Henry Miller on Television* is presumably a lost film.

Saturday Night in London was taped while Schiller was vacationing in London. He took a camera and an NBC microphone to the streets and asked Brits what they thought about *Saturday Night Live*. Of course, *Saturday Night Live* didn't air in England—not then, and not now. Schiller made the film in 1977, and while Chevy Chase, Gilda Radner, Dan Aykroyd, John Belushi and company were already stars in the United States, they had not yet appeared in any big movies that had carried over to the rest of the world. In Great Britain, as well as any other country aside from the United States, they were unknowns.

Schiller's trick? With some of the people, Schiller asked them to repeat specific lines. With others, he asked them what they thought of *Monty Python*. Then when he returned to New York, he dubbed over his questions so it seemed like he was asking them about *Saturday Night Live*. Watching prude old British ladies in particular talk about the show is a hoot.

©Schillervision

One traditionally-clothed security guard at Buckingham Palace even talks about how magnificent the Muppets were, even though they had already left the show the year before. It's surprising that the guard was willing to talk. Schiller also tried to interview a silent guard on horseback. While holding his microphone up, the silent guard struck Schiller's hand. The guard hit very hard, and Schiller was frightened by it. The scene obviously did not make it into the final cut of the film.

Another interviewee really gets into it, hilariously delivering the line "The *Saturday Night* show is the only thing that has given me nothing...and made it stick." Other interviewees speak specifically about the cast members: Teenagers talk about how sexy Laraine Newman is; one man says that Aykroyd is a brilliant actor; bobbies mention that their favorite cast member is Gilda—or as they say it, *Gilder*; and a group of kids sitting on a ledge say that they love Billy Murray. One lady says they are all great...but adds that she is certain that they are all gay.

Saturday Night in London manages to pack a lot of jokes into just one minute, but it's not at all like Schiller's other movies. Like *Henry Miller on Television*, it's the type of film that was more likely to have come from Gary Weis, since Schiller's films were more like miniature movies. For whatever reason, *Saturday Night in London* never aired. But it must have gotten a big laugh from the cast when they saw it.

Finally, *Search for Âkâsa* is an old-fashioned serial with a look and story line similar to Frank Capra's *Lost Horizon*. Credited as Tex Ritter in the opening titles, Schiller stars as Tex Carter, an Indiana Jones-like adventurer in search of Âkâsa (pronounced *Akasha*), the eternal record of time, in Katmandu in 1947. Of course, *Search for Âkâsa* was made before *Raiders of the Lost Ark*.

In order to find it, Tex Carter visits a place called Boris Restaurant & Bar, where he and owner Boris drink vodka before getting down to business. Boris warns him not to proceed any further in his journey. "It's very dangerous," Boris explains in a strong accent. "Even Hitler had sent an expedition in the late thirties. And what's happened to him? The son of a bitch is dead."

Tex Carter believes that Boris is hiding information from him, and forcefully demands the texts that might reveal the location of Âkâsa. Boris angrily replies that he won't find them, and the film ends there. It promises a follow-up of Tex Carter's

©Schillervision

further adventures in his search for Âkâsa next week, although Schiller never intended for multiple episodes. He merely pretended that it was part of a serial.

Schiller shot the film in Nepal, where he was visiting his brother. Boris was a real person—Boris Lissanovitch—who lived there, and his Bar & Restaurant was the actual location they used. Tex Carter is an interesting creation—both a precursor to Indiana Jones and a call back to the classic adventure serials of the past. He always wears his big white hat slanted so that you never get a clear look at his face, and also wears sunglasses. When Carter sits down at the table with Boris, Boris asks him why he doesn't take his hat off, but Carter says he'd rather keep it on. Schiller normally has the look of a funny person and generally does not look like a slick leading man. Nevertheless, in *Search for Âkâsa* he is cleverly disguised and believable as such.

The film is heavily scratched in order to match the visual quality of a neglected serial. Schiller shot everything on Super8 and added all dialogue and sound when he returned to the United States. He really went to town with the title cards, which also look very authentic with the bold, three-dimensional title. They were hand-drawn by a friend.

The film is stylish and accurately recreates the black-and-white adventure films of the past, but it suffers from a lack of humor. Aside from the concept, there are only a few jokes. The other problem is that it is very long. Schiller himself admits that his best shorts are the shortest ones. *Search for Âkâsa* has too much unnecessary back story and starts off too slow. The opening credits are exactly like those in a real motion picture—except a real motion picture runs for about ninety minutes. At a length of nearly four minutes, it is easy to lose interest before *Search for Âkâsa* is over, let alone before the opening credits are done with. It might have worked better at two minutes, like most other *Schiller's Reels*.

One other film did air, but not until after Schiller had left *Saturday Night Live*. *L'Art est Ficiel*, or *Art is Ficial*, as it is translated in English, premiered on November 7, 1981. Schiller already had the raw material but did not put it together until 1981—more than a year after leaving the show. *Search for Âkâsa* was also intended to be shown around this time, but it never made it to air.

©Schillervision

L'Art est Ficiel is disguised as a documentary for French television, which Schiller narrates with a strong French accent. The subject is the nonexistent "poet, Dadaist and literary dog" Maurice Blaget, who lived from 1901 until 1957. The film shows the bearded, middle-aged artist at his home in Avignon in 1951. He is frustrated by the presence of a camera, although he doesn't always seem to notice because he's usually drunk. He sits in his backyard and throws empty bottles to the floor. The narrator says he does this when remembering all the better artists he once knew but was now rejected by. The narrator then goes down a long list of artists including fellow Dadaists Max Ernst and Marcel Duchamp, surrealist (and also one-time Dadaist) André Breton, filmmaker Jean Cocteau, Salvador Dalí, Henry Miller and many others. With every name, Blaget throws down more bottles.

Blaget makes daily pilgrimages to the nearby chateau La Coste, a ruin of the castle that was home to the Marquis de Sade in the late 1700s. On his way up the hill, the half-mumbling, half-singing Blaget is passed by French women who recognize him but are taken aback by his haggard appearance. Once in front of the castle, Blaget stands and blurts out his nonsensical, unintelligible Dadaist poetry while moving his arms about like a madman. It appears as if he is trying to talk to someone in the chateau. In his narration, Schiller jokingly mentions that the castle has been empty for over five hundred years. Of course, the Marquis de Sade lived there as recently as the late 18th century.

The film then flashes forward to Paris in 1956, where Blaget is spending his last days in *the bughouse*—the mental institution. He is sick, neglected and full of self-pity. In between coughs, Blaget grunts a few words, which he then writes down in a notebook. "Quelle heure et-il...et pourquoi?" (What time is it...and why?) Blaget then comes to the nonsensical realization that "after all, art is ficial." He takes a moment to think about what he has just come to realize, and then starts screaming out of his window: "Art is ficial, vous entendés? Art is ficial!"

Schiller had invented the mythological Dadaist poet Maurice Blaget years earlier. He thought up the character with his friend Hans Hartmann (who plays Blaget in *L'Art est Ficiel*) in Copenhagen at the age of twenty. Schiller wrote stories that referenced the character, and finally used him in *L'Art est Ficiel*. Blaget also appears in Schiller's feature film *Nothing Lasts Forever* as a chain-smoking art test administrator at the Port Authority. Blaget is played by a different actor and looks nothing like his earlier incarnation—in *L'Art est Ficiel*, Blaget is gaunt and bristly, while in *Nothing Lasts Forever* he is plump and greasy. Nevertheless, Schiller insists that the Blagets from *L'Art est Ficiel* and *Nothing Lasts Forever* are one and the same. *Nothing Lasts Forever* even references to Blaget's time spent in Montmartre as a failed artist.

As far as hidden layers, which one might expect from *L'Art est Ficiel*, there aren't any. The title simply stems from the word *artificial* and has no hidden meaning. As for the character, the last name sounds a lot like the word *blasé*, which is fitting since Blaget is pompous and nonchalant. "It's a play on the nihilism and certain bleak European Albert Camus stuff that was going on at the time," Schiller adds. "It's abstract nothingness." Camus, the French philosopher who lived around the same time that Blaget would have, was an existentialist and a self-proclaimed absurdist. Although he has sometimes been categorized as a nihilist, he was in fact very critical of nihilism, stating that it was one of the biggest problems in the twentieth century. In his lifetime, Camus disparaged the writings of the Marquis de Sade. In effect, Blaget's spouting of Dadaist poetry in front of chateau La Coste echoes Camus' critiquing of de Sade.

L'Art est Ficiel can be seen as both a take-off and an homage to the films of Robert Snyder. Snyder's films were similar portraits of artists shown in their natural habitats, partaking in their daily activities, and reflecting on their lives and careers. Parody is often seen as a sign of respect.

L'Art est Ficiel is also a satire of inadvertently droll French television documentaries. High on clichés and dim-witted in their pretentiousness, documentaries from France (and, in general, the rest of Europe) are often dry in their presentation, and as a result, filled with unintentional humor. Especially with his French voice-over, Schiller mocks the ostentation of the *documentaire*.

But as is the case with a number of other *Schiller's Reels*, *L'Art est Ficiel* is a film that will fly over the heads of many *Saturday Night Live* viewers. Most won't realize how the film is making fun of French television, or they won't know anything about the Dadaist movement. In their defense, *L'Art est Ficiel* demands a few viewings in order for the joke to fully sink in, even for those with some grounding in art and history. Upon first viewing it, it is hard to determine what Schiller is trying to do with the film. Ultimately, the joke is in the presentation and not merely in the notion that 'art is ficial.'

Chapter 6

Looking Back In Anger

There is no doubt that Schiller's short films were clever, and they were always well-received at the show. But sadly, they have gotten lost in the crowd. Today, most of them are largely forgotten because Schiller usually didn't put any of the cast members in his films. The short films of Gary Weis, which didn't always utilize the cast either, suffered the same fate. For the cable and syndication markets, Schiller's films were frequently cut out. Because a ninety minute show is harder to program, Broadway Video cut the episodes down to sixty or thirty minutes. Since Schiller's films rarely featured cast members, his shorts rarely made it onto the compressed episodes, and for many years it was tough to see Schiller's work. Other *Saturday Night Live* filmmakers have had the same experience.

But Schiller did make four classic star-driven shorts between 1977 and 1980. His third and most popular short, *Don't Look Back in Anger*, starred John Belushi. *La Dolce Gilda*, his fourth film, starred Gilda Radner and also featured John Belushi, Dan Aykroyd and Laraine Newman. His eighth, *Perchance to Dream*, starred Bill Murray. And his tenth, *Java Junkie*, starred Peter Aykroyd.

Don't Look Back in Anger is the short film that Schiller is most famous for—at least among today's audiences. A black-and-white vision of the future, it

©Schillervision

is very funny, but unfortunately has become ironic and anti-prophetic in that the exact opposite of what it predicted happened.

In *Don't Look Back in Anger*, Schiller again applies his trademark time capsule humor. Not only does the film envision how John Belushi will look back on his experiences at *Saturday Night Live* decades in the future, but Schiller also makes the film look like something from the past.

Tom Schiller claims to have the ability to look at certain people and see what they will look like when they become old. John Belushi was someone that he could vividly envision with gray hair and wrinkles, so he came up with the idea of an old Belushi, decades in the future, visiting the graves of his fellow cast mates who have fallen before him. Belushi liked the idea, so Schiller began work on it.

Don't Look Back in Anger starts with John Belushi, made-up to look as if he was ninety years old, sitting in an old-fashioned train compartment. The scene is under-exposed and the film is purposely scratched like the infamous old newsreels in the opening of *Citizen Kane*. The train stops and Belushi gets off. He walks onto a snow-covered cemetery and faces the camera to describe that he has arrived at the 'Not Ready for Prime Time Cemetery.'

"They all thought I'd be the first to go," he tells the audience. "I was one of those live-fast, die-young, leave-a-good-looking-corpse types. Well, I guess they were wrong." He then walks over to the specific gravestones. For each grave, Belushi names the cast member and describes what they did after *Saturday Night Live* ended,

©Schillervision

as well as how they died. The first one he approaches, ironically, is Gilda Radner, who died of cancer in 1989. According to Belushi, Gilda Radner and Laraine Newman died of old age, Jane Curtin died of complications during cosmetic surgery, and Garrett Morris died of a heroin overdose. Chevy Chase was the first to go, right after his first movie with Goldie Hawn, while Bill Murray lived the longest, reaching the ripe old age of thirty-eight. The last grave that Belushi goes to is that of his closest friend Dan Aykroyd, who according to Belushi was gruesomely killed in a motorcycle crash. Belushi had to identify his body by his webbed toes.

"The *Saturday Night* show was the best experience of my life. And now they're all gone, and I miss every one of 'em," Belushi emotionally declares. "Why me? Why did I live so long? They're all dead." After a short pause, he continues in a sly voice: "I'll tell you why. 'Cause I'm a dancer." The Yiddish song 'Roumania, Roumania' by Aaron Lebedeff plays and Belushi dances on the graves of his cast members as the camera zooms out to reveal the entire graveyard.

Belushi gives an exceptionally convincing performance, and according to Schiller, it was almost eerie how well he played the part. "When we shot it," Schiller recalls, "he went to every grave stone perfectly the first time with no rehearsal or anything."

"Tom Schiller shot his films at unusual times and in the worst of weathers," says costume designer Sheila Kehoe. "When he was doing *Don't Look Back in Anger* with John Belushi, that snow was real. The blizzard that had provided all that realistic snow had closed down Brooks Van Horn, the costume company that provided the costumes for *Saturday Night Live*. We were all behind in our assignments. I had just met Tom that week and had pulled a couple of coats and hats for John to try on. Tom called that Saturday to see if he could bring John by for a fitting." That was the first time the two worked together. Kehoe eventually became the official *Schiller's Reel* costume designer and was also the costume designer for *Nothing Lasts Forever*.

Don't Look Back in Anger is another film in which Schiller manipulates time. The manner in which it was shot, the film scratches, Belushi's old-fashioned mustache and garb, the fact that he travels by train—all make this film that is set in the future look as if it were produced in the thirties or forties.

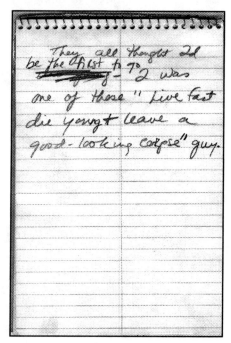

Laila Nabulsi's production notebook.

Don't Look Back in Anger first aired on March 11, 1978. Exactly four years later, on March 11, 1982, friends and family attended a memorial service for John Belushi in New York, six days after the actor died. Despite the unavoidable irony that surrounds it, *Don't Look Back in Anger* is very amusing. "It was hilarious then and it's still funny now. And, of course, ironic," says Dan Aykroyd. "It's an impression of what could be in another dimension. In another dimension, perhaps Belushi does live on."

Originally, *Don't Look Back in Anger* was nearly twice as long. Early on, the film was referred to as *Belushi at 90*. Part of the opening scene, which consisted of additional footage of Belushi sitting in the train and a montage, was cut from the film to keep it from running too long. In the deleted footage, Belushi is in the train together with a young man named Tom, played by Tom Schiller. Belushi is reading the obituaries in *The New York Times* and tells Tom how he outlived Jagger, the Beatles, Dylan—even Phil Lesh. Belushi tells about how he became a big star of the stage and screen. After *Saturday Night Live*, Belushi moved to Hollywood and made fifty-four films (twenty-three of which were Samurai movies). Tom asks if he also knew Chaplin, and Belushi confirms that he, indeed, did know Chaplin. Geraldine Chaplin. Belushi then tells about his experiences on Broadway in his five thousand

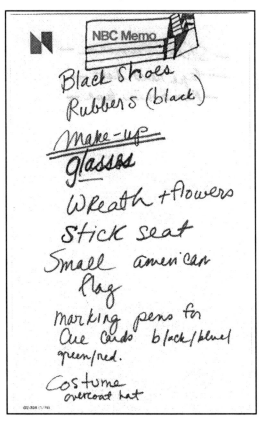

NBC Miscellaneous Expense Voucher

This form must be prepared in accordance with company policy and the instructions on the reverse side.

PAGE 1

Receipts must be attached for each item of expenditure of $10.00 or more.

Employee Name	Employee No.	Department	Date
TOM. SCHILLER .		SAT. NITE	FEB 14, 78

Date	Description (Include Items, Place, Business Relationships and Business Purpose. See specific instructions with respect to each of the above headings on reverse side.)	Amount
	ALL ITEMS FOR BELUSHI FILM	
2-16-78	PROP "WREATH" (receipt att)	10 80
2-10-78	MAKE-UP + MUSTACHE (2 receipts att)	42 50
2-9-78	PROP "FLAG" AMERICAN (receipt att)	2 25
2-11-78	PROP "GLASSES" (receipt att)	35 00
2-11-78	PROP "GLASSES (receipt att)	6 00
2-1-78	MAP OF JERSEY LOCATION HUNT no receipt	1 19
2-13-78	TRAIN TICKETS FOR CREW (7 PERSONS) ROUND TRIP TO SUMMIT (receipt att)	18 20
2-2-78	PROP "STICK-SEAT" (receipt att)	16 19
2-13-78	2 FLAGS CANADIAN PROP (receipt att)	1 80
2-15-78	PROPS "GOLASHES" FOR CEMETERY 2 PAIR (receipt att)	12 95
2-13-78	TOLLS (HOBOKOKEN STATION LOCATION SHOOT) 6 receipts att	3 00
2-11-78	BATTERYS FOR TAPE RECORDER FOR LOCATION MUSIC (receipt att)	3 43
2-13-78	NEWSPAPERS - PROP	1 06
2-13-78	PLUS-X FILM - STILLS (receipt att)	5 00

Total amount expended (write out)   continued, page 2 —   Dollars

Settlement (To be signed at time of submission to cashier)		Date	Amount
	Cash		
	Advanced		
	By Company		
	Balance due to company (To be returned with this voucher)		
Recieved or made settlement Date	Balance due to employee Reimburse by ☒ Cash ☐ Check		

I hereby certify that I have incurred all the expenses above on behalf of the company and that they are directly related to and/or associated with the active conduct of the company's business.

Account distribution			Amount

2-21-78

Signed   Date
Approved   Total

GE-28 (12/76)

NBC Expense Voucher

performances of the one-man show *Hal Holbrook Tonight*. Of course, Holbrook had made a name for himself with *Mark Twain Tonight*, but according to Schiller, nobody seemed to get the joke.

Belushi then dozes off and dreams of his Broadway success, how he was knighted, and how Broadway was renamed Belushi Boulevard. Then the train whistle wakes him up as he reaches his stop, Rosebud. The film then continues much like it does in the final version. The opening scenes were filmed and

Date	Description	Amount
	NBC Miscellaneous Expense Voucher	
	Receipts must be attached for each item of expenditure of $10.00 or more.	PAGE 2
	Employee Name Tom SCHILLER. Employee No. Department SAT NITE (CONT) Date FEB 14, 1978	
	Include Items, Place, Business Relationships and Business Purpose. See specific instructions with respect to each of the above headings on reverse side.	
	ALL ITEMS FOR BELUSHI FILM	
2-14-78	CAR RENTAL FOR TRANSPORTATION TO HOBOKEN STATION WITH CREW + SHOOTING LOCATIONS. (receipt att)	31 60
2-14-78	PARKING FOR CAR ON LOCATION SHOOT (receipt att)	6 36
2-13-78	GAS FOR CREW'S CAR (receipt att)	5 00
2-13-78	JUDY JACKLIN GRIP ASSISTANCE ON LOCATION	10 00
2-13-78	TRAIN CONDUCTOR VOICE OVER (copy release att) no receipt	10 00
2-14-78	LEE AUSTIN MAKEUP MAN (receipt att) 2 DAYS WORK @ 50 DAY	100 00
2-15-78	STEVE FISCHLER AND JOEL SUCHER FOR SOUND RECORDING 2 DAYS AND ASSISTANT WORK (receipt to come)	300 00
2-17-78	JUDY IROLA 2 DAYS CAMERAWOMAN AND CAMERA RENTAL (receipt att)	450 00
2-14-78	LAILA NABULSI PRODUCTION ASSISTANT WORK att. ADVANCE (receipt att.)	100 00
2-13-78	MEAL FOR CREW ON LOCATION HOBOKEN STATION (receipt att)	35 13
2-13-78	MEAL FOR CREW ON LOCATION (receipt att)	13 85
2-15-78	LUNCH CREW CEMETERY SHOOT (receipt att)	18 70

Total amount expended (write out) one thousand two hundred + twentyfive dollar and fifty two cents 1224 52

Settlement (To be signed at time of submission to cashier)

Cash
Advanced By Company
Balance due to company
(To be returned with this voucher)
Balance due to employee
Reimburse by ☒Cash ☐Check

Recieved or made settlement _____ Date

I hereby certify that I have incurred all the expenses above on behalf of the company and that they are directly related to and/or associated with the active conduct of the company's business.

Account distribution

Signed   2-21-78   Date
Approved

GE-28 (12/76)   Total

NBC Expense Voucher

Schiller had selected stock footage to use for the dream montage, but Schiller ultimately decided to shorten the film.

Other notable differences in the Master Script include Belushi's description of Bill Murray's death. In the finished film, Belushi explains that Murray died happy because he had just grown his mustache back, while in the shooting script he says "he died happy…in the saddle, if you know what I mean." Also, Chevy Chase's gravestone was supposed to be a big, lavish tomb with lots of flowers. In the original script, Belushi explains that Chase's *Foul Play* co-star Goldie Hawn still sends flowers from Beverly Hills each day. Furthermore, Belushi's comment about Dan Aykroyd's webbed toes (which Aykroyd really does have) was also a last-minute addition.

After John Belushi passed away in 1982, it was tough for his widow Judith to watch any of his appearances on *Saturday Night Live*, *Don't Look Back in Anger* included. But as she learned to deal with her loss, she was able to enjoy watching the show again like everybody else. A few years later, she took on the task of compiling all of John's greatest bits into *The Best of John Belushi*, a videotape and television special.

Judith Belushi Pisano thought *Don't Look Back in Anger* was great and wanted to include it, but Warner Home Video, the distributor of the videotape, had their doubts. "I already knew it was an important piece of his," says Pisano, "but Warner Brothers tried to talk me out of it." The film is not provocative or offensive—it's simply ironic. She persisted, and the film made it on. When *The Best of John Belushi* was released in 1985, it became the biggest non-theatrical release to date. It was *Saturday Night Live*'s first *Best Of* compilation released on tape, and the success of the title led to an enormously lucrative series of video tapes and DVDs.

At the same time, Judith Belushi Pisano was working on a book chronicling her struggle of how to deal with the loss of her husband. She had the idea to write her own book not long after John's death. It was to be culled in part from her diaries. Her working title was *Don't Look Back in Anger*, but she first participated in Bob Woodward's biography *Wired: The Short Life and Fast Times of John Belushi*, published in 1985. Even though Woodward spoke to hundreds of Belushi's family members, friends and co-workers, the book has been dismissed as an unfair and inaccurate portrait.

The release of *Wired* was a disappointing experience for her, and suddenly the title *Don't Look Back in Anger* rang even truer. Ultimately, she decided to change the title. "I began the book with an idea of what I thought it would be, and the original title reflected that," Pisano says. "At first I so wanted to get to the place where I could look back and not be angry or sad. And I did. But when I was done with the book it seemed like the journey reflected much more than that."

Pisano kept the title as *Don't Look Back in Anger* during most of the writing process, but eventually changed it to something more honorable and without the inherent sense of cautionary bitterness: *Samurai Widow*.

Like most of the cast and writers on *Saturday Night Live*, John Belushi and Tom Schiller had been good friends. The two of them regularly visited a Turkish/Russian bathhouse, which inspired a scene in Schiller's later film *Nothing Lasts Forever*. During the first season of *Saturday Night*, some of the cast and crew went on vacation to

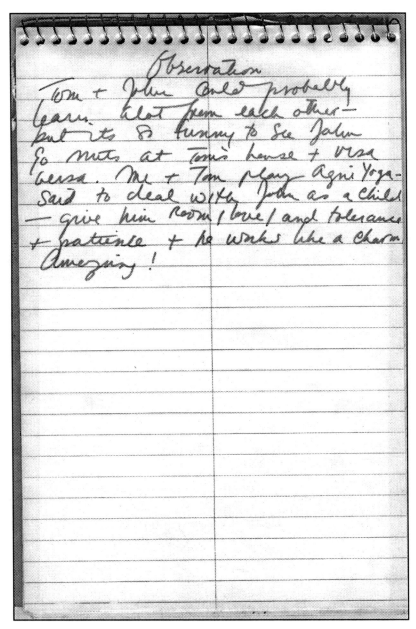

Laila Nabulsi's production notebook.

Jamaica when they had a week off. John and Judith Belushi, Dan Aykroyd, Paul Schaffer and Howard Shore went, as did Schiller. It was their first real outing. Later, the Belushis also rented a house in Long Island for the Summer, and Schiller would visit and stay with them as a houseguest. "He's one of those perfect houseguests," Pisano recalls.

John Belushi by Tom Schiller

Don't Look Back in Anger is Tom Schiller's most popular short film. It is probably the film that has been seen most, and it is certainly the film that Schiller is most recognized for. It's undoubtedly among his best works as well. The film is emblematic of Schiller's style and the themes that recur throughout his works, and it is both humorous and poignant. *Don't Look Back in Anger* is the definitive *Schiller's Reel.*

Chapter 7
Star Vehicles

Schiller's next film, *La Dolce Gilda*, is his favorite out of all the *Schiller's Reels* he has done and it has a mood similar to that of *Don't Look Back in Anger*. Both films are very funny, but at the same time a cloud of sadness hovers above them because the stars of the films died at young ages.

Shot in a style similar to Fellini's *La Dolce Vita*, *La Dolce Gilda* stars Gilda Radner in the title role and also features Dan Aykroyd, Laraine Newman and John Belushi. It follows movie star Gilda Radner at the *Saturday Night Live* after-party, where she has fun but is never left alone. The stars arrive in a Cadillac while the paparazzi—a term coined by Fellini in *La Dolce Vita*—flash and snap their pictures.

Once inside, everyone wants to play with and be around Gilda. Partygoers whisper in her ears. Dan Aykroyd, who plays a character by the name of 'Marcello' and is dressed up to look like Marcello Mastroianni, tries to convince her to leave the party with him. He then jumps on top of another girl and begins riding her like

©Schillervision

a rodeo horse. Laraine Newman plays Lina Wertmüller, the outspoken Italian director whom she had played before on *Saturday Night Live*, including in one of Schiller's
Bad Theater sketches. Even Gilda's mother shows up—a forceful lady who is as
heavily-accented as she is heavy. She begs of Gilda to come home with her.

The partygoers act as if they are appearing in a real Fellini movie, complete
with overdubbed dialogue. They all speak in Italian accents while a sad-faced mime
looks on. Despite all the attention and excitement surrounding Gilda, she still
feels lonely. At dawn, she leaves the party and the mime follows her outside with
a balloon. "I love to play," Gilda wistfully exclaims while facing the camera, as
Nino Rota's melancholic accordion theme from Fellini's *Amarcord* plays in the
background. "But every time we play, you win." As she walks away, the mime faces
the camera and gently opens up his tuxedo to reveal a heart cut out of paper on his
white shirt. The camera follows his balloon as he lets it float away into the sky.

Schiller filmed *La Dolce Gilda* after the live show at one of the clubs that
regularly hosted the *Saturday Night Live* after-parties. It does a very good job of
capturing the atmosphere of Fellini's *8 ½* and *La Dolce Vita*, which are the two
specific films that Schiller modeled it after. The characters are dressed up in
elegant attire and quip aphorisms like "the early Fitzgerald was good, but then
came an orgy of voodoo-realism." *La Dolce Gilda* also features Fellini's signature
close-ups of mouths with the dialogue dubbed slightly out of synch.

However, it is not merely a take-off. It stands up well on its own by revealing
the holes that fame and admiration cannot fill. Gilda has a good time, but there is

a part of her that is lonely and sad. One interpretation is that this part of her is represented by the plaintive mime that follows her everywhere. Like a number of other *Schiller's Reels*, *La Dolce Gilda* does not have a punch line. It merely has a few jokes throughout, courtesy of the Felliniesque eccentrics at the after-party.

La Dolce Gilda was shot at One Fifth, the restaurant where *Saturday Night Live* held its official after-parties for many years. After the show ended, the cast members either dressed up while still at Rockefeller Center or rushed to Schiller's house—actually, Laila Nabulsi's mother's house in Washington Mews, since Schiller had been renting it from her. The cast and crew met up at the house where all the costumes had been set up. Once dressed, they hurried over to One Fifth, which was right around the corner.

Many familiar faces can be found at the party in *La Dolce Gilda*. *Saturday Night Live* fans should be able to point out many of the writers, like Brian Doyle-Murray, who is dressed up as a padre, and other regulars like Judith Belushi. Tom Schiller's brother also appears, wearing a turban. The mime is played by Steve Brennen, a friend of Laila Nabulsi's who was actually a clown at Barnum & Bailey's

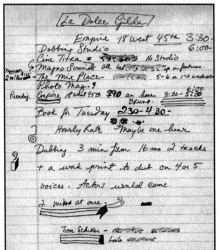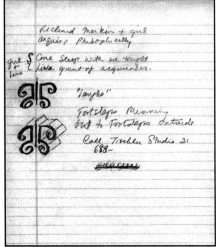

Laila Nabulsi's production notebook

NBC Expense Voucher

circus. Schiller and Nabulsi made up note cards with lines of dialogue that the extras were supposed to repeat, and gave one card to everyone in the film. They also made 'thank you' cards, which were handed out at the end of the party.

The only regular cast members missing were Bill Murray, Garrett Morris and Jane Curtin. Bill Murray attended most after-parties, but for some reason did not attend when *La Dolce Gilda* was shot. He was not written into the script, either. Garrett Morris and Jane Curtin rarely showed up for the official parties—Morris usually had his own post-show events set up, while Curtin preferred staying home with her husband over the late-night pandemonium that was a *Saturday Night Live* after-party. John Belushi was not supposed to be in the film, but he showed up in costume. Schiller had envisioned the film just for Radner, Newman and Aykroyd. Belushi was not part of the script but wanted to

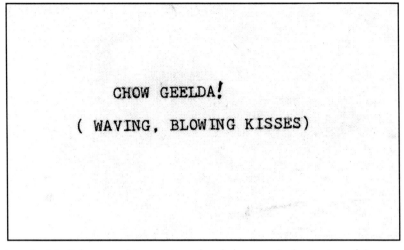

CHOW GEELDA!

(WAVING, BLOWING KISSES)

A card with dialogue and instructions, handed out at the beginning of the party

be in it anyway, so he came along with Radner, Newman and Aykroyd in the Cadillac. Since the Cadillac arrival had been pre-arranged so that Schiller would be there in advance with the camera ready when the stars arrived, Schiller had no choice but to include Belushi in the film.

After everything had been shot at the party, Schiller, Nabulsi and their crew took Gilda up the West Side Highway and shot the closing scene at dawn. They had to be there at the exact moment that the sun came up. When they got the shot, Schiller treated everyone who worked on the film to breakfast at the Empire diner.

Everybody looks back on making the film with fondness. Schiller was able to combine the legendary *Saturday Night Live* after-party experience with his love

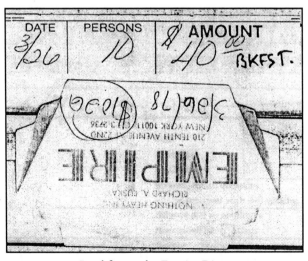

Breakfast at the Empire Diner

A 'Thank You' card handed out at the end of the party.

for Fellini. "It was just beautiful," says Dan Aykroyd. "We understand that there's culture outside of America, and we're not only going to do scenes about Americans. To touch Italian cinema that way was great."

Making *La Dolce Gilda* was an opportunity for Tom Schiller to produce an homage to his idol, Federico Fellini. A few years after it aired on *Saturday Night Live*, Schiller had the opportunity to meet Fellini when he was vacationing in Rome. Fellini was shooting a film at Cinecitta Studio in Rome, so Schiller went up to the gate and asked if he could meet him. He said that he was a friend of Paul Mazursky and Henry Miller, so he was allowed on the set.

Meeting Fellini was an amazing experience. Schiller told Fellini about *La Dolce Gilda* and they arranged a screening. Fellini was amused by the little homage and said 'carina'—Italian for 'pretty' or 'sweet.' "He said it had the atmosphere of some of his films," Schiller recalls. The two directors kept in touch for the next few years.

Perchance to Dream, a black-and-white piece starring Bill Murray, is one of Schiller's best films. It is also Bill Murray's favorite of all the *Schiller's Reels*—but of course, he starred in it. Murray plays a homeless drunk who, though unnamed in sketches, was known around *Saturday Night Live* as The Honker. Honker appeared regularly on the show whenever a sketch called for a homeless person or a drunk. Murray created the character years earlier and used it in his auditions.[9]

Perchance to Dream shows Honker's serious side—it shows that he too has dreams and aspirations. On a cold, snowy night, he wanders around outside a stage door and sits down on the steps. He then finds a small bottle of liquor buried under the snow. Honker's narration is unique—he talks to himself in his

©Schillervision

mind, but half of the time he just talks out loud. Given the fact that Honker is persistently drunk and possibly schizophrenic, it's a clever technique.

Honker takes a sip from the mysterious drink, but it knocks him out almost immediately. He awakens, suddenly clean-shaven, his face covered in white theatre make-up and his hair combed neatly. He is the star of a play and is led to the stage by a crowd of directors, costumers and stagehands. He is hesitant at first, but then begins a soliloquy culled from the most famous lines of *Henry V* and other works by Shakespeare. He has turned from a bum into a convincing Shakespearean actor. After his soliloquy, the crowd applauds and throws roses at him. An attractive young co-star rushes to his side and begins to kiss him.

But then he begins to wake up. He is no longer kissing an attractive young co-star, but instead kisses a nightstick that is being shoved in his face. The police officer standing in front of him is the same person that directed him on stage, only now he is telling him not to loiter. Just as Honker stumbles away, he comes across a rose, pristinely sitting on the ground, and picks it up. "What the hell is this? A rose, right," he mumbles. "But what if they didn't call it that? It would still be just as beautiful."

Perchance to Dream was shot at the Entermedia Theatre, once a famed Jewish theatre which later became an off-Broadway venue and eventually a movie theater. Brian Doyle-Murray was supposed to play a monk, but he was unable to make it to the shoot due to scheduling difficulties.

Photo by Christopher Zuk

Perchance to Dream is one of Schiller's bittersweet films. Bill Murray's Honker character is worth a few laughs throughout, but there is no real punch line. It is a good example of what sets Schiller's films apart from the many other films that appeared on the show. The film is captivating, warm, heartfelt and, simply put, sweet.

But *Perchance to Dream* is also about the concept of the comedian wanting to become a serious actor. While it might have been funny to see the goofy Bill Murray recite lines from Shakespeare in 1979, today it is easier to take the acting more serious because Murray has successfully made the move to drama. The film is prophetic in that it mirrors the journey that Bill Murray has gone through himself. Murray co-wrote and starred in an adaptation of W. Somerset Maugham's *The Razor's Edge* in 1983, but critics and audiences were not ready for his dramatic debut. His performance was panned by critics, and the film was a financial disap-

pointment. Years later he tried again with the comedy *Rushmore*, which had some dramatic elements, and he has since established himself as a talented dramatic actor—ultimately earning an Academy Award nomination for *Lost in Translation*.

"It shows a side of the comic actor," Schiller says of *Perchance*, and the performances in his short films in general. "Not dramatic, but it shows another dimension of their acting ability or their comic ability." With *Perchance to Dream* in particular, Schiller showed Murray in a different light, but the same goes for Gilda Radner in *La Dolce Gilda* and John Belushi in *Don't Look Back in Anger*.

Many comedic actors over the years have had the desire to move from comedy to drama, and the cast of *Saturday Night Live* is no exception with many of the stars that have passed through the show taking on serious roles. Dan Aykroyd was the first to earn a Best Supporting Actor Academy Award nomination for his dramatic turn in 1989's *Driving Miss Daisy*. Robert Downey Jr. was nominated for *Chaplin* and Joan Cusack for *Working Girl* and *In & Out*. Randy Quaid had already been nominated for a Supporting Actor Oscar for *The Last Detail* more than a decade before he joined the cast. *Perchance to Dream* captures the ambition of the comedic actor, which is not always apparent when they are cracking jokes and making funny faces.

Photos by Christopher Zuk

©Schillervision

Peter Aykroyd and Teri Garr star in *Java Junkie*, an excellent short film that accurately recreates the look and feel of *films noirs* of the 40s and 50s. The film was modeled after Billy Wilder's 1945 Best Picture Oscar winner *The Lost Weekend* starring Ray Milland. It also has a bit of the cautionary melodramas of the 1930s in it—anti-marijuana films like *Assassin of Youth* and *Reefer Madness* where smoking dope turns teenagers into maniacs. Peter Aykroyd's character is led into a similar kind of hysteria when he becomes a coffee addict in *Java Junkie*.

In terms of pacing, *Java Junkie* takes after Otto Preminger's 1955 film *The Man with the Golden Arm*, in which Frank Sinatra plays a heroin addict. Schiller also used Elmer Bernstein's dark, frenetic jazz ensemble score from that film. For some reason, *The Man with the Golden Arm*'s copyright had lapsed so the film has been in the public domain for many years, allowing Schiller to use it freely.

Teri Garr. Courtesy of Neal Marshad Productions.

Java Junkie starts off innocently with Peter Aykroyd, as Joe, walking into Franklin Restaurant, an old-fashioned diner on West Broadway and Franklin Street in Tribeca, for a cup of coffee one morning. In a typical *film noir* narration, Joe mentions that his girlfriend Betty wants to break up with him and that he has just lost his job. What starts as an innocent cup of coffee quickly stacks up to several dozen cups. Teri Garr plays the friendly waitress who happily keeps serving him more and more coffee, until the cups start stacking up and she begins to look concerned.

Joe spends almost the entire night at the diner, until the entire counter area in front of him is filled with empty coffee cups and the waitress tells him that they are out of coffee. Joe is escorted out by the short-order cook and he goes on a quest for

©Schillervision

more caffeine. He scours coffee shop after coffee shop until he becomes delusional and has horrible visions of coffee, much like a drug-addict would of drugs. He imagines a sultry female in a mink stole on the street seducing him with a cup of coffee and laughing at him. Joe then strolls along the New York sidewalks following the imaginary woman, screaming for coffee. Thankfully, he is soon able to get a fix when he walks into yet another coffee shop, grabs the coffee pot and proceeds to drink directly out of it while police sirens sound.

The police find Joe on the street and check him into Maxwell House, a rehabilitation center where caffeine addicts are locked up until they are completely decaffeinated. Seven weeks later, Joe has recovered and revisits Teri Garr at the coffee shop. With everything in his life under control—a new job and his girlfriend Betty wanting to see him again—he is no longer tempted by the coffee and excitedly orders a cup of hot water.

Java Junkie is enjoyable mostly for its style. Aykroyd does a good job of playing the innocent man who becomes an addict. It is a double-sided affair as he plays both the upstanding citizen who innocently enters the coffee shop with a newspaper under his arm and politely orders a cup of coffee, as well as the strung-out addict who suffers withdrawal hysteria. *Java Junkie* looks a lot like the films it spoofs, and accurately pokes fun at the way drugs were presented on film in the past.

Peter Aykroyd joined the *Saturday Night Live* team in 1979 as a writer and featured performer. He and Schiller understood each other's humor and collaborated a number of times, both on the show and later in several film projects.

Courtesy of Neal Marshad Productions.

"He jokingly referred to me as his Mastroianni, and he was my Fellini," Aykroyd remembers.

"I think Peter Aykroyd is an excellent actor," Schiller says. "He has just the perfect face and the look for that kind of a guy in *Java Junkie*. You think you've seen him before."

"He was a big fan of a sketch that I wrote called *Speci-Pak*," Aykroyd recalls, "which was kind of a metal hard-shelled case for separated digits or body parts, when you rush to the hospital with them to have them reattached. We worked on one sketch in particular called *Los Beatolos Cubanos*, the Cuban Beatles." *Los Beatolos Cubanos* was an advertisement for an album by a band that performs Cuban versions of popular Beatles songs. Bill Murray played their manager, Rizzy Baldero, and the band consisted of Garrett Morris, Paul Shaffer, and Aykroyd and Schiller. "It was his idea," Aykroyd adds. "He resonated with me and I played guitar and sang."

Peter Aykroyd later appeared in Schiller's films *From Here to Maternity* and *Flapjack Floozie*, and he made a cameo in *Nothing Lasts Forever*. He has the ability to play 'the straight guy' very well in comedic situations, but can also be silly and make people laugh like that. He has a sense of familiarity. In *Java Junkie*, he captures a bit of Ray Milland's essence from *The Lost Weekend*—of the rational man who is lead into madness because of an addiction—although that was not his intention. In fact, Aykroyd had never seen the film, and Schiller didn't mention that that film was the inspiration.

Aykroyd is from Canada, so he had to try to disguise his Canadian accent to play the all-American *film noir* hero. He does it well until the end, when he has to say the line "Well, they found me that night and threw me into this place, Maxwell House." American English and Canadian English are similar, but some of the most famous differences are that Canadians sometimes add 'eh' to the end of a sentence and instead of saying 'about' and 'house,' they say 'aboot' and 'hoace.'

When it came time to record Aykroyd's voice-over narration, Schiller had to ask him several times to say 'Maxwell House' as Americans do, but it kept coming out as 'Maxwell Hoace.' Aykroyd kept trying to say it right, but in the final film he still pronounces it with a bit of a Canadian accent.

"It was a fun shoot—it was great to work with Tom on that," Aykroyd recalls. "He's very enthusiastic about his work, so you really get taken up in his energy and enthusiasm. He's a good director—he's able to speak to the performing side of an actor."

Schiller shot *Java Junkie* in the late fall of 1979 in Tribeca. A three-day shoot, *Java Junkie* was Schiller's most ambitious project. All of his other films had taken just a day or two to shoot, but with *Java Junkie* he had many different locations and some night shots. Nevertheless, he and Laila Nabulsi had everything under control. It was cold out and a bit rainy, but the many exterior shots required for the film were completed within reasonable time.

"One of my favorite genres is the *film noir*," says Schiller. "I looked at a lot of old movies, and I also had an associate who was a known camera guy, Neal Marshad. He was instrumental in getting a lot of great camera angles and shooting at night. I remember the shot where a woman is beckoning Aykroyd with a cup of coffee. He lit that with the headlights of a car, which I thought was rather interesting."

Schiller asked his close friend Teri Garr to play the friendly, old-fashioned waitress in *Java Junkie*.

"He just asked me if I wanted to be in it, and I said 'of course,'" Teri Garr remembers. "He's the best. He affected my life in a great way. He's like a teacher, a learning guru."

Peter Aykroyd. Courtesy of Neal Marshad Productions.

"She's wonderful," says Schiller. "She's not conceited—she's a real human being, totally professional, and she added a lot to the character. She knew exactly the attitude of that character to play that 1940s, 1950s kind of gum-chewing waitress."

Java Junkie was the last short that Schiller got to make with Laila Nabulsi at his right hand. Shortly after the film was completed, she left for Colorado to live with her boyfriend, Hunter S. Thompson. Thompson had been trying to get her fired by harassing Schiller, albeit in a humorous manner. He would call Schiller at home at odd hours and inopportune times with hopes of irritating him so much that he'd get rid of Nabulsi. Schiller was amused by the attempts, but they were all to no avail. Nabulsi eventually left on her own.

"He was a pain in the neck," Schiller remembers of Thompson. "But a good pain in the neck."

After *Java Junkie* aired on *Saturday Night Live* in 1979, Schiller submitted it to numerous film festivals. The film was selected to be in the National Endowment for the Arts 'Short Film Showcase.' Shot on 16mm, it was blown up to a 35mm print so that it could be shown in any theater. In New York City, it even played together with David Lynch's *Eraserhead*. It won a Special Jury Award at the 1980 Houston International Film Festival, and also earned awards at the Chicago Film Festival and the Athens International Film Festival.

Java Junkie is Schiller's most stylish and well-crafted short from the classic era of *Saturday Night Live,* and is heightened by its clever concept.

Tom Schiller left *Saturday Night Live* at the end of the fifth season in 1980 along with almost all of the cast and writers. Everybody left. Part of the reason why Schiller left was out of loyalty to Lorne Michaels. The other part of the reason was that five years had been long enough, and it was time to take a break. It was time to move on to bigger and better things. Like making a movie.

Chapter 8
Lorne's Movie Deal

"Would the three of you like to make a movie?" Lorne Michaels asked Tom Davis, Al Franken and Jim Downey one day in 1980 or 1981.

"Just way open-ended like that," Davis recalls. "The three of us spent a couple of weeks in the Hamptons not thinking about the movie. There was no specific schedule or anything and we doddled around, and Schiller got his script in right away."

Franken, Davis and Downey, the "trio of disaster" as Davis jokingly calls them, procrastinated their way out of a chance of a lifetime. Downey, who still writes for *Saturday Night Live*, has been known to submit sketches in the afternoon on Saturday, and Franken and Davis were not exactly early risers themselves. "We jammed on it and it probably took us a year to write it, which is ridiculous," says Davis. "We should have taken six months, but we fucked up."

Following the successful run of *Saturday Night Live*, all the Hollywood movie studios were looking to make 'the *Saturday Night Live* movie.' Nobody knew exactly what it was, but it was going to star a number of *Saturday Night Live* cast members. Chevy Chase was a star thanks to *Foul Play*. John Belushi was a smash in *National Lampoon's Animal House*, and made a great team with Dan Aykroyd in *The Blues Brothers*. Bill Murray was in the summer hit *Meatballs*. Warner Brothers had the right idea with *Caddyshack*, which teamed Chevy Chase and Bill Murray with veteran comics like Ted Knight and Rodney Dangerfield. But all studios were looking for the next big thing: A movie with *Saturday Night Live* stars and the trademark *Saturday Night Live* humor.

When *National Lampoon's Animal House* became the most successful motion picture comedy in history, a number of the Not Ready for Primetime Players became highly sought-after movie stars. As such, Lorne Michaels also became a highly sought-after movie producer, even though he had nothing to do with *Animal House*. Michaels and all of the cast and writers left the show in 1980 to pursue further careers in movies and television, but before then Michaels had already been making the rounds with the Hollywood movie studios. Paramount made an offer for a nine-picture deal, which Michaels passed on. Warner Brothers had something less long-term—a three picture deal. Michaels signed with Warner Brothers and developed several projects, but aside from a filmed version of Gilda Radner's Broadway show *Gilda Live* directed by Mike Nichols, none of the films came to fruition.

He then signed a deal with MGM and several *Saturday Night Live* writers started developing projects and writing screenplays. Tom Schiller wrote a script. Don Novello, better known as Father Guido Sarducci on the show, worked on a script entitled *Man Called Sporcaccione*. The projects were not even limited to comedy: "There was a modern version of *Pride and Prejudice*, which Lorne was always keen on doing," recalls John Head, who consulted on several projects. "It was one of his favorite books, so Elia Katz did a version of that, and then I later did a version of that as well. It was a pretty faithful adaptation of the book, only updated."

But the potential project that got the most interest and excitement from Michaels and MGM was *Nineteen Eighty-Five*, a starring vehicle for Dan Aykroyd and Bill Murray that was written by Al Franken, Tom Davis and James Downey. Michaels himself was also heavily involved with the writing of *Nineteen Eighty-Five*. In terms of budget, *Nineteen Eighty-Five* would have been a big science fiction comedy in the vein of *Ghostbusters*, which Aykroyd and Murray made a few years later. But in terms of concept, it was more like Woody Allen's futuristic comedy *Sleeper*— incredibly funny, but not a big summer popcorn tent-pole. *Nineteen Eighty-Five* was a spoof of George Orwell's *1984*. Director Michael Radford was preparing a sincere adaptation of Orwell's novel at the same time with actors John Hurt and Richard Burton, although it did not make it to US theaters until early 1985. Franken, Davis and Downey's idea was that their film would be produced in 1983, released in 1984, and have the title *Nineteen Eighty-Five*. "That was a big part of what was making us laugh," says Tom Davis. "We wrote a script that I do like in this day, but very few people who have read the script like it."

Nineteen Eighty-Five was set in a domed society in a post-apocalyptic future. Franken, Davis and Downey were clearly influenced by films like *THX-1138*, *Logan's Run* and *Planet of the Apes*. After a nuclear armageddon, a large community of survivors live in a giant domed structure under the leadership of The Big Brothers. With the exception of The Big Brothers, none of the survivors have an inkling of what their life before the big explosion (referred to as The Big Thing) was like because their minds were erased. The entire society is controlled by the government under the strict scrutiny of The Big Brothers— two nerdy scientists who took charge after the nuclear explosion, thanks largely to the mind erasure technology they invented. Under their rule, love is illegal. Even masturbation is regulated by monthly coupons. All citizens are monitored at all times by computerized cameras—except when a masturbation coupon is redeemed for twenty minutes of privacy. Leaving the Dome is also illegal. But most importantly, the State is never wrong.

 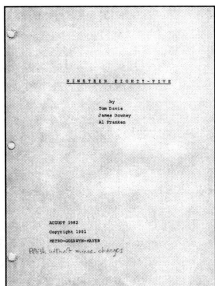

The main characters are three thoughtcops: Endicott, Sutton and Circle. Thoughtcops enforce the law by taking action whenever a citizen says or does something wrong. While Aykroyd and Murray were set to appear in *Nineteen Eighty-Five*, it never got far enough to determine who were going to play Endicott, Sutton and Circle. Franken, Davis and Downey were also big fans of Robert Klein, whom they considered for a part.

The story begins when Sutton is due for new shoes. Like everything else, the distribution of clothing is controlled by the State. Sutton picks up his shoes at the Footwear Dispensary, a small room with a computerized vending machine, but gets one shoe that is too small. The shoe barely fits and is very painful for Sutton to walk around in. Plus, Sutton cannot use his old shoes because he had to discard them before he could get a new pair. The computer has clearly made a mistake, but to say anything about it is a thoughtcrime and will lead to Sutton's arrest. Sutton is afraid to say anything to anybody and tries to convince himself that he has a mental condition that leads him to believe that one of his shoes doesn't fit.

Meanwhile, Endicott meets a female citizen named Saratoga, and it is hinted that the two knew each other before the Big Thing. Saratoga has some knowledge of what is going on behind the scenes at the State and tells Endicott about it. Endicott does not arrest Saratoga, but he's still skeptical. He finally realizes that something is afoot when he learns about Sutton's situation. After finding himself unable to deal with the pain, Sutton makes an attempt to escape. He immediately is caught and his mind is erased.

Endicott later finds out that the government did make a mistake—The Ministry of Shoes and Socks was forced to cut its budget after construction of a new Dome was not coming along fast enough in time for its 1986 deadline. As a result, they randomly distributed smaller shoes to citizens. After learning about this, Endicott finally believes what Saratoga has been trying to tell him all along.

According to the State, the world outside the Dome is uninhabitable because of toxic gas. Saratoga is convinced that that is a lie perpetuated by The Big Brothers, so she and Endicott plan their escape. With help from Circle, the two are able to leave the Dome and briefly wander through the outside world—which turns out to be the remnants of Washington D.C. Endicott and Saratoga are able to breathe without any trouble and make love on the lap of Abraham Lincoln at the Lincoln Monument. Suddenly, they are attacked by mutants—evil human survivors of the Big Thing who are covered in cauliflower-like tumors that make them look like The Elephant Man. Endicott wants to return to the Dome, but Saratoga argues that it's possible to live in the outside world. Endicott disagrees, and they end up heading back in.

The film ends with a resolution to the budget problem that is keeping the new Dome from being finished in 1986. On New Year's Eve, everybody is ready to ring in the New Year: 1985. The year simply repeats itself, giving the State an extra year to finish the Dome. Of course, the State never makes mistakes, so for any citizen to say anything would be a thoughtcrime.

The film's ending is anticlimactic. The story ends almost as if nothing has happened—good does not overcome evil, and Endicott and Saratoga resume their lives in a world of forbidden love. It's a fascinating conceit, and with Franken, Davis and Downey's humor infused throughout, *Nineteen Eighty-Five* had the potential to be unlike anything else. But it clearly was not what big summer movies were made of.

"It was very funny," says Michaels. "We were very close and wanted to work together." MGM expressed a definite interest in the film, and they sent back notes and suggestions for improvements. The outlook seemed bright from the initial feedback they got, and the entire crew was looking forward to working together. The studios were looking for 'the *Saturday Night Live* movie.' *Nineteen Eighty-Five* seemed to be it, and MGM had it.

"But MGM at that time was in deep financial crisis," Michaels adds, "which I wouldn't have been sophisticated enough to read into or understand. What really was going on was I think they weren't authorized to make any movies."

While MGM had insufficient funds, *Nineteen Eighty-Five* did carry an enormous price tag, and the budget simply had not been worked out to their satisfaction. *Nineteen Eighty-Five* would have required expensive sets, costumes and special effects. For example, all of the cars in the film are AMC Pacers—the only existing automobiles in the year 1985. It was an expensive joke. Plus, Lorne Michaels had another problem: his deal with MGM was going to expire unless he made a movie before a specific date. Everybody wanted to do *Nineteen Eighty-Five*, but it wasn't anywhere near ready to be rushed into production.

The other projects had not progressed well, either. All were in the early stages of development and the scripts just hadn't crawled up far enough in the process. The exception was Tom Schiller's project. Schiller had everything planned out and had it developed almost entirely by himself. His script was fully fleshed out and he had storyboarded every scene. He knew exactly what he wanted, and was ready to go into production. And best of all, it wasn't an expensive project.

"We needed to get a picture in production by a certain date in order to maintain this deal with MGM," says John Starke, who was hired by Michaels to oversee his projects, including *Nineteen Eighty-Five*. "And Tom, being the most organized guy in the world, had storyboards. He had made the movie in his mind, so his little picture kind of came out of the woodwork and was the one that we could go right into production on."

With the deadline looming, Michaels championed Tom Schiller's project, a unique science fiction comedy script called *Nothing Lasts Forever*. "Lorne was very tenacious and enthusiastic," says Boaty Boatwright, the head of East Coast productions at MGM at the time. "He was constantly talking about Tom who he believed, as we all did, would become this very stylized director."

Michaels' idea was that Schiller's project would be a small, low-budget comedy. It was an off-beat little comedy script with elements of science fiction and musical numbers that could be produced for significantly less than the production costs of an average studio film. But Michaels and MGM had different ideas about the term 'low budget.'

"I believe I said to the person who was running MGM, 'If you leave him alone and you let him work the way he wants to work, then it would be a new voice and it would be great,'" Michaels recalls. He believed that Tom Schiller's script could be made for between $400,000 and $500,000—a very low budget for a studio picture. Michaels envisioned that MGM would put up the money and just leave them alone with it. He figured that he and Schiller would have creative freedom. After all, Michaels was used to overseeing every aspect of his productions as he had in his television career. But MGM turned it into a bigger production because stars from *Saturday Night Live* were involved, albeit to a limited extent. "I think that it then got elevated into a greater sense of production, a larger budget, and became a more important film at the studio," Michaels remembers. "The studio thought of it as a low-budget comedy that they could make a lot of money with, like Woody Allen's first films. Because the level of casting was so good, I think that somewhere in the middle of it, the studio tried to make it into more of a mainstream picture. And I think that's where the tension started."

Before winning Oscars for *Annie Hall* and moving into drama with *Interiors*, Woody Allen made a string of slapstick comedies, each for about two million dollars or less—films like *Take the Money and Run*, *Bananas*, *Everything You Always Wanted to Know About Sex * But Were Afraid to Ask*, *Sleeper* and *Love and Death*. Allen usually added a couple well-known actors to the ensemble and created his own niche with his unique voice. When you went to see a Woody Allen film, you knew exactly what to expect. The films did very well, but best of all, not too many studio dollars were at risk. Tom Schiller had a similarly unique voice present in his work—and the *Nothing Lasts Forever* script in particular—so it seemed that everyone envisioned the same eventual career path for him as well.

The other example Michaels threw around at MGM was another comedy auteur, Albert Brooks. The West Coast's version of Woody Allen, Brooks' 1979 feature directorial debut *Real Life* was a lot like the short films he made for *Saturday Night Live* in 1975. Despite taking a bit more time between directing projects, it led to a similar filmmaking career: 1981's *Modern Romance*, 1985's *Lost in America*, 1991's *Defending Your Life*, 1996's *Mother* and 1999's *The Muse*. Each undoubtedly has the distinct Albert Brooks touch, and all were produced with modest budgets.

Thanks to Lorne Michaels' continuous insistence, MGM gave *Nothing Lasts Forever* the green-light. "That movie would never have been made if it hadn't been for Lorne Michaels," says Boaty Boatwright. "He was the one, with some help from me, that pushed it through. He really was the one that was always, always telling us what a genius Tom Schiller was."

"They wanted to make something from the people of *Saturday Night Live*," says Michaels. "And I was more than happy to vouch for Tom because I think he's brilliant, and as long as the expectation was that it wasn't the big summer release picture, it was going to be not unlike the first film that Albert Brooks did, *Real Life*. My sense was that if the expectations of it were low and it was just judged on that level, and they were careful with it and distributed it properly, that it would be successful."

When MGM production head Freddie Fields finally gave *Nothing Lasts Forever* the green-light, Lorne Michaels and Boaty Boatwright called Tom Schiller from Los Angeles to give him the good news. Schiller could not wait to get off the phone so he could find out if Jose Ferrer wanted to be in his movie. Ultimately, Ferrer was unavailable or not interested, but some of Schiller's other childhood favorites, including Sam Jaffe and Imogene Coca, did make the cut.

Schiller and Michaels are lucky that the film was made in the first place. That it was made at the troublesome MGM, of all studios, is a miracle.

1970 marked the beginning of the end for MGM, when the rags-to-riches Las Vegas hotel and casino mogul Kirk Kerkorian bought the studio. Kerkorian did not put a lot of money into MGM, instead focusing his funds on expanding his hotels and casinos, opening the MGM Grand Hotel in 1973. Franchises like *James Bond* and *Rocky* provided the bulk of the studio's income. In 1981, Kerkorian acquired United Artists (MGM and United Artists eventually merged in 1983 to become MGM/UA). The gargantuan purchase sent MGM into the red, and aside from *James Bond* and *Rocky* the studio had very little income. Add to that a number of high-profile clinkers, and it's safe to conclude that MGM was in trouble. Under Kerkorian's ownership, the studio continued to crawl on hands and knees for many years.

A number of regime changes followed the United Artists acquisition. Head of production Freddie Fields was demoted by former Paramount honcho Frank Yablans and the New York offices were eventually closed. *Nothing Lasts Forever* was one of the last projects given the green-light by Fields before he lost his position.

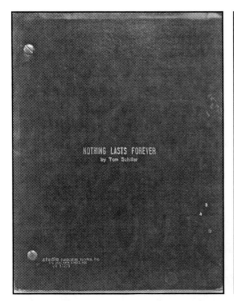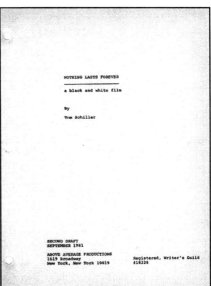

The *Nothing Lasts Forever* script.

The MGM executive in charge of production for *Nothing Lasts Forever* was Boaty Boatwright. Normally the head of East Coast production, it was the first time that she had been given that position on a film. In addition, Lorne Michaels was a first-time movie producer and Tom Schiller was a first-time feature film director. This was all new to them.

With MGM in the middle of a regime change, they were left alone for most of the shoot. "We sort of were in limbo land as far as we were left to our own vices," says Boatwright. "There was no-one that we were really reporting to at the time. I don't think anybody from MGM ever came near the set while we were shooting, which was unusual, particularly for a movie that had so many new people involved with it."

The budget kept rising during pre-production and negotiations, and it became a bit more than Lorne Michaels had bargained for. Once filming began, the budget was approximately two-and-a-half million dollars—still a relatively low budget for a studio motion picture, and the equivalent of an eight-to-ten million dollar movie today. As the budget went up, the studio started meddling with the picture more than Michaels had hoped they would. His vision was that they would leave Schiller alone with a small budget and let him make whatever creative little film he wanted to make.

Many of the events and characters in *Nothing Lasts Forever* Tom Schiller took directly out of his own life. The journey that Adam Beckett, the main character in *Nothing Lasts Forever*, undertakes in part mirrors what Schiller went through growing up. Schiller jokingly claims that *Nothing Lasts Forever* is 125% autobiographical.

As original as *Nothing Lasts Forever* may seem, Schiller did not come up with the title. Some years before, in the late 1970s, Schiller found himself in the hospital where he met an animated French immigrant named Oscar Haimo. Haimo was a legendary mixologist—a barman extraordinaire—who had penned books about mixing drinks in the 1940s. His *Cocktail and Wine Digest* (also known under the title *The Barman's Bible*) was the leading resource on how to prepare everything from Absinthe cocktails to Zombians. It was a guide that both amateurs and professional bartenders used to learn how to put together even the most exotic drinks. For many years, Haimo even held the position of president of the International Bar Manager's Association.

When Schiller met Haimo in the hospital, Haimo was in his seventies but still very energetic. He excitedly told Schiller about his self-published 1953 autobiography. Entitled *Nothing Lasts Forever*, it took its title from a quotation from the *Book of Solomon*. Haimo's father often spoke those words to keep hope alive in the Paris Ghetto.

Haimo's story is both heartbreaking and inspiring. The book chronicles his upbringing in poverty in the ghettoes of Paris in the early twentieth century. Haimo enthusiastically tells how he left school at an early age to work, how he traveled the world with numerous tough jobs, and how he became the world's leading expert on mixology.

Haimo also discusses the tragic life of his sister Mischka, a successful night-club dancer in Paris, to whom he dedicates the book. She had promise and was popular, but eventually became a drug addict and a prostitute. Even worse, she lost her legs in a terrible accident and took her own life at a young age, leaving behind a loving husband. His sister's story is one of many heartbreaking stories that Haimo recounts in *Nothing Lasts Forever*, but at the same time, Haimo's way of telling it is unintentionally funny. Haimo's writing style in both his *Cocktail*

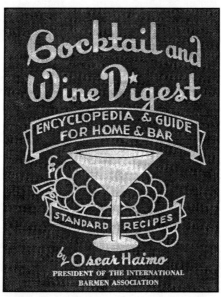

The cover of *Nothing Lasts Forever*. The cover of this book, *Nothing* Lost *Forever*, is both a spoof of and an homage to Haimo's cover.

and Wine Digest and *Nothing Lasts Forever* is naïve, to put it lightly. He was relatively new to English. Moments that are intended to be tragic or dramatic become funny because of his odd word choices. Plus, a lot of old French adages are translated word-for-word, the meaning and humor ending up lost in translation.

His story also takes drastic, unexpected turns that are both shocking and hilarious. At one point, out of the blue, Haimo commits a murder. It was a man who had tormented him, and Haimo claims that he ruthlessly killed him out of revenge. Haimo addresses his shame and remorse for the situation, but does not refer back or express any lasting regret later in the book. Haimo describes the act as something terrible, but because it comes totally out of left field, the way in which he recounts it is hilarious. Towards the end of the book, it is revealed that the man actually lived and Haimo was not a murderer. Instead of expressing relief for the fact that he was not a murderer and that a man whom he thought dead was still alive, Haimo merely talks about his happiness to be able to return to France again, where he believed he was wanted for murder. The entire murder subplot gives the book a bizarre tone.

Even the book's cover, which Haimo designed himself, is overly dramatic. It features a photo of a woman with a field of flames behind her and the *Nothing Lasts Forever* logo above. For a book that interprets the term 'nothing lasts forever' as positive, that hardship will not last forever, the flames on the cover infer the opposite, that all that is wonderful must come to an end, too. Nothing lasts forever, not even life.

Nevertheless, the book is engaging as a whole—in part due to Haimo's unintentionally humorous style of writing. There are some stories that do not make much sense, but overall, the book is an engaging and inspiring story of survival.

"To me it was always a little tongue-in-cheek," says Schiller, describing both *Nothing Lasts Forever* and *Cocktail and Wine Digest*. "It's a Frenchman trying to write in English, which can sometimes be amusing."

In addition to writing and publishing the book himself, Haimo also provided the artwork. Each chapter starts with one of Haimo's illustrations. The drawings are cute, but again, they show a hint of Haimo's childlike innocence and naïveté. Schiller enjoyed the book and often gave out copies of the book to friends as a gift. Haimo would sign and inscribe them for him. It's typically Schiller—to give someone a little-known book written by an obscure 1940s mixologist.

But what Schiller loved even more about the book was its bold logo and its title, *Nothing Lasts Forever*. It is such an inspiring phrase for anyone who finds himself in a rut. A bright light at the end of the tunnel.

Nothing Lasts Forever was the first feature length screenplay that Schiller ever wrote. He knew nothing about the rules of screenwriting and had never read a book on how to write a script. Instead, it is from watching great films and reading classic books that Schiller learned how to tell a good story and ultimately write a screenplay.

As such, Schiller's script does not follow any formulas. In terms of the rules of storytelling and screenwriting, *Nothing Lasts Forever* is questionably structured. The main character, the protagonist, does not overcome any hurdles in order to reach his goal of becoming an artist. Plus, he takes hardly any actions to move the story along. The secondary characters move him from scene to scene. Joseph Campbell would probably find it confusing.

Even the love story in the film makes little sense. Adam's love interest is not introduced until the last third of the film. Furthermore, it is a pre-arranged relationship which does not develop in any way. Adam meets her and they immediately fall in love, as if they have known each other for years. Even though it's romantic, there is nothing else to the relationship.

Alternatively, *Nothing Lasts Forever* can be seen as a statement against formula. One could make the point that it argues against boundaries imposed by the rules of storytelling. That is why it stands out so much and why it has made a memorable impression on the few that have seen it. *Nothing Lasts Forever* is like no other film. In that regard, Tom Schiller's film is a masterpiece.

Chapter 9
Meet Adam Beckett

Casting for *Nothing Lasts Forever* took place in New York, where the film was also to be shot, in early 1982. Lois Planco was the casting director, although Tom Schiller was heavily involved in casting as well. Schiller cast every single part—both speaking parts and extras—himself. They held open auditions and cattle casting calls where anyone could come in. Hundreds of New Yorkers walked through the doors and Schiller hand-picked the people who he felt looked right. The film was supposed to look like it was set in the 1930s, so Schiller carefully selected anyone who had the typical 1930s look. Schiller specifically looked for people with interesting faces and rough features.

Some of the bit players and extras were odd characters. The crew was not always comfortable working with these eccentric non-actors. They were not professionally trained, so Schiller and the rest of the crew had to be very patient with them.

"He cast every one of those parts himself," says Boaty Boatwright. "They all did it because Tom was so ingenuous and so infectious."

The search for an Adam was a long journey that took many months. Adam Beckett, the lead character in the film, was supposed to be like Tom Schiller when he was a young man, since much of the film was autobiographical. Through the open casting calls, there were auditoriums filled with potential Adams. At first, they were looking for a fresh, unknown face. When they could not seem to find the right match, they tried looking at better-known actors. For example, a year before casting on *Nothing Lasts Forever* started, a young actor by the name of Timothy Hutton had broken through in Robert Redford's *Ordinary People*, even winning an Academy Award for his performance. So, they all went to go see *Ordinary People* to see if Hutton might be a possibility.

Zach Galligan first came in to audition early in 1982—around January or February. He would later go on to star in Joe Dante's *Gremlins*, but at this time was a relative unknown. He had been going to auditions for less than a year at this point. It was a standard audition—nothing out of the ordinary—for 'the *Saturday Night Live*' movie, as he referred to it. "I thought I did reasonably well," Galligan recalls. "But then I didn't really hear anything."

Shortly thereafter, Galligan saw an audition notice in *Variety* and figured that he had not gotten the part and that they were still looking for someone to play Adam. He put it out of his mind.

To his surprise, Galligan was called back a few weeks later, on April 6th,

1982. In the morning he auditioned for another movie, *Risky Business*, which did not go well. He initially felt that his second audition for *Nothing Lasts Forever* did not go very well either. The odd and unusually long audition started with Schiller putting on some classical music and asking Galligan to mimic his hands as if he was playing along on a player piano. Galligan had no opportunity to practice and in his mind did not do a good job of pretending to play the piano.

Schiller began asking him about his hair, which was longer at the time, and whether he was willing to cut it. Schiller then had him read some dialogue. At the end of the audition, Galligan was puzzled. "I remember walking out thinking that was an unusual audition and that Tom was an unusual guy," Galligan recalls.

Schiller sent Galligan outside to wait. New York was in the middle of a blizzard, and the snow was stacked on the ground over one foot high. Schiller came out and talked to him for a bit.

"Wow, this is so wild," Galligan said to him.

"You're never going to forget this day," Schiller said.

"Yeah, I imagine you're right," Galligan replied, under the impression that Schiller was talking about the snowstorm.

"No, you're never going to forget this day, because this is the day that you got your first lead in a feature film," Schiller said. Galligan was excited but stunned. He did not know what to say or what to do. Should he hug him?

"But you know it's going to be a lot of work," Schiller said, quickly becoming serious.

Galligan raced home and surprised his mother. "Guess who got 'the *Saturday Night Live* movie?'" It was a chance of a lifetime for Galligan, who was still in high school. He was in his Senior year and had to miss the last month of classes in order to do the film. Thankfully, the school let him do the film as his Senior project, allowing him to graduate along with the rest of his class.

Schiller picked Galligan for a number of reasons. "He seemed like a perfect kind of preppy, sort of snobbish upper-East Side New York kid," Schiller recalls. "He didn't seem like a movie star, but he had a sort of egotistical quality that I found important for someone who thinks he's going to be an artist."

Additionally, Galligan's left ear was missing some cartilage, which made it stick out a little. "That's another reason I liked him," Schiller says. "Because he had an odd ear." Galligan had surgery to correct it a few years later.

Some of the actors that Galligan beat out in his auditions were Matthew Broderick, Matthew Modine and Sam Robards, all of whom went on to successful acting careers as well. None of the four contending actors had a lot of acting experience, but Zach Galligan was the youngest and the latest to have entered the world of auditions. Broderick in particular would have been a more commercial choice, but at that point, no one could have known how all of their careers would have turned out. Another actor under consideration was Griffin Dunne. Schiller met with Dunne and discussed the role, but did not have Dunne come back for an audition. Schiller was set on casting Galligan.

"He was so willing and so charming and so nice," says Boaty Boatwright about Zach Galligan, "and certainly not without talent."

Co-producer John Head preferred Matthew Modine, who was also up for the part. "Zach Galligan was okay, but I thought that Matthew Modine might have been better," Head recalls. "It was really before he'd done anything, and he was the one who impressed me most in his audition."

John Starke shares that opinion. "I would have thought Matthew Modine would have been better," he says, "but I thought it was a great opportunity for Zach, and he was nice. He was that kid."

Tom Schiller, on the other hand, was very happy with his choice. "Zach Galligan was very easy to work with—a neat guy," Schiller says. "He got it completely."

"As I was watching it I kept thinking it should have just been Schiller playing the part," says Galligan's co-star Bill Murray. "It was Schiller he was playing. I didn't learn that myself until I was much older when I was having trouble playing a particular part, so I'm not surprised he didn't think 'Well, I should just play Tom Schiller here, be like him…'"

Zach Galligan did know that he was playing Tom Schiller, and it is obvious from his performance—at least to anybody who knows Tom Schiller.

"The earnestness only works if you're amused by the earnestness of the character," says Murray of Galligan's work in the film. "You have to understand it in the light of the world, but just being so young, you can't be expected to know what that means. In a way, he was younger than the character, but the character was written with the hindsight of history. It's more informed than the actor would be."

Galligan was eighteen and did not have a lot of acting experience. He probably would not have been able to get the part down on his own, so Schiller spent as much time as possible with him in order to mold him into a young Tom Schiller. In the weeks leading up to the start of production, Galligan spent a lot of time talking and reading lines at Schiller's apartment in the Village. Schiller told stories of his adventures and experiences at Desilu, in Europe and at *Saturday Night Live*.

Schiller and Galligan also practiced mimicking various piano pieces on Schiller's player piano. Schiller loved to pretend he was a great pianist and became so good at faking it that he recognized the notes on the music roll as they came through. "I would go down to his house and it had a player piano in it," Galligan recalls. "Tom would sit down and play the player piano, and he was really amazingly good at getting some of his favorite pieces. It just made me think that he was eccentric, because I imagined him sitting at the player piano pretending to be a concert pianist when he couldn't really play—which I thought was an interesting hobby."

Schiller has long been obsessed with player pianos, to the point of housing one in his *Saturday Night Live* office.[10] The piano plays an important part in *Nothing Lasts Forever*, and while Galligan did not need to be able to play the piano, he did need to know how to mimic it. Whenever he is seen playing in the film, it had to look like he was really playing the piano. Each day Galligan sat in front of the piano at his house and listened to a tape so he could practice Chopin's 'Polonaise opus 53' and 'Winter

Wind opus 25,' which are the pieces Adam Beckett plays in the film.

> - *Learn the story.*
> - *Learn piano look.*
> - *Cultivate innocence + non-snottiness.*

In addition to the piano being a recurring symbol of Adam's desire to become an artist, homeless people also figure largely into the plot of *Nothing Lasts Forever*. In the film, Adam shows kindness towards the derelicts he encounters. Most people look upon the homeless with disdain, disgust and pity, but Adam is supposed to be gentle and understanding. To prepare Galligan for that connection, Schiller took him out for walks around Greenwich Village with a stack of dollar bills. Whenever they came across a homeless person, Schiller would hand Galligan a couple dollars and tell him to go up to the homeless person and politely offer some money. Galligan walked up, handed over the dollar bills, and when he came back Schiller asked him to remember the feeling.

Schiller also gave Galligan a piece of paper that said 'cultivate innocence and non-snottiness,' so that Galligan remembered what mindset he needed to be in. "I went to a prep school and we were raised to think that we were the crème de la crème of Manhattan," Galligan recalls. "I'm sure I carried some of that attitude with me. I think Tom was very clever with the way that he manipulated me. He was basically making me be Adam before I had to be Adam."

Galligan had to convey a sense of humility, which was tough for an opinionated young Manhattanite. "I was really young, and there was just a ton that I didn't really know about the world," Galligan recalls. "I basically got to school and that was it. That was all I knew about the world. I didn't have a whole lot of experience and I certainly didn't have any sense of gratitude about how the other ninety-nine percent of the world lived. So he instilled that into me, too."

Overall, Galligan plays the role well. He is very young and has an innocent quality, but, as Schiller put it, with a hint of egotism. Adam Beckett is a rather passive character—he does not do much in this film, as it is actually the supporting characters who move him from point to point in the story. Nevertheless, Galligan is able to convey the quality of a leading man through his performance.

Zach Galligan as Adam Beckett.

Chapter 10
The Making of *Nothing*

Lorne Michaels was not a hands-on, always-on-the-set producer. He generally keeps everything under control, but in this case he wasn't the one giving directions—at least not to Tom Schiller. That job went to his friend John Head, who is credited as Co-Producer. Essentially, John Head and John Starke were the nuts-and-bolts producers. Starke was involved with the budgeting, scheduling and hiring, while Head was more involved with the actual production and keeping a first-time director in line. Head was on-board very early and was there for every pre-production meeting with Tom Schiller and Laila Nabulsi. "Lorne wanted me to be involved in it," Head recalls. "But he didn't have the time, or perhaps the inclination, to be involved on a day-to-day basis. So he asked me to do that."

Head worked closely with Production Manager John Starke, who is also credited as Associate Producer, and the two made a great team.[11] "I was a freelance production manager in New York," says Starke. "I was interviewed for and took a position with Lorne Michaels to oversee a number of films that he had slated in production for MGM.

"One of the things Boaty Boatwright said to me, which I always thought was kind of funny, was that she wanted to welcome me aboard," Starke adds. "And I thought, I'm welcomed aboard by Boaty Boatwright..."

Fred Schuler, who had previously worked with John Cassavettes on *Gloria* and would later work on *Fletch*, was the cinematographer. Schuler made his start in the business as an assistant cameraman to Haskell Wexler and started working as a director of photography on American films in the 1970s. Before *Nothing Lasts Forever*, he had done mostly comedies, such as *Easy Money* with Rodney Dangerfield, *Arthur* with Dudley Moore, and *Stir Crazy* with Richard Pryor and Gene Wilder. But his most recent film was Martin Scorsese's *The King of Comedy* with Robert DeNiro and Jerry Lewis. He was a hot commodity, and *Nothing Lasts Forever* was a much smaller film than anything else he had shot over the past few years. Schiller screened the 1939 film *Intermezzo* for Schuler to give him an idea of what he wanted *Nothing Lasts Forever* to look like. *Intermezzo* was the remake of a Swedish film from 1936 starring Ingrid Bergman. The 1939 *Intermezzo* remake also starred Bergman, in her first American film role. Schiller liked the black-and-white cinematography in *Intermezzo*, so that is what he asked Schuler to recreate.

MGM executive Freddie Fields convinced Schiller to shoot the entire film in color. Fields argued that color can always be changed to black-and-white, but black-and-white can never be reversed to color. Schiller wasn't happy with the pressure to do the film in color, but in retrospect, he is glad that he shot it that way. There are a couple scenes where the film gradually dissolves from black-and-white to color and vice versa. Had only the color segments been shot with black-and-white film, this would not have been possible. The color film stock gave Schiller flexibility.

Schuler was German, so Schiller would sometimes joke around on the set. Schiller would speak in a fake German accent and refer to the two of them as 'Schiller and Schuler.' Schuler seemed amused, but was known to roll his eyes at times. Overall, the two got along well. "Freddie's a very professional, Germanic kind of guy," John Starke says of Schuler. "In some ways, they were an odd pair, but Freddie understood what Tom wanted to do. They had a good relationship."

To provide the music, Lorne Michaels' longtime friend Howard Shore was brought on board. The two had known each other since childhood in Canada, and Shore was involved with the *Hart & Lorne Terrific Hour* on Canadian television. Shore was also the musical director at *Saturday Night Live* while Michaels and Schiller were there, and he had some film composing experience from scoring two of fellow Canadian director David Cronenberg's films. For *Nothing Lasts Forever*, Shore was going to be involved throughout production. He was even on the set during some of the shoot, which is rare for a film composer to do. Cheryl Hardwick, who had also been involved with the *Saturday Night Live* Band since the beginning of the show, was also involved with the music. Hardwick arranged some of the musical numbers.

Tom Schiller's drive to make his movie was intense. He would do anything to make sure it was what he wanted it to be. He was the auteur, and he was at times uncompromising. This was his baby. But he was not tyrannical. To most of the cast and crew, it was wonderful to work with him. They look back fondly on their experience in making this film and have a lot of respect for him. Schiller really wanted to make this movie, and his passion to get his vision onto the screen was inspiring. But there were a few exceptions.

Early on, a disagreement took place between Schiller and Lorne Michaels. On one of the first days of shooting, Schiller was ready to start a scene involving Adam Beckett in the train compartment. Everything went along fine, until Schiller felt a tap on his shoulder. He turned around and it was Lorne Michaels. Michaels started making suggestions. He should stand a little closer to this, You should have him say the line like that…Schiller was not happy. He was not about to let Lorne Michaels co-direct his movie, so he looked at him and said "Hey! You said that I should make a Tom Schiller movie. Now let me direct it." Michaels walked away, and for the rest of the shoot, the two barely spoke to each other. In retrospect, Schiller admits that he might have handled this situation in a more diplomatic way.

Fortunately, not a lot of the crew seemed to take notice of what had just taken place, and not everybody noticed the strained relation between the two throughout the rest of the shoot. Even if they did, it was kept hush-hush and it certainly had no effect on the mood on-set—which was generally pleasant. "Lorne was very good about that. He's so diplomatic that you couldn't tell," Boaty Boatwright recalls. "Lorne never let anybody know—certainly not the rest of us who were there to work for him."

"Lorne has an amazing ability to read people," says John Starke. "He knew that he would only get so far with Tom. It was Tom's vision, and he didn't put up for any alterations. Lorne didn't separate himself from the project, but he didn't spend as much time there as he has on other projects."

"Lorne is the best," adds Boatwright. "He wasn't an early riser, but he was the one that everybody looked to to pull it together. And he certainly was the reason, as was Tom, that all those actors wanted to be there. I can see why Lorne has had this longevity of being one of the great producers."

Michaels noticed that Schiller had a very different way of working compared to other studio filmmakers. "The way Tom had worked at *Saturday Night Live* was that there were almost no boundaries, other than length and the idea that he would be completely responsible for it, which he loved," Michaels remembers. "So after the first few I really didn't see his films until dress rehearsal. And so, I think he was used to that sort of autonomy. While they were shooting *Nothing Lasts Forever*, if he felt he got everything he wanted and there was another four hours left on the day, he'd say 'I think we got everything.' John Starke would call up and say 'he stopped shooting at three o'clock in the afternoon and say 'I'm done.'" MGM was more used to endless amounts of coverage—a less personal approach. It wasn't the way a normal studio picture had been done. He did an incredible job of holding his own, but I think it was a first-time director.

"Tom had never worked on that scale before," Michaels adds. "For the first time, he was commanding a set and commanding a movie."

"He kept thinking he was making the next *Wizard of Oz*," says Boatwright. "It wasn't. But he loved it, and I've never seen anybody have so much fun working as Tom did. He laughed during every scene. He thought everything was the perfect way to shoot. He really, really wanted to make that movie. He was having so much fun that I sort of pretended like he was going to be the other side of the coin of Woody Allen."

"I can only imagine what sort of pressure he was under," recalls costume designer Sheila Kehoe. "Here was MGM thinking they were getting *Animal House II*, and there was Tom with this little gem of a black-and-white art film, being told that he should shoot it in color."

"None of us had ever done this before," Boatwright adds. "This wasn't *Saturday Night Live*. We were making a movie for MGM."

Principal photography began on April 21ˢᵗ, 1982 at Filmways Studio in New York. Shortly before, Federico Fellini made a phone call to Tom Schiller to wish him good luck. Despite having to deal with the recent loss of John Belushi, a dear friend of several cast and crew members, everyone seemed eager to get to work.

Nothing Lasts Forever

The opening credits sequence, accompanied by Howard Shore's enchanting orchestration, is exactly like that of any motion picture released before 1960. It features the old-fashioned titles with almost everyone from grip to make-up getting their credit. For the past thirty or forty years, opening credits usually only feature the cast, the producers, the writers, the editors, and the director, and a small handful of other people. Before that, films had no end credits, so all credits were listed in the opening.

The camera closes in on a relief-model of the planet Earth, goes through the clouds and finally arrives at sold-out Carnegie Hall. Inside, Adam Beckett, played by the young and then-unknown actor Zach Galligan, beautifully continues the *Nothing Lasts Forever* theme—an orchestration of Frédéric Chopin's 'Polonaise opus 53 in A Flat'—on a grand piano. After he finishes his performance, he runs off distraught, while the audience calls for an encore. The audience is a mix of stock footage from the 1947 Edgar G. Ulmer film *Carnegie Hall* and new footage of only the people in the first few rows that was shot by Schiller. Schiller shot this new footage at the Savoy Theater, while the stock footage of the rest of the audience was actually from inside Carnegie Hall.

Adam goes to his dressing room where a seasoned stage manager and a number of other old men try to convince him to go back to the stage. Adam insists that he can't go back to the stage and that he will no longer have any part in it. Eventually, the men convince Adam to go out there, one last time, for an encore.

As he sits himself down in front of the grand piano again, he slowly begins playing Chopin's 'Winter Wind Étude.' But after a few notes, Adam dramatically lifts his hands to reveal that he is playing on a player piano. He is a fake and cannot take the deception anymore. The audience goes wild and the upper-class, elegantly dressed elderly in the first few rows jump over each other to rush to the stage. They begin to attack him, nearly tearing him to shreds. One man rips the music roll out of the piano and begins wrapping it around Adam, at which point he wakes up.

Adam, riding inside a train cabin in Sweden, is jolted awake when the conductor asks him for his ticket. The conductor, played by John Garson, asks him in English but replies by saying 'alstublieft' (a Dutch word meaning 'here you are'). Just as Schiller traveled through Europe to find himself as a young

Tom Schiller with actor Walt Gorney

man, so did Adam Beckett. A man sitting across from him tells Adam that he was having a nightmare. The old man, a wise Swedish architect, recites an old nonsense rhyme that used to haunt him as a young man: "Snip snap snorum, hej kakalorum."[12] Almost out of nowhere, he asks Adam what he wants to be in life. Adam replies that he wants to become an artist, but that it hasn't been working out for him. Adam has tried painting, writing and playing piano, but did not show promise in any of those areas. The architect tells him that he should go back to America and gives Adam a word of advice to set him on his journey: "You will get everything you want in your lifetime, only you won't get it in the way you expect." According to Schiller, an architect on a train actually told him that when he lived in Copenhagen. With those words, Adam's journey begins. It is not a Hero's Journey, but an Artist's Journey.

This opening scene was intended to last longer. At the end of the scene, Adam would have run to a nearby window with his writings in hand and declared: "I hereby end my staying here for my return to the United States. I pray to God, the Buddha, James Joyce, Ramakrishna and Jesus the Christ that I will become an artist, no matter what," upon which Adam throws his papers out the window. This extension of the scene would have intensified the beginning of Adam's journey. Ultimately, Lorne Michaels and MGM cut the scene, perhaps because of its religious connotation.

The acting in *Nothing Lasts Forever* is very old-fashioned. Schiller tried to recapture the look and feel of the film and television that he grew up with, so the performances had to be hackneyed and exaggerated as well. Zach Galligan plays Adam Beckett as an innocent child embodied in a young man. Even though he has just spent a considerable amount of time outside of the United States, there is little trace of his worldliness. Adam Beckett is about as naïve as somebody who has spent his entire life in a small town. He is amazed by everything he sees, and when he later enters New York, it appears as if he has never been there before.

Many other actors in the film also give similarly theatrical performances, but it is rarely used as a method of emanating humor. There are a few moments later on in the film where Adam Beckett becomes angry and trashes a room out of frustration, and it is so forced that it is funny. But that is one of just a few instances where old-fashioned acting styles are used to garner a few laughs. *Nothing Lasts Forever* is not a spoof of 1930s and 1940s film. It's a respectful recreation, so the performances are not so over-the-top that they generate too much attention.

After the opening scene that introduces the viewer to Adam Beckett and his vow to become an artist, the film employs stock footage of an airplane from the 1940s to convey Adam's flight back to the United States. An old-fashioned Fox Movietone newsreel narrated by actor Paul Frees covers a hundred-day bus drivers' strike in New York which has affected transportation and employment to the extent that The Port Authority has taken complete control of the city.

Originally, the newsreel would have also mentioned that an earthquake devoured the entire state of California, but this was another part of the film that was excised. The earthquake would have explained why Adam did not return to California, where he presumably is from. Paul Frees, a legend in the voice-over world, is excellent as the pompous, deep-voiced newsreader. The original cut of the film includes the Fox Movietone logo, but because it was tough to clear with 20th Century Fox, it has been replaced by a Universal International News logo in other versions.

With the city in disarray, Adam has trouble entering the city even though he already has a place to stay lined up—his aunt and uncle's apartment. Once he has arrived, he immediately has to show his portfolio in order to enter through the gates as an artist. Adam has no portfolio because he is not sure yet what kind of artist he wants to be. He hopes to find his inspiration in the city itself, but only those who have shown promise in the arts are allowed to enter without having a definite source of income. The woman at the gate is lenient and allows Adam to enter, but under the condition that he has to take an art test at the Port Authority Artist Testing Center within 48 hours to prove whether he really is an artist.

In Schiller's script, Adam was to have traveled from the Port Authority gates to Manhattan by tugboat. On the tugboat, Adam befriends the captain, who was going to be played by actor Drummond Erskine. The scene would have been too complicated and expensive to shoot. Since it was of limited importance to the rest of the story, the scene was dropped.

Once Adam has arrived in Manhattan, his Aunt Anita, played by singer Anita Ellis[13], and Uncle Mort, played by comedian Mort Sahl[14], welcome Adam to their Manhattan apartment. Aunt Anita and Uncle Mort are having a party in their apartment, which almost doubles as a night club. They are happy to see Adam, although they are mostly preoccupied with entertaining their other guests. Anita Ellis also takes a few moments to sing 'It's Only a Paper Moon,' one of several musical numbers in *Nothing Lasts Forever*. Anita and Mort's maid Lu (played by Clarice Taylor of *The Wiz* and *The Cosby Show*) shows much more affection and enthusiasm when she sees Adam. Adam confides in her that he is in New York to become an artist, and Lu is confident that he will succeed. Adam's aunt and uncle, on the other hand, do not have as much faith in him.

The entire party and all scenes set in Uncle Mort and Aunt Anita's luxurious apartment were shot in just one day at Anita Ellis' actual East Side apartment, right by the East River and Carl Shurz Park in Manhattan. Schiller loved the elegant look of the apartment and asked if he could use it in the film. Ellis was apprehensive about the production taking place in her own apartment, but allowed for it anyway. She was glad that shooting was completed in one day.

Mort Sahl was a well-known and respected stand-up comic, but he had limited film acting experience. He wanted to rehearse his scenes over and over again with Zach Galligan to make sure that he got his lines down right. He was not very comfortable, but his uneasiness is tough to notice from his performance. Sahl was also insistent on using his own clothes. Costume designer Sheila Kehoe had asked him to come to a fitting, but Sahl was certain that his own designer suit would be fine. Schiller was very detailed in explaining how he wanted the other party guests to dress, so Mort Sahl does stick out a bit.

With a supporting cast of talented comics like Mort Sahl, Dan Aykroyd, Bill Murray, Imogene Coca and King Donovan, it's surprising that there is hardly any improvisation in the film. The dialogue in the shooting script and the final film are almost exactly alike.

"You were always free to do that," Bill Murray recalls about the subject of ad-libs in *Nothing Lasts Forever*. "It was really trying to get the tone of what Tom wanted in the scenes. There was the odd line, but improvisation is not like 'Oh, I'm just gonna have an idea here and make up an entire scene.' That happens sometimes, but most of what the ability to improvise is is to be able to create transitions—to be able to create the endings and beginnings of scenes and to be able to dove-tail. It's a kind of re-writing that enables you to bravely enter and exit situations. That's what improvisation means to me.

"With Schiller, though, it was always loose and if you said something good, he knew it," Murray adds. "He was paying strict attention to it, watching you fiercely. You really felt like you had a lot of responsibility. However you wanted to dial it in, you could do it. You could go for anything, and you had absolute freedom and responsibility."

Tom Schiller was very specific about Adam Beckett's wardrobe. Schiller's trademark outfit consisted of a comfortable pair of brown walking shoes, jeans, a white buttoned-down shirt, and a black corduroy blazer. Schiller wanted Adam to wear the exact same outfit. With Galligan cast just two weeks prior to production, it was not easy to find the right outfit. Since Schiller generally purchased his clothes in Europe, costume designer Sheila Kehoe had to have the jacket tailor-made.

Kehoe had worked with Lorne Michaels and Tom Schiller before as a costume designer on *Saturday Night Live*. Schiller even referred to her as his own Edith Head. "I was the one they sent to run to Bloomingdales at the last minute for fashion accessories added in the late edition of *Weekend Update*," Kehoe recalls. "Literally run. I clocked in at sixteen minutes in good weather. It was usually my job to go down to the make-up and costume rooms the second Lorne came up with the new order and break the bad news if there was a next-to-impossible quick change. I always felt like a doctor coming out of surgery breaking bad news to the relatives. Considering Lorne's impression of me from *Saturday Night Live*, I was very grateful that he allowed me to do Tom's movie.

"When *Nothing Lasts Forever* got the green-light, I was probably the last person MGM would have thought to have hired as a designer, since I had very little film work to my credit. But I did have *Schiller's Reel* and I worked for scale, so I suppose that was prerequisite enough for everyone." The *Nothing Lasts Forever* shoot was stressful for her because the budget and schedule were very tight.

Kehoe did not have as much experience as some of the other art and costume department crewmembers. In fact, Kehoe was in charge of others who had more experience than her, so it was a tough and sometimes awkward situation for her. On the other hand, Kehoe felt fortunate that her support had so much experience. Colleen Atwood, a future Academy Award-winning costume designer for *Chicago*, was her assistant. Also valuable were wardrobe supervisor Lee Austin and his assistant Patricia Eiben.

"I was both boosted and challenged by working with all three of them," Kehoe says. "Colleen Atwood was my assistant, and she had more film experience than I had. I think everybody was a little bit nervous about having me. I had never done a feature film before. It was a leap of faith on everybody's chart to let me do it, because I was certainly not the main costume designer on *Saturday Night Live*. So I wanted a crew around me that knew what they were doing."

Finding a replica of Schiller's vintage corduroy jacket for Zach Galligan proved to be a challenge. "I couldn't put things into work like Adam's black corduroy jacket without an 'Adam' to put it on," Kehoe recalls, because Galligan was not cast until a few weeks before the shoot began. "This was one of the details that Tom was very, very specific about. It had to look like the vintage one that Tom himself wore. Nothing was exactly right. Brooks Brothers had the best cut, but in every color but black. Finally, after Zach got cast, I convinced Tom to part with his own well-worn jacket for a few days so my tailor could take a pattern from it."

Since Kehoe had built up a repertoire with Schiller, they had established somewhat of a vocabulary. "There is sort of a SchillerVision dress code," Kehoe recalls. "It usually is referential to great classic black-and-white films. Having worked with Tom on *Saturday Night Live* and on his reels, I knew some things shorthand." As such, it was easy for Kehoe to figure out how Schiller wanted the party guests at Uncle Mort and Aunt Anita's to dress, as well as numerous other costumes in the rest of the film.

On his way to the Port Authority Artist Testing Center the next morning, Adam shows kindness to a homeless man in the park by handing the old bum a few coins. This is one of several instances in the film where Adam shows kindness to strangers, which Schiller had already prepared Zach Galligan for. The Port Authority then announces to the entire city via loudspeakers that the workday has begun. A variety of stock footage from the Depression era is stuck together in a montage alongside new footage of people waiting in lines. Schiller also included an arial shot of a small model of a busy New York intersection in which ants run around. Since the ants are so small, they almost look like people.

Once he arrives at the Artists Testing Center, Adam has to sit in the waiting room. The waiting room is filled with interesting, colorful characters, including Toulouse Lautrec (played by Erick Avari, a recognizable character actor). Adam is given the art test by a Frenchman by the name of Maurice Blaget—the same literary dog from *L'Art est Ficiel*, but this time played by a different actor. John Garson, who also played the conductor in the opening train sequence, plays Blaget. According to Schiller, when he let Garson read the script, Garson told him that he'd like to play the conductor and Maurice Blaget, so Schiller gave him both parts. Blaget leads Adam into a little room where he has three minutes to draw a portrait of a blasé nude woman, while the chain-smoking Blaget amusingly peeks through a peephole. All that the perplexed Adam is able to draw of the nude model is a black pubic triangle with his name signed beneath. It's not good enough for Blaget, so Adam is given a uniform and is sent to work for the Port Authority at the entrance to the Holland Tunnel. He is given the monotonous job of tracking damaged automobiles that try to pass through.

Adam's supervisor at the Holland Tunnel is Buck Heller, played by Dan Aykroyd. Heller takes his job very seriously and seems to enjoy it. He likes working with the cars and will go to great lengths to make sure that no damaged vehicle enters the city. But he is the opposite of Adam. Heller is a bold, gruff and burly man, while Adam is a submissive youth. Adam is perplexed when Heller gives him his gun. He has no idea why he might need a gun in telling damaged vehicles to turn around and return. "Don't be such a pussy, Beckett," Heller replies.

"He asked me to do a part, and that's an automatic Yes," Aykroyd recalls. "Anything Schiller brought to any of us, because we had such respect for his talent and love his work. He's got that kind of power. He's one of those people that comes along and I think he's got the pull of Woody Allen. He hasn't used it yet to that extent, but I think he could."

Schiller had written the part specifically for Aykroyd, and asked him to be in it. Aykroyd was paid scale—the minimum allowed by the Screen Actors Guild—and only worked one day on the film. It was essentially done as a favor. Nevertheless, he took the part very seriously and was focused in delivering his lines as best as possible. Zach Galligan was impressed by his technique. Before each shot, Aykroyd repeated his lines over and over until he found a rhythm.

"I was very surprised that Aykroyd could just come on the set and act, just like nothing happened," Schiller recalls, referring to the recent loss of Aykroyd's best friend.

Chapter 11
The Distinguished Derelict

After work, Adam wanders around the city. As he walks past Carnegie Hall and dreamingly looks at the placards, he meets a starving homeless man played by actor Paul Rogers, and gives him his cup of coffee and roll. This is the second time that Adam has shown kindness towards the homeless. The homeless man is very grateful and tells Adam that his name will one day be up on the Carnegie Hall marquee.

Veteran British stage actor Paul Rogers was cast to play the part of Hugo, the gentle homeless man who leads Adam to the Inner Sanctum. Casting director Lois Planco had heard about him, so Tom Schiller and Laila Nabulsi went to see Rogers on Broadway where he was the lead in *The Dresser*. After sneaking in at intermission and witnessing the second half of the play, Schiller was impressed.

"I was always a little intimidated by him because he was just a grand, great actor," Schiller says. "He came out of the English acting school and here I was, like this pipsqueak from L.A. trying to direct him."

Rogers had dislocated his shoulder so one of his arms was in a sling. His costume had to accommodate his injury, so his arm is covered underneath his coat. Nevertheless, it is tough to notice any sign of Rogers' injury in the final film. Furthermore, since he was still performing in *The Dresser*, his contract specified that he was not allowed to grow a beard for the part. Hugo is a bearded homeless man, so the make-up department had to neatly attach a beard each day.

Rogers was a consummate actor and gives an excellent performance. He never stumbled over his lines and in each take, he repeated his lines in the exact same way. Seeing a homeless man who is a polite British gentleman is highly unusual, yet in *Nothing Lasts Forever* it works. But Paul Rogers was a last-minute casting decision. Schiller had written the part for his friend John Belushi, who passed away on March 5, 1982—just six weeks before filming began.

Nobody will ever know how Belushi would have played the part. His version of Hugo would have been a polite, refined British gentleman as well, because that's the way the part had always been in Schiller's early drafts of the screenplay. He certainly was a versatile actor and highly capable of playing it as such, but he would have probably added his own qualities to the character. Nevertheless, there is no way to replace John Belushi by casting a similar actor. Nobody was like him and any attempt at trying to imitate him would likely have ended in disaster.

"I remember calling him at home and asking his wife to wake him up," Schiller recalls. "He was sleeping at four in the afternoon when I asked him to be in the film. That was the last time I ever spoke to him."

Shortly before his death, John Belushi had a slate of upcoming films. The one he wanted to do the most was *Noble Rot*, a script he worked on with Don Novello. Louis Malle also had a script for him that would have followed that, and Dan Aykroyd had written three scripts set for the two of them, including *Ghostbusters* and *Spies Like Us*.[15] Belushi's contract was with Paramount, and he wanted to do *Noble Rot* next. It was a project that he was passionate about, but Paramount CEO Michael Eisner pressured him into doing another movie first, *National Lampoon's Joy of Sex*, which Belushi was absolutely not looking forward to. (*Joy of Sex* ended up being made not very long thereafter, and it was a critical and financial trifle.)

But Judith Belushi Pisano is certain that *Nothing Lasts Forever* was something he would have enjoyed. It would have only taken a few days or a week to shoot, but she believes that he would have happily done it for Tom Schiller.

When John Belushi died, *Nothing Lasts Forever* was in the middle of pre-production. Laila Nabulsi, who lived in Colorado at that time with her fiancé Hunter S. Thompson, came to New York for the funeral and to comfort her friends. Since she had worked with Schiller before on *Saturday Night Live*, she stuck around to work as Production Associate on *Nothing Lasts Forever* and stayed with Judith Belushi Pisano.

The pre-production meetings that followed shortly after Belushi's death were particularly tough on Nabulsi. Schiller, Nabulsi and John Head had numerous meetings at Schiller's apartment, but there were also meetings at Broadway Video in which Lorne Michaels, John Starke, Howard Shore and others were in attendance. During one such meeting at Broadway Video, Lorne Michaels commented about a cartoon that was in *The New Yorker* or the newspaper. The cartoon was about angels in heaven, and John Belushi was mentioned in it. To Nabulsi, the comment came over as cavalier, and she walked out of the meeting upset.

"There were times when you would be working and it was fun," Nabulsi recalls. "But there were moments when something would remind you. I remember running around the city with Tom and there was a poster of John. Stuff would just come up. It was great that there was work to do, but personally, I couldn't sustain it because everything was so upsetting." Nabulsi returned to her fiancé in Colorado halfway into the production.

"Looking back, I regret that I let Tom down, professionally and personally," Nabulsi says. "But I was young and filled with grief."

Nabulsi was missed on the set. Zach Galligan, who spent much of his time with Schiller and Nabulsi, felt safe around her. Thankfully, Schiller's assistant Dianne Dreyer was a great asset to the production and helped fill the void that Nabulsi left.

A number of cast and crew members had been close to John Belushi in the past, and his death affected the mood on the set in some regard. "I think everyone was of two minds," says Zach Galligan. "The sensation I got was that everyone was glad to be back at work. Going to work takes your mind off painful things and allows you to do things that you love. At the same time everyone was sort of not dealing with it. You could tell that Aykroyd was more subdued, as you would expect someone to be six weeks after losing his best friend."

"I think John's death affected the mood all over that group of people, very strongly and very effectively, for quite a while," says John Starke.

"John was a dear friend of many, naturally, and he created a big void," recalls Peter Aykroyd, who makes a brief appearance in *Nothing Lasts Forever*. "It took a lot of us a while for the grieving process to happen, slowly."

"Of all the people that I wanted to work with, unfortunately, Belushi was really the one that I wanted to work with most," Zach Galligan recalls. "I grew up obsessed with *Animal House*, and Belushi was just the funniest. To me he was sort of the star of *Saturday Night Live*. I really wanted to work with Belushi, and that's why I one time asked Tom what part Belushi was going to play, and he told me Hugo. And that made perfect sense to me. It's hard for me to even think what else Belushi would have played."

When Dan Aykroyd shot his scenes, he was obviously still dealing with his recent loss. He did not make himself available to anybody. Nevertheless, he was excited about doing the part and was very specific about how he wanted Buck Heller to be dressed. "He wanted to make sure that his costume was going to be what he wanted it to be," recalls Sheila Kehoe. "He called me and left a number on my machine, and said 'Don't give this number to anyone, under pain of death,' because he really was in hiding."

Aykroyd could have taken the character in many directions, and he wanted some control over the way he looked. There might not have been a lot of improvisation on *Nothing Lasts Forever*, but an actor can bring an awful lot to his character and mold it into many different shapes and forms without changing a single line of dialogue. Aykroyd specifically wanted to wear a hardhat with goggles over it. Kehoe had envisioned Buck Heller with motorcycle pants, but Aykroyd wanted a rubber suit, which fits the character well.

"As part of the *Saturday Night Live* design team, I had total respect for Danny on visuals," Kehoe says. "The Coneheads, after all, were his vision. Though I don't always approach design as 'tell me what you want,' with Dan Aykroyd I was happy to comply."

The next morning, Aunt Anita and Uncle Mort are about to leave on a holiday to Bali. Uncle Mort and Aunt Anita are the type of upper middle-class sophisticates who have the audacity to travel to Indonesia while New York City is crumbling. Before leaving, Mort says that he has contacts at Columbia University and can get Adam into Art School there. Adam politely declines because he wants to do it his own way. He decides to move out of the luxurious apartment and spends the day trying to find a new place to stay.

Adam walks in and out of apartment building after apartment building. He has no luck finding anything until he comes across an old place where artists used to stay. The hotelier, a peculiar old man played by Bert Wood, says that there is one room open in the attic. It's a cheap, dusty room that used to belong to a painter, who one day disappeared and left the room as it is. The room is filled with junk and covered with dust. There is one painting in particular that Adam notices, a curious drawing of a beautiful young lady. The hotelier offers to clean out the room before moving in, but Adam insists that he wants to keep it the way it is. The hotelier then humorously adds that the artist who used the room before him was an artist by the name of Dufy.

As was the case with many of Schiller's unusual casting choices, Zach Galligan and Tom Schiller had a tough time containing their laughter when shooting certain scenes. Some *Nothing Lasts Forever* cast members were not professional actors or had little experience, so the rest of the cast and crew had to exercise patience in dealing with them. Some were also very old, such as Bert Wood, so it was hard for them to learn and say their lines, or they had an eccentric way of delivering their lines that caused others to crack up. To use strange and eccentric people as extras and for minor speaking parts was a trick that Federico Fellini used in most of his films as well.

The next day at work, Adam meets maintenance worker Mara Hofmeier, played with a German accent by Dutch actress Apollonia Van Ravenstein. Mara also failed the Port Authority art test under Maurice Blaget, and is also trying to become an artist. She is involved in the art world—having once been an extra for Fellini—and allows Adam to follow her as they try to discover which art form is the right one for Adam to pursue.

Van Ravenstein was a model who moved from Eindhoven, the Netherlands, to New York City at age eighteen. She was a successful model throughout the 1970s. She appeared in one movie prior to *Nothing Lasts Forever*, playing the title role in Frederick Wiseman's *Seraphita's Diary*. "I chose her because she was part of the Andy Warhol group, the group that represented fake SoHo artists," says Schiller. It was exactly the art scene that Schiller tried to satirize. "To me, she looked perfect for that style of blasé kind of cool people. She represented those cold women—all fashion and severe cheekbones."

Dan Aykroyd enjoyed working with her. "She was very exotic and a beautiful find," he says of Van Ravenstein. "She didn't have to do anything for a living back then, and she did the movie because she loved the script and saw the fun in it."

"I don't think she liked acting too much," Schiller recalls. "I think she was successful as a model. That was her thing." Essentially, Apollonia Van Ravenstein is making fun of her own crowd—the Warhol group and the SoHo art scene—but she did not seem to mind the self-mockery. "I think she had enough of a sense of humor that she accepted it," Schiller adds. "I don't think she was offended by it."

Even though Van Ravenstein was just as worldly as Mara Hofmeier, she was not as brash and cold towards the cast and crew. "I liked Apollonia, although I was very intimidated by her," says Zach Galligan, who was eleven years younger than Van Ravenstein. "I didn't know what to make of her, but she was much nicer than her character."

Apollonia Van Ravenstein at age sixteen in Eindhoven, the Netherlands.
Photo courtesy Jan de Waal.

Adam and Mara discuss art at a new age espresso bar. The bar itself is an example of the film's creative set design. The floor is diagonal, the espresso machine is extra large and extra loud, and nauseating clips from the surrealist Buñuel/Dalí collaboration *Un chien andalou* play on television sets placed in the background. In the espresso bar, Mara explains that she had more success being an artist in Paris. There she was respected, while in the United States, she feels that aspiring artists are treated like communists. Adam asks her why she moved from Germany to the United States, and Mara gives a convoluted reason, but claims that she's ultimately a Dadaist at heart.

Tom Schiller makes an uncredited cameo as Mara's sleekly dressed friend who walks by and tells Mara about a new installation at the Futaba Gallery in SoHo. The character is an art phony and tries to incite Mara to give him a dollar. Mara tells him to leave, but Adam tries to be friendly and gives him some money.

As part of their quest to find out what art form Adam excels in, Adam and Mara first check out the live exhibit *Lifewalk 5000* at the Futaba gallery. Adam is amazed how everyone around him at the event marvels at a shirtless man walking on a treadmill and counting to one million. Adam is bewildered by the performance piece, but the patrons next to him seem to be taking an interest—one girl next to him even wears a *Lifewalk 5000* sweatshirt and counts along as Klaus Wiener marches on. "*Lifewalk 5000* was typical of happenings of the era," Schiller says. "It was inspired by the pseudo art world of New York City in the 1980s—the SoHo downtown art scene with fake artists who had gallery openings and exhibitions of stuff that I felt was the emperor's new clothes."

Next, Adam and Mara go to a rock performance of a band made up of Schiller's friends Peter Aykroyd, Judith Belushi Pisano and Rhonda Coullet. The band does not sing and only makes noise by randomly banging on their guitars. "I was a member of an art band," Peter Aykroyd recalls. "We stood at a wall of speaker cabinets stacked 12 feet high, one on top of the other. They were kind of tetering, we had them stacked so high. We were called Wall of Sound. It was no lines, no need to perform, other than just standing there making noise with the guitar and kind of having a solid face."

The scene was shot just weeks after John Belushi had passed away. Aykroyd and Coullet were both close friends of Belushi. Shooting the scene was a fun distraction for them, and the scene is a great example of the bad art that Mara was fanatic about.

One short scene that was cut from the film would have offered another example of Adam's art exploration. In the scene, Adam and Mara visit a gallery of Air Art. All that hangs in the gallery are empty frames.

The next morning at Mara's apartment, the two are making love, but Mara stops because *Battleship Potemkin* is on television. She watches the film on a television set the size of a wristwatch while Adam gets ready to go to work. The idea of a larger-than-life film like *Battleship Potemkin* being viewed on a one-inch television screen is amusing in itself and Mara's stopping to watch the film is typical of her pretentious character.

Additionally, *Potemkin* is an important film and grand in scope, but many will disagree on how great it really is. It is a film that is screened at film schools and recognized as a landmark that everybody who is interested in the art of filmmaking must see, but aside from Sergei Eisenstein's remarkable editing techniques used in the film's Odessa Steps sequence, many of today's filmgoers have found it tedious. It is a film that today is strictly for film history enthusiasts because it is not enjoyable when seen outside of its political and historical contexts. In this regard, Mara's need to watch *Potemkin*, even on a miniature screen, over having sex again symbolizes how she possibly refrains from having her own judgments and instead adapts to the viewpoints of her peers.

Shooting the love scene proved to be quite an experience for Zach Galligan. Galligan was eighteen years old. He had a steady girlfriend and was not completely comfortable being in bed in his underwear with a topless supermodel. But Apollonia Van Ravenstein got into the part more than she needed.

Before shooting the scene, Galligan and Van Ravenstein rehearsed in their underwear. Once it was time to shoot, Van Ravenstein already had her top off. Galligan knew that the scene called for it, and even though he was not comfortable with it, there was no problem when they rehearsed it like that. But Galligan started becoming nervous when he noticed that Van Ravenstein also took off her panties. He quickly walked over to Tom Schiller.

"You know, you might want to tell Apollonia that she doesn't need to be fully nude," Galligan told him.

Schiller forcefully grabbed Galligan by the arm. "She's fully nude?!" Schiller humorously acted as if he was surprised. "Well, if she does not need to do that, I'm going to tell her that she…" and then he paused. "Wait, wait. I'm not going to tell her anything," Schiller said as he patted Galligan on the back with a mischievous look in his eyes. "Just go and have a good time and enjoy yourself."

Once the crew was ready to start the scene, Schiller grabbed his megaphone: "Sensuous grinding, Action!"

Zach Galligan was scared to death and tried his best not to get excited, but Apollonia Van Ravenstein was not nearly as repressed. She seemed to be enjoying herself.

Even though Mara makes a few more appearances in the film, this point marks the separation of Mara and Adam. This is the first time that they are at odds. At this moment in the film, it becomes evident that Adam and Mara were not made for each other. Mara lives for art, but it appears that she is merely caught in the scene. She is a mentor to Adam, but she only shows him what he does not like.

At work, Hugo, whom Adam encountered in front of Carnegie Hall, pays a visit. The old homeless man invites Adam to follow him if he truly wants to become an artist. Hugo takes Adam to the Inner Sanctum of The Illusion of New York City, and as the two go down the elevator and enter the underground area, the film magically turns from black-and-white to color. To open the door, Hugo recites the same Swedish nonsense rhyme that the Swedish architect told Adam about in the opening of the film: Snip snap snorum, hej kakalorum!

As Hugo speaks those words, the film changes. Not only does black-and-white become color, but the film from this point on is no longer grounded in reality. Up until this moment, everything in the film was somewhat realistic, if not always as plausible. But from this moment on, the film becomes a surreal science fiction fairy tale. Exactly half-way into the film, Snip snap snorum marks the turning point.

Before Adam can enter the Inner Sanctum, he has to be purified by fire. A group of heavy, sweaty old men with only towels around their waists who look as if they came straight from Fellini's *Roma* rapidly take off Adam's clothes, wash him and shove him into the oven. Adam quickly awakens. He is now fresh and reborn inside the Inner Sanctum.

The entire scene of the Chamber of Purification, which Adam has to go through in order to enter the Inner Sanctum, was inspired by the Turkish-Russian bath house on 12th Street that Schiller and John Belushi went to. Visitors go in for a steam, then get into the ice cold water, and then are rubbed down with soapy oak leaves. It was a hip thing to do while Schiller and Belushi were at *Saturday Night Live*—to go for a *schwitz*.

"An old friend of mine named Kenny Vance used to take me down there and we'd hang out, take a steam, and then later eat Russian food," Schiller remembers. "It was a very colorful, interesting scene. All of these fat, old Jewish and Russian men were there, just like I had in the movie. Belushi also used to come down there once in a while, and I'd go with him."

Zach Galligan did not enjoy shooting the Chamber of Purification scene, because he had to be undressed down to his underwear while sweaty old men rubbed him all over his body with the soaked oak leaves.

The Inner Sanctum is part Fellini extravagance, part *Wizard of Oz*. A whole new world has opened up for Adam. This is the real New York, while everything seen before in black-and-white was an illusion. Humanity is controlled from within the Inner Sanctum as homeless people look over every soul in New York City. Needless to say, *Nothing Lasts Forever* was made more than fifteen years before *The Matrix*.

Father Knickerbocker, played by Sam Jaffe (*Gunga Din, The Day The Earth Stood Still*) in his last screen role, keeps an eye on everything that happens in the world. He is more or less the king of the homeless and oversees everything while holding onto a big staff, which he uses as a cane. He plays an extremely old wise man, but *Nothing Lasts Forever* was not the first time that Jaffe played such a part. Almost fifty years earlier, he required a lot of make-up to play the two hundred year-old high llama who similarly monitors all that is going on in Shangri-La in Frank Capra's 1937 classic *Lost Horizon*. It was this film that inspired Tom Schiller to cast the veteran performer in *Nothing Lasts Forever*, for which the 91 year-old actor needed little make-up.

'Wetdown' by Andrew D. Schwartz

Jaffe was very frail. He was barely able to walk, and it was very tough to get him to climb up a few steps. Thankfully, he was constantly chaperoned by his younger wife, actress Bettye Ackerman. Jaffe was hard of hearing so he had two big hearing aids in his ears, which Schiller had neither the heart nor the courage to ask him to take out for filming. "It didn't matter," Schiller says. "He was highly professional and really wonderful, and I was honored to work with him."

The crew had to be patient with Jaffe because he had some trouble getting his lines straight. Whenever he forgot one of his lines, he would stomp his staff on the floor, making a loud noise. John Starke had trouble scheduling Jaffe because of issues with insurance. Since Jaffe was in such poor health, Starke had to schedule him for consecutive days. Nevertheless, Sam Jaffe was very sweet and everybody enjoyed the opportunity to work with him. Jaffe died of cancer less than two years later.

Father Knickerbocker explains that Adam was called to the Inner Sanctum to bring light and love into the world. He will be a master, like many others before him. Hugo tells Adam more about these so-called masters and says that they sometimes come back to visit. He gets particularly excited about the fact that Walt Whitman visited the Inner Sanctum just a week earlier.

Knickerbocker explains the aberrant nature of humanity by showing civilization through the ages via clips from D.W. Griffith's *Intolerance*. Humanity needs guidance, he says. He clarifies that their work has spread all over the world, but not yet on the moon. He sends Adam to the moon to fall in love with a young native woman named Eloy, Creature of Light, of which he shows Adam a picture. It turns out that Eloy is the exact same girl depicted in the painting that Dufy left behind in Adam's new apartment. If Adam can prove that he is able to love her, he will become a true artist. Adam is then presented with a golden lyre, which he proudly holds in his hands. Knickerbocker says that the lyre—referred to as The

Sam Jaffe as Father Knickerbocker.

Gift of Music—is a symbol of his promise that Adam will become an artist.

The film returns to black-and-white and Adam is now holding a sewer lid instead of The Gift of Music. Excited about the spiritual experience he has just had, Adam pays Mara a visit to tell her all about it. Mara thinks he is crazy and tries to kick Adam out of her apartment. Adam thought that they were in love, but she tells him that love does not exist. Adam quickly finds out why Mara is not letting him into his apartment: She is cheating on him with *Lifewalk 5000* artist Klaus Wiener, who cluelessly stumbles out of the shower, still counting.

```
NOTHING LASTS FOREVER"  #1963
M.G.M. - c/o Broadway Pictures              DAY/DATE  MONDAY, MAY 17, 1982
1619 Broadway, Room 905                     DAY OF SHOOTING    20th
N.Y., N.Y. 10019              CALL SHEET    CREW CALL  7A @ Filmways Studio
                                                      246 East 127th Street
                                                      N.Y., N.Y.
         PRODUCER:  LORNE MICHAELS   CO-PRODUCER:  JOHN HEAD   DIRECTOR:  TOM SCHILLER
RODUCTION MANAGER:   JOHN STARKE     1ST ASST DIRECTOR:  FRED BERNER   2ND ASST DIR: MARK McGANN
```

SET DESCRIPTION	SCENES	PGS.	CAST	LOCATION
INT/CELESTIAL CHAMBER - NITE	104,105	1	1,6,15	Filmways Studio
				246 East 127th Street
INT/CELESTIAL CHAMBER - NITE	106	1/8	1,6,15	(betw 2nd & 3rd Avenues)
INT/CELESTIAL CHAMBER-VIEWING SCREEN - NITE	107,108,109	1 6/8	1,6,15	N.Y., N.Y.

CAST	# CHARACTER	M/U	ON SET	TRANSPORTATION
Zach Galligan	1 Adam	7:30A		P/U @ 7:10A
Lauren Tom	2 Eloi	HOLD		
Apollonia Van Ravenstein	3 Mara	HOLD		
Paul Rogers	6 Hugo	7:30A		P/U @ 7A
Clarice Taylor	7 Lu	HOLD		
Sam Jaffe	15 Father Knickerbocker	7:30A		P/U @ 7:10A
Walt Gorney	20 Theatre Manager	HOLD		
Edwin Cooper	21 Old Timer	HOLD		
Marc Alderman	39 Man on Treadmill	HOLD		

STANDINS/EXTRAS	PROPS	SPECIAL INSTRUCTIONS
S.I. Adam @ Studio @ 7A	Hugo's cane	
S.I. Hugo @ Studio @ 7A	ticker tapes	
S.I. F.Knickerbocker @ Studio @ 7A	confetti	
	F.Knickerbocker's walking stick	
2 twin bums)	blackboard	
3 black bums)		
2 women bums) @ Studio @ 7A		
1 bum angel)		
9 gen bums) 18 gen bums @ Studio @ 7:30AM		

```
DIRECTOR    P/U @ 6:40A    STILLS    8A         WARDROBE       7A
1ST A.D.         7A        SCRIPT    7A         HAIR           7A
2ND A.D.       6:45A       ELEC      7A         MAKE/UP        7A
TRAINEE        6:45A       GRIP      7A         OTHER
P.A.'s         6:45A       PROP      7A         TEAMSTERS  per M. Hourihan
DIR.PHOTOG.      7A        SOUND     7A         COFFEE & for 65 @ Studio @ 6:45A
CAMERA           7A        SCENIC    7A                  for 35 @ Studio @ 6:45A
```

ADVANCE SCHEDULE	TRANSPORTATION
TUESDAY, MAY 18, 1982	All trucks per M. Hourihan
Int/Celestial Chamber-Viewing Screen-Nite,	P/U Tom Sthiller @ 6:40A
Sc 110,111,112	P/U Zach Galligan @ 7:10A
WEDNESDAY - FRIDAY, MAY 19,20,21, 1982	P/U P.Rogers @ 7A
Int/Carnegie Hall-Nite, Sc 9,20,21,6,23,24,200,	P/U S.Jaffe @ 7:10A
204,205,213,215,199,201,203,207,210,212,	Van leaves 86th St & 3rd Ave @ 6:45AM
11,13,15,17,19,25,26,27,202,208,209,214,	
12,14,16,22,198pt,8,10	

Chapter 12
Riding a Bicycle Blindfolded

A couple of weeks into the shoot, Peter Aykroyd asked Tom Schiller how everything was coming along. "It was the first major motion picture he had directed," Aykroyd recalls, "and he said that it was like riding a bicycle with a blindfold on, with everybody coming up to him and asking questions from every department, and having to make snap decisions from his own intuition."

In 1931, while shooting the film *Skippy*, director Norman Taurog needed star Jackie Cooper to cry in three different scenes. The eight year-old Cooper, appearing in the title role, already had a lot of experience making films but did not know how to get himself to cry in front of the cameras. He tried, but couldn't dredge up the tears. Taurog became frustrated and got furious, yelling at the little boy with hopes that it would induce tears. This only made Cooper angry rather than sad. Then, he asked a different boy to walk around on the set in Cooper's costume, leading Cooper to believe that he had been replaced. The tears quickly began to flow and Taurog got his shot.

For the next scene where Skippy had to cry, Cooper again was unable to produce tears on demand. The trick of making him believe that he was going to be replaced was not going to work a second time. Since Cooper appeared in the scene with a dog with which he was getting along nicely, Taurog told him that the dog was going to be shot. Again, the tears began to run down the boy's cheeks.

The third time around, Cooper feared what Taurog was going to do to him next, and was able to cry on his own.

The *Nothing Lasts Forever* shoot went along smoothly. It was late in the Spring and the weather outside was beautiful. It was a wonderful time to work in New York City. For Zach Galligan, the film came along nicely. Everybody was incredibly nice to him—aside from Bill Murray, depending on his mood—and Galligan was learning everything about making a motion picture when he was not in front of the cameras. He was having the time of his life.

117

At first he was a bit intimidated by the fact that he was doing a big movie with big stars. He was worried about whether everyone was happy with his performance and was not entirely sure if he was doing everything right. But now, after everything was going so well, he felt more and more confident that he was playing his part right. At this point, he was certain that he'd nailed it.

The scene they were shooting today was part of the opening dream sequence. Adam Beckett has just faked performing Chopin's 'Polonaise' on the player piano in front of an unknowing sold-out crowd at Carnegie Hall. But he has run off the stage to his dressing room, upset and distraught. Six tuxedoed old-timers follow him in and the stage manager tries to convince him to go back on stage to perform the 'Winter Wind Étude.'

"What's the matter, Adam? You've got to go back out there, you know?" the old stage manager, played by Walt Gorney, exclaims. Meanwhile, the audience can still be heard cheering in the background, crying for an encore.

"But I can't go back out there," says Adam.

Then one of the other stagehands, played by actor Edwin Cooper in his very last performance, tells him that it's only an encore and that he'll be done in a few minutes. Adam reluctantly agrees, but says that it will be the last time he ever performs.

The room looks like an authentic Carnegie Hall dressing room, but it was in fact two walls set against each other in the front of the Savoy Theater, which housed the Carnegie Hall interior set. But with the right camera angle and proper lighting, it looks like a genuine 1930s dressing room like in the *Gold Diggers*, *Broadway Melody* and Fred and Ginger movies of the time.

They did some rehearsing, and Schiller seemed content with it. The crew gets ready for the first take.

"Action!"

Zach Galligan, Walt Gorney and Edwin Cooper do the entire scene.

"What's the matter, Adam? You've got to go back out there, you know?"

"But I can't go back out there." Galligan delivers his lines in a straightforward manner, as he had just done in his rehearsal.

"Cut!"

Schiller walks over to Galligan. "Listen. You've got to realize something," he said. "You're a tortured artist and the idea of going out there and doing something that you don't believe in is a terrible thing. The last thing you want to do is go out there and be a phony."

"Okay, I got it," said Galligan.

So, they tried the scene a second time. Take two.

"Alright, let's go. Roll camera," Schiller says. "Action!"

"What's the matter, Adam? You've got to go back out there, you know?"

"But I *can't* go back out there!"

"Cut!"

Schiller again is unhappy with the take. He approaches Galligan and says "You're not upset enough."

Galligan thought he had the part nailed, but now he begins to have his doubts.

"You've got to be really, really upset," Schiller said.

"Well, okay…" Galligan agreed. Take three.

"Action!"

"What's the matter, Adam? You've got to go back out there, you know?"

"But I *can't* go back out there!"

"Cut, cut, cut, cut.

"Come here with me," Schiller said, and they walked outside. The two stand underneath the scaffolding of the Savoy Theater. "Listen, I don't know what's going on with you, but you're just not doing it. You've got to be angrier! Much angrier!!"

Galligan begins to cry and Schiller quickly realizes it. "But listen, you've got to do this."

"But I tried my best, I tried."

"Okay, okay, let's go back in." Schiller swiftly gets everybody back on the small dressing room set and is ready to roll again.

Meanwhile, Zach Galligan is losing his mind.

"Action!"

"What's the matter, Adam? You've got to go back out there, you know?"

"But I *can't* go back out there!"

They finish the scene with Galligan practically in tears.

"Cut! Thank you. That's exactly what I wanted!"

Galligan quickly stumbles off confused and upset. Schiller follows him and puts his arm around him.

"That was great!" he says in a much friendlier tone than before. "Film lasts forever. You'll always be able to see it. Remember when I told you that I wasn't gonna let you down, that I wasn't gonna let you be embarrassed on-screen? This was great. What you were doing before was not. Everything I said before, I didn't mean it."

Twenty-two years later, Zach Galligan can only laugh when looking back at it. "I was very lucky to have Tom as my director for my first film, because he really did a good job of shepherding me along, with the exception of this incident where he felt he had to badger me into tears," Galligan says. "He was really good and supportive. He won my trust over by making me believe that he was really doing this for my good as well as for his own good. I think he really kept his word, which is one of the reasons why I have so much fondness for him."

Schiller had an enormous knowledge of film history and utilized old-fashioned tricks like getting angry with Zach Galligan in order to make the film that he wanted to make. Schiller learned that Orson Welles would often treat his cast badly when he wanted them to effectively play sad or angry characters. "I hear stories about other directors who did that to people in the old days," Schiller remembers. "But I'm not sure that was a very good thing I did. I cringe now when I think of it. I was a fledgling director."

Of course, Schiller also applied Federico Fellini's tradition of putting as many interesting, odd-looking faces on the screen as possible. He also tried having one actor count to a hundred, and then later re-dubbing it in English—another legendary Fellini trick—although it had embarrassing consequences.

But Schiller did not limit himself to the actors. He also used old forced perspective tricks from German expressionist films from the 1920s.

"He really does know a lot about film," says Schiller's friend Bill Murray. "Most people have never seen *Nothing Lasts Forever*, of course. Even if they have seen Schiller's movies on TV, I don't think they realize his film knowledge. Even stuff like crazy perspective shots. He hired dwarfs to be in the background of the shot, so it looked like they were further away than they were. It's somebody else's old idea—some old movie man like Pabst did that a long time ago. And Schiller just decided to do that in his flick, too."

Directors like F.W. Murnau (*Nosferatu*), Robert Wiene (*The Cabinet of Dr. Caligari*), Georg Wilhelm Pabst (*Pandora's Box*) and Fritz Lang (*Metropolis*) famously used this technique to make small sets look much bigger. By utilizing forced perspective, Schiller was able to construct a modest set and make The Inner Sanctum look like a big, endless space. Objects that appeared to be far in the background were not that far at all, but the set was designed to fool the audience into thinking otherwise. Plus, Schiller placed little people further down so that it looked like they were people of normal size far in the background. The trick works. The Inner Sanctum looks like a giant abandoned train station, while the set was much smaller in reality.

Photo by Andrew D. Schwartz

Chapter 13
A Trip To the Moon

Adam wanders through New York City, confused about what has just happened to him. His girlfriend just broke up with him and he was led to believe that he is supposed to go to the moon. He returns to his apartment and trashes the place. Seeing Zach Galligan try to break objects and knock over a table are humorous because it is completely unexpected from his character. Up until this point in the film, Adam has consistently been gentle and kind. It is almost as if he is unable to do anything bad, so when he throws over a table in his room, it comes off as awkward.

After leaving his apartment and running through a thunderstorm, Adam arrives at a bus stop and gets on a bus. He does not care where it is going, and just gets on—slipping past two flight attendants. Bill Murray plays Ted Breughel, the hostile flight attendant in charge of the trip. Schiller named the character after one of his favorite artists, Pieter Bruegel the Elder. Despite only appearing in the second half of the film, Breughel is the film's antagonist. "Bill and I were friends, so I guess he just did it because he was friends with me," says Schiller. Murray appeared in the film as a favor to Schiller and was paid scale.

"He just talked about this movie he was going to do and he kept saying there was a part for me," says Murray. "I didn't quite understand what it was."

Like Dan Aykroyd, Bill Murray was eager to act in Tom Schiller's movie. "He was asking people to be in his movie and his movie was going to be different than *Animal House* and *The Blues Brothers*," Murray adds. "It was going to be something that was a little bit more of an art movie. That was sort of the cheese. It wasn't going to be a big budget movie but it was going to be something we were going to be proud of when it was all over, yet we weren't going to break the bank making it."

Bill Murray worked on *Nothing Lasts Forever* for about a week. While he enjoyed working with Schiller, doing the film was exhausting. At the same time that he shot *Nothing Lasts Forever*, he also worked on Sydney Pollack's *Tootsie* alongside Dustin Hoffman and Teri Garr. For John Starke, it was tough to work around Murray's *Tootsie* schedule, but they were able to secure certain dates and times and Murray just came in and had fun. "There wasn't a lot of waiting on the movie," Murray recalls. "People worked really fast. Everything was very well thought out and scenes were funny. I could relate to them. I think even the extras felt very excited to be involved with this because you could tell it was something different." Often, Murray would work a day on *Tootsie* and then the next day on *Nothing Lasts Forever*. One time Murray even worked on *Tootsie* the entire day and then came in to shoot some scenes for *Nothing Lasts Forever* at night. It was obviously exhausting, but he was in good spirits. Most of the time.

On one of the shooting days, Murray almost got into a fight with a co-star. Thankfully, this was an isolated incident and overall, Bill Murray was a pleasure to work with. It started with a famous Fellini trick that Schiller heard about, so he was going to try to apply it in his film. Fellini's scripts were always changing, so whenever he was filming, he often had his actors simply count to ten or to a hundred. Then in post-production, the dialogue would be looped with whatever script Fellini wanted. Schiller was intrigued by this technique and decided to try it with one of the characters in the film, a Lunar Shopping Observer. Unfortunately, the actor had come in with his character completely worked out. He was a bit offended when Schiller asked him to simply count to a hundred. He found it embarrassing to do in front of the other actors, so he almost left the set. Schiller slowly began to see that what he had asked the actor to do was not correct. He started to feel horrible about it, and realized that he made a mistake.

But Bill Murray didn't let it end there. He told the actor that he should be doing what the director wanted and that he was not a good actor. Murray taunted the actor in front of everybody, leading to an awkward situation. Schiller didn't know how to stop Murray, and it almost erupted into a fight between the two performers. The actor left and was replaced by a look-alike. "I learned one thing," Schiller says. "You don't tell an actor to count to a hundred unless you're Fellini and you're working in Rome."

Murray often joked around and made everybody on the set laugh, but Zach Galligan did not know what to make of him. At times, Murray was very kind to him, almost treating him like a little brother. He would grab Galligan by the neck and give him noogies, just like his famous Nerd character Todd DiLaMuca did to Gilda Radner's Lisa Loopner on *Saturday Night Live*. Once when Galligan was sitting in his director's chair and listening to his walkman, Murray walked over and could hear from the bleeding headphones that Galligan was listening to the theme from *Chariots of Fire*. Murray told Galligan to take the headphones off and started singing lyrics to the instrumental score, which he invented on-the-spot.

They run by the ocean
They run by the shore
They run almost as fast as a chariot of fire

Murray followed his impromptu performance with a bow. "*Chariots of Fire*, ladies and gentlemen, *Chariots of Fire!*" he said, and the crew began to applaud.

"When he was in the mood to entertain, he would do it," Zach Galligan recalls. "Most of the time, people would find it very amusing and would enjoy it. He would just do these things spontaneously."

Murray's jokes were a welcome diversion to the entire crew, but there were times when the crew was under pressure and needed to finish certain shots on time. Some of the crewmembers would roll their eyes. *Can we just shoot this thing now?*

Zach Galligan watched *Saturday Night Live* religiously, so he was a big fan of Bill Murray and loved working with him. But there were days when Murray withdrew himself. "He is obviously a complicated guy. He does not have the reputation of being the sort of 'sunny disposition' kind of guy," says Galligan. "There were times when he was very nice to me—very generous and funny…the Bill Murray that I had always hoped that I would work with. And then there were times that he was sullen and unhappy and kind of moody. You didn't really know which Bill Murray was going to show up on the set that day. My whole relationship with him left me very confused."

"He was just a high school or college kid," says Murray about his young co-star. "I don't think he really knew how to enjoy himself as much as he could have at that time—how much fun you could have making movies. But he was a nice kid."

"When you're eighteen, adults can intimidate you pretty easily," Galligan adds. "They can make you feel nervous, and make you feel stupid and all sorts of things. This was my first big role in a movie, and I didn't really know what I was doing. I probably tried to cover that up with plenty of false bravado. I really wanted to worry about it as little as possible. And sometimes Murray made it easy for me."

Alternatively, Galligan believes that the way Murray treated him was possibly intended to help his performance. Since Murray played the villain in the film, Galligan was supposed to hate him. There needed to be a sense of conflict between them. By palling around on the set together, Murray and Galligan were not establishing that friction. Galligan believes that Murray purposely acted with hostility towards him so that the friction between them could carry over to the screen. As a result, when Galligan had to shoot the scenes in which he was supposed to hate Ted Breughel, he did not need to do much acting.

Many months later, Zach Galligan was a student at Columbia University (the same school that Adam Beckett passed on in *Nothing Lasts Forever*) and Dan Aykroyd and Bill Murray were there to shoot some scenes for *Ghostbusters*. This was before *Gremlins* was released, and since the release of *Nothing Lasts Forever* was in limbo, Galligan was still a virtual unknown. Crowds of students were looking on from behind blockades as the Ghostbusters shot their scenes and waited around. Galligan recognized his co-stars so he tried to climb around the blockade. A security guard stopped him, but Aykroyd and Murray were quick to recognize the intruder. "It's that kid!" Murray yelled, quoting one of his memorable lines from

Nothing Lasts Forever. Both actors motioned to the guard for Galligan to come over, and they were incredibly nice to him. There was not a single trace of the previous hostility that Galligan had felt from Murray.

While Ted Breughel and another flight attendant, Freida Shimkus, help the passengers climb aboard the bus, Adam sneaks onboard without the two of them knowing it. The bus is destined for Miami Beach, and all of the other passengers are senior citizens. Before getting ready for take-off, Ted Breughel takes a moment by himself outside the bus to say a little prayer.

Freida Shimkus is an older flight attendant with a strong German accent. She is played by Andrea Coles, a non-actor who showed up at the cattle call audition dressed in the same flight attendant's uniform that she wears in the film. Schiller was impressed, so he cast Coles for the part of Ted Breughel's stewardess.

As Breughel addresses the passengers and welcomes them aboard, he realizes that a young man has made it into one of the seats. He asks Freida how that happened, but she has no idea how he got on the bus, either. Breughel whispers to her that he will have to come along on the trip because the bus is already pressurized for take-off. Breughel then tells everybody to fasten their seatbelts. He walks by all the passengers to make sure that everyone has their seatbelt fastened, but when he comes to Adam, he takes a harsh tug at Adam's seatbelt so that it is painfully tight.

The sign on the front of the bus switches from 'Miami Beach' to 'The Moon.' Finally, the bus takes off into the air like an airplane. Adam has no idea where the bus is going so he looks out of the window, surprised that the bus is launching into the air. Once the bus has stabilized and is gently cruising through space, Freida Shimkus serves the passengers a Lunartini. Adam takes a small sip from the alcoholic beverage but is disgusted by the taste.

On the on-board monitor assembled into the back of the seat in front of him, called Luna Vision, Adam turns through the channels. He finally settles on a station which is showing a clip from *I Love Lucy*—a reference to the television show Schiller's father is most famous for. It's a clip from the show's most famous episode, *Job Switching*, in which Lucy and Ethel work at a candy factory. The clip shows the two of them stuffing chocolates into their mouths and clothes because the conveyor belt moves too fast. Adam watches the clip and smiles.[16]

All the passengers are dressed in 1950s outfits. MGM had recently shot the film *My Favorite Year*, which was set in 1954, so costume designer Sheila Kehoe used some of those vintage outfits as the basis for the passenger suits.

Once the bus is in the air, everyone staggers into a spacious lounge area located in the back. Of course, the lounge is about a dozen times the size of the bus itself. The passengers also magically change their outfits as they enter the lounge, so that they look like they are dressed for a special occasion. "Continuity be damned!" Schiller told Sheila Kehoe. Their outfits mysteriously change once again when they land on the moon.

Most of the Lunarcruiser senior citizens were non-actors, or had done some acting when they were younger—decades earlier. A few had been extras on *Saturday Night Live*. Because they had little to no acting experience, it took some patience to deal with them, but overall they were very excited about being in a film. Still, it was tough on a low-budget film with a short shooting schedule. Certain crew members were sometimes worried about how the film would turn out once it was finished.

"He had a lot of people who hadn't had that much experience, and at the same time there were a lot of elders that weren't necessarily actors," says Bill Murray. "Their rhythms were very different. We would both know when something in a scene hadn't worked right, but if what I was doing was right Tom would just nod, like 'Don't worry, you're right there. I'll fix this other part.' Then he'd give directions to somebody else."

Sheila Kehoe remembers fitting one of the old ladies in the Lunarcruiser for a dress. The zipper was on the side of the dress, so the old lady had to pull it over her head in order to put it on. Halfway through, the lady became claustrophobic and started screaming. Kehoe had to convince the old lady that the dress looked good on her and that she needed to put it back on for the next day of shooting.

One of the more animated Lunarcruiser passengers is actor Calvert DeForest, better known from his appearances on *Late Night with David Letterman* as Larry "Bud" Melman. DeForest had just began making appearances on Letterman's new show a few weeks before principal photography on *Nothing Lasts Forever* started, but was not yet the recognizable face that he is now. At that point, he had appeared in adult films as a nerdy comic relief character who (thankfully) did not take off his clothes. He came to the cattle casting call and was one of the peculiar-looking people that Schiller hand-picked to be in his film. On the set, crew members would refer to him as 'Froggyman' because his thick horn-rimmed glasses made him look like a frog. DeForest was only sixty years old when he made *Nothing Lasts Forever*, but because he looked so much older and talked like a senile person, he blended in with the other senior citizens.

Eddie Fisher, playing himself, performs in the lounge and sings one of his signature songs: 'Oh! My Pa-Pa.' The singer, then in his fifties, was dressed and covered in make-up to look a little younger than he actually was. Fisher had appeared on many television shows but had done very little acting in feature films. In 1982, he was in a self-admitted career slump and Schiller wanted to introduce Fisher to a whole new generation of moviegoers. Given his career situation at the time, Fisher might be the type of person to perform on a trip to the moon—not unlike 1950s crooners who perform on cruise ships. Schiller was also a close friend of Eddie Fisher's daughter Carrie, so they already knew each other. According to Schiller, Fisher enjoyed making the movie, but after filming was completed admitted to the director that he was unhappy with the way in which 'Oh! My Pa-Pa' was sped up. He had to sing it differently than normal and thought it was disrespectful to the song. Nevertheless, Fisher was a good sport in making fun of himself, his numerous affairs and his career situation. *Nothing Lasts Forever* was made before it became hip for actors like William Shatner to make fun of their own image and their sagging careers. Shatner almost turned it into an art form, but Eddie Fisher was not as much at ease in making jokes at his own expense. In a scene in which Fisher confides with one of the Lunarcruiser lounge stewards, he asks how it all came to this—singing on a bus to the moon. The old Lunarcruiser steward suggests that it is because he had so many affairs. You can see from Eddie Fisher's gaze that he is not comfortable in putting himself down like that. Nevertheless, Fisher told Schiller that he had a lot of fun making the film.

In his lifetime, Fisher has probably performed 'Oh! My Pa-Pa' at least a thousand times. Nevertheless, Fisher insisted that Howard Shore stand right next to the camera and mime the lyrics to him as he sang it. Whether it was because the song was sped up or because Fisher did not know the lyrics, Schiller was surprised. 'Oh! My Pa-Pa' was one of Fisher's trademarks. Schiller did not understand why Fisher needed someone to mouth the lyrics to him.

After Fisher has performed, the passengers are led into another big area—the galaxy deck dining room. In the dinner lounge, an elegant senior citizen played by Imogene Coca sits at Adam's table and explains that nobody is supposed to know about their lunar travels. The government established a secret base on the moon in the 1950s. She says that the passengers on the bus have chips implanted in their brains so that whenever they want to tell their friends and relatives at home about their trip to the moon, the word 'moon' is automatically replaced by 'Miami.' Coca explains that the children and grandchildren of the senior citizens on the bus are beginning to suspect that they are becoming senile, so they are not completely surprised when they return from their trips and start talking about the craters of Miami. Breughel, who suspiciously keeps an eye on them, quickly interrupts and tells Adam not to cause any trouble.

Schiller had been an admirer of comedienne Imogene Coca from when she performed with Sid Caesar on *The Show of Shows* in the 1950s. "When I was a little boy I used to see her on TV and I just loved her and thought she was funny," Schiller says. "And she was terrific in the film." Coca was incredibly funny, causing Schiller and Zach Galligan to break out in laughter. In one memorable take, Coca flubbed

---

M.G.M. - c/o Broadway Pictures
1619 Broadway, Room 905
N.Y., N.Y. 10019

DAY/DATE   MONDAY, April 26
DAY OF SHOOTING   4th
CREW CALL 7:30A @ Filmways
246 East 127th St.
(betw 2nd & 3rd Ave

CALL SHEET

PRODUCER: LORNE MICHAELS   CO-PRODUCER: JOHN HEAD   DIRECTOR: TOM SCHILLER NY,NY
PRODUCTION MANAGER: JOHN STARKE   1ST ASST DIRECTOR: FRED BERNER   2ND ASST DIR: MARK McCANN

SET DESCRIPTION	SCENES	PGS.	CAST	LOCATION
INT/BUS - NITE	129	1 -/-	1,18,46,48,49,50	Filmways Studio
INT/BUS - NITE	A128	3/8	1,18,46,48,49,50	246 East 127th S
INT/GALAXY DECK - NITE	159 - 162	2 2/8	1,46,57,58	(betw 2nd & 3rd
INT/GALAXY DECK - NITE	163	6/8	1,18,46,57,58	N.Y., N.Y.

CAST	#	CHARACTER	H/U	ON SET	TRANSPORTATION
Zach Galligan	1	Adam	7:30A	8A	P/U @ 7A
Bill Murray	18	Breughel	7A	8A	P/U @ 6:15A
Calvin deForest	46	Eyeglass Passenger	7A	8A	rpt to studio @ 7A
Andrea Coles	48	Stewardess	7A	8A	" " 7A
King Donovan	49	Lunartini Man	7:30A	8A	" " 7:30
Dortha Duckworth	50	Lunartini Woman	7A	8A	" " 7A
Imogene Coca	57	Mattie	8A	9:30A	P/U @ 7:40A
Avon Long	58	Porter/Steward	8:30A	9:30A	rpt to studio @ 9A

STANDINS/EXTRAS	PROPS	SPECIAL INSTRUCTIONS
S.I. Adam @ studio @ 7:30A	mini seat belts (sc 129)	
S.I. Mattie @ studio @ 9A	microphone (sc A128)	
9 passengers @ studio @ 7A		
5 passengers @ studio @ 8A	after dinner service)	
S.I. Breughel @ studio @ 7:30A	coffee & chocolates) scs 159-163	
1 bartender @ studio @ 8:30A	piano)	
	postcard "Eden Roc")	
	pen)	
	chime)	
	coffee urn)	

DIRECTOR	P/U @ 7A	STILLS	8:30A	WARDROBE	7A
1ST A.D.	7:30A	SCRIPT	7:30A	HAIR	7A
2ND A.D.	6:45A	ELEC	"	MAKE/UP	7A
TRAINEE	6:45A @ 86th @ 3rd	GRIP	"	OTHER	
P.A.'s	6:45A	PROP	"	TEAMSTERS	per M. Hourihan
DIR. PHOTOG.	7:30A	SOUND	"	COFFEE & for 75 @ studio
CAMERA	7:30A	SCENIC	"		@ 6:45A

ADVANCE SCHEDULE	TRANSPORTATION
TUESDAY, APRIL 27, 1982	All trucks per M. Hourihan
Int/Skylounge - Nite, Sc 152-158	P/U Tom Schiller @ 7A
Int/Galaxy Deck-Galley - Nite, Sc 164	P/U Zach Galligan @ 7A
	P/U Bill Murray @ 6:15A
WEDNESDAY, APRIL 28, 1982	P/U Imogene Coca @ 7:40A
Int/Testing Cubicle-Day, Sc 77,81	van leaves 96th St & 3rd Ave (NW corner)
Int/Adam's Studio-Day, Sc 94	@ 6:45A
Int/Adam's Studio-Day, Sc 89	
Int/Adam's Studio-Nite, Sc 115	

'One Hour Lunch' by Andrew D. Schwartz

her lines. When she could not remember what to say, she improvised—even to the degree of changing the name of her character. In the final cut of the film, there are a few odd pauses when Coca speaks. When she introduces herself to Adam Beckett, she says "My name is Daisy...Schackman. I'm from Dayton...Ohio." Throughout much of the scene, Zach Galligan can be seen trying to disguise his laughter. In the script, Coca's character was written as Mattie James, but Schiller loved Coca's delivery of the flubbed line so much that he used that take.

Even though Coca only appears in one scene, she was on the set a lot because her husband, King Donovan, also played a Lunarcruiser passenger. Donovan was a well-known actor from the 1950s, so he is one of the more recognizable passengers. Imogene Coca and King Donovan were together on the set whenever one of them had to shoot a scene. Shortly after shooting *Nothing Lasts Forever*, Imogene Coca played Aunt Edna, a memorable supporting part alongside Chevy Chase in *National Lampoon's Vacation*, immortalizing the actress to a new generation.

After Ted Breughel interrupts Adam's conversation, Daisy Schackman excuses herself and leaves. Breughel angrily tells Adam that while he has no idea how he ended up on the bus, he needs to watch himself when the bus lands. Breughel says that he'll keep an eye on him, and warns him to stay with the group and not to wander off. Bill Murray had not played a character as hostile as Ted Breughel before in a film. Many of his characters up to this point had an underlying arro-

The bus has landed.

Ted Breughel with a lunar traveler.

gant quality to them, such as John Winger in *Stripes* and Tripper Harrison in *Meatballs*. They were snide but good-natured characters. Ted Breughel, on the other hand, is more direct in his hostility. It is hidden behind a façade so that the other passengers do not notice it, but Breughel does not spare Adam Beckett of his scrutiny. Even though he is strict towards the senior citizens on the bus, he is very hostile towards Adam and later in the film completely loses his temper. Breughel is, beyond a doubt, the bad guy of *Nothing Lasts Forever*.

Murray used his personal experiences of traveling and his encounters with attendants who did not have a service mentality as a basis for his character. "I have been treated badly, so it was easy to form a character who has just resented anyone who was younger than himself who was free to travel. He was forced to work and even though he was on the plane, he wasn't going anywhere," Murray recalls. "I've been treated badly on various types of transportation in my life and

I've always felt that inherent schoolteacher mentality where there are teachers that resent you because you're going to graduate this class, and they're going to be there next year. There are some that don't belong in the transportation business and that's why they stick out. They have the job and they have the position but they don't have the grace."

Once the bus is ready to land, the passengers return to their seats and they all put on their lunar protective sunglasses. The glasses look like normal black sunglasses (or grey, for the ladies) but with a grid of holes in the lenses. "They came from this health food store near where Tom lived growing up," recalls Sheila Kehoe. "It was like going on a scavenger hunt finding the place. They were these dark glasses with pinholes on the lenses which were supposed to exercise the eyeball and improve your vision. We needed to exaggerate the pinholes by painting a grid on the lenses, but the idea was one of those Schiller touches that would be impossible to just come up with on your own."

Upon landing on the moon, the film once again turns to color. The set looks intentionally like that of a B-movie from the 1950s, and the background was actually taken from the 1956 film *Forbidden Planet*. During the twenty-five years since *Forbidden Planet* was made, MGM kept the backdrop safely rolled up. It was a mountain backdrop from the planet Altair-4, only the green skies had to be covered with black felt because the sky on the Moon was supposed to be black.

Hula dancers greet the senior citizens as they exit the bus. The lunar natives look and act suspiciously like Hawaiians, because when Schiller was a child, a family vacation to Hawaii made a lasting impression on him. The Hula dancers sing a welcome song in their native language, while Ted Breughel translates the lyrics into English.

"I was like nine or ten years old, and our family used to go to Hawaii for Christmas," Schiller says. "This is exactly what happened when you got off the airplane at the airport. There would be Hawaiian women and they'd throw leis around you, and it was just intoxicating and magical for a child ten years old, such as I was. And that stuck with me a lot. So, the idea that people would have that on the moon to fool visitors and lure them to the shopping—that struck a chord."

One of the moon natives is Eloy, whom Father Knickerbocker told Adam of earlier. Eloy is played by twenty-two year-old actress Lauren Tom, best known for her later roles in *The Joy Luck Club* and *Bad Santa* and her voice work in the animated series *Futurama*. It was her very first film role, and Schiller told her that she had the part at the audition.

"Tom wanted me to sound a bit exotic, being from the moon and all, and I had no idea how to do a Chinese accent," recalls Lauren Tom, a second generation Chinese American. "So I copied my friend John Lone's (*The Last Emperor*) accent. I remember thinking I better practice the way he speaks because I might be able to use it one day. He said some sentence about Lipton tea and I practiced it over and over again to get the rhythm and timing."

"She was just perfect for the part," Schiller recalls. "She just immediately did a voice that I remembered from when I was little watching corny science fiction movies like *The Time Machine*. She symbolized that for me, and she was perfect."

"Tom and I really hit it off. We just clicked and he actually told me I had the part right then and there at the audition," adds Lauren Tom. "That had never happened before, and has never happened since. I was hysterical with excitement. I thought I was going to become a gigantic movie star."

"I remember one time walking into her dressing room to talk to her," says Zach Galligan, "and she and all of the girls were in there practicing the Hula dance. They wanted to run the Hula dance by me to see what I thought. I liked that because it was a lot of really attractive women dancing just for me. We really had a good time, and she laughed a lot. She was fun."

"I thought that she was very sweet, and did a good job," says John Starke. "She was very sweet and pleasant to deal with. Because of some of the characters that Tom had brought in, you're emotionally hoping that you can get through the day because there were very few professionals. There's a hundred people that you're paying on any movie crew, and you're hoping that all the non-professionals do what they're there to do, in the time constraints."

"I remember I had to learn a Hawaiian dance for the part," Lauren Tom recalls. "If you look really closely, you can tell what a novice I was, because as soon as we land on the moon, I look for my mark and then I jump on it. This was my first movie. I was just happy to be there and was trying not to screw up too much."

Lauren Tom worked on the film for a couple weeks and enjoyed the work. However, she did not always get along with one of her co-stars. "Bill Murray liked to tease me about being the 'young starlet' or something like that," she recalls. "It bothered me a bit. Actually, I thought he was sort of an ass."

"Actresses, what are you gonna do?" Murray jokingly exclaims. "No, I liked her. She was good and well prepared and worked hard. I thought she did a good job. I didn't have a problem with her—I was trying to loosen her up."

"Years later, we worked again on a film called *With Friends Like These* and I liked him a whole lot better," adds Lauren Tom. "I think he was a different person then than he is now. He's just so much more evolved and more in his own sense of himself. He seemed like a much happier person that second time around."

The name 'Eloy' comes from 'Eloi,' Hebrew for 'God' or 'Godly.' Eloi is also the name of one of the two futuristic races that humans have evolved into in H.G. Wells' *The Time Machine*. As a child, Schiller was a big admirer of the films of George Pal, including his film adaptation *The Time Machine*. The Eloi were the suppressed, kind-hearted race, while the Morlocks were the race of ruthless oppressors. As such, Eloy is a fitting name for Lauren Tom's character, because according to Father Knickerbocker, she is a creature of light.

Zach Galligan's portrait of Lauren Tom.

Lauren Tom and Zach Galligan inside Eloy's geodesic dome.

Schiller wrote the character in the script as Eloi, but when the MGM legal department returned his script with all kinds of notes on potential copyright infringements, they told him to change it to Eloy. H. G. Wells wrote *The Time Machine* in 1895 but didn't die until 1946, so the copyright had not yet lapsed. The rights to character names lay with his estate, so Schiller had no problem in making the minor spelling modification. It was one of the legal department's legitimate concerns, as opposed to some of the more inane notes filed in their report. Schiller was particularly amused by one comment: 'Of course, a bus cannot really fly unless it has wings.'

Schiller wanted Adam Beckett to be pre-occupied with Eloy in some way, even though the characters do not meet until the last third of the film. To do this, Schiller tried to get Zach Galligan to become obsessed with Lauren Tom. Before shooting began, he had him draw a portrait of her as Eloy.

The purpose of bringing senior citizens to the moon is strictly for marketing tests. The so-called 'Lunar consumer adventure' is reminiscent of Disneyland nostalgia in several ways. The passengers are taken away in trams and are given a tour of a giant shopping center, the Copernicus Consumer Zone, as if it's a Disneyland attraction. A song about shopping on the moon plays in the background. Schiller wrote the song together with Howard Shore. It was a take-off of a song that Schiller remembered from childhood visits to *The General Electric Carousel of Progress*—a long gone Disneyland attraction that started as an exhibit at the World's Fair. *The Carousel of Progress* was a slowly-spinning theatre that introduced visitors to an American family (brought to life through the wonders of audio-animatronics) in four different stages of history. The song in the tram scene that Schiller and Shore wrote is a spoof of 'There's a Great Big Beautiful Tomorrow' by the Sherman brothers.

Along the way to the Copernicus Consumer Zone, old-fashioned animatronic astronauts are stationed alongside the road planting a United States flag. The movements are anything but fluid, much like in *The Carousel of Progress* attraction, or *Great Moments With Mr. Lincoln,* another old Disneyland ride in which an audio-animatronic Abraham Lincoln gives a history presentation. Originally, there were also supposed to be animatronic cavemen, but that idea was cut because it would have added too much to the budget. Additionally, the printed color film is very saturated so that it looks like a 1960s episode of *Disneyland*, the television series which Walt Disney personally introduced each week.

Before Adam boards the tram, he briefly exchanges a few words with Eloy, whom he recognizes from the painting in his apartment and the picture that Father Knickerbocker showed him. Adam tells her that he must talk to her, but Eloy warns that it's too dangerous to talk while Ted Breughel is watching. She says that they will speak later. Breughel quickly walks over and pushes Adam away so that he doesn't stop the flow of passengers leaving the bus.

As the trams enter the Copernicus Consumer Zone, they pass a giant screen on which a man welcomes the senior citizens to the moon. The man on the screen is renowned soap-maker Dr. Bronner, whose soap labels contained words of wisdom. Schiller had struck up a correspondence with Dr. Bronner long before and asked him to make a short appearance in his film. The doctor's appearance is one of the many reasons that the film is so quirky and offbeat, because the reference is incredibly obscure. Dr. Bronner, who passed away in 1997, was not a household name but his line of Magic Soap products was popular at specialty stores, and he was well-known as creator and spokesman. The idea of someone like Dr. Bronner appearing on a giant screen to welcome senior citizens to the moon is such a random concept that contributes to the overall creativity of the film. Schiller taped Dr. Bronner's appearance on video and also had him read some of the more provocative uses of his soap. It can vaguely be heard in the background when Adam jumps off the tram and hides behind a crashed Russian space probe (which has a label on the back reading 'Ajax Prop Co').

There was supposed to be a scene that took place inside the Copernicus Consumer Zone, but it was too expensive to build the sets. The scene would have involved the senior citizens rushing through the aisles and grabbing as much as they could and stuffing it into their shopping carts. Then they would try to run as quickly as possible to the check-out with their overflowing carts, while Adam would only buy an orange. Since it would have cost too much to build the interior of the Copernicus Consumer Zone, the scene was not filmed.

After Adam has jumped off the tram and has been reunited with Eloy, they sneak off to Eloy's quarters, which is a small geodesic dome constructed with bamboo and filled with plants. Schiller had known Buckminster Fuller when he was younger and was fascinated by everything he learned about the geodesic dome structure. As a result, he decided that the lunar natives live in geodesic domes.

Once inside the dome, Adam says that he wants to return to earth and take Eloy with him, but Eloy says that it is impossible. She says that they will be caught anyway, so they should enjoy their moment together while it lasts. She offers Adam some Lipton tea and they drink together. They start singing a song called 'Nothing Lasts Forever' and eventually embrace.

Zach Galligan provided his own vocals, but Tom Schiller and Howard Shore wanted Eloy's singing voice to be incredibly high, as if it was from a 1940s musical. "Howard Shore was auditioning me to sing on the soundtrack, and I couldn't do it because it was written so high," Lauren Tom recalls. "My range was more of like a Broadway belt—really loud, but low—and not that kind of serial high soprano voice. So I remember feeling really disappointed that I couldn't do what he was asking me to do." Singer Mara Beckerman, who has an extremely high soprano voice, ended up providing Lauren Tom's singing voice.

Galligan had rehearsed his singing at Howard Shore's apartment over one or two days. "He was always cool to me because he knew that I had a pretty limited musical experience," Galligan remembers. "What he wanted me to sing was so high. Basically, he wanted me to sing falsetto, which most people are not very good at. I remember the session because it was the first time I ever put on headphones and heard my voice back in the cans. I didn't really like what I heard, and apparently neither did Howard, because if you listen to it, I'm barely audible on the soundtrack. They wanted me to sing something that I just did not have the vocal range to sing, so they were kind of stuck with it and they did the best that they could."

The film boasts excellent art direction courtesy of Woods MacIntosh, who did the same duties a year earlier on *The World According to Garp*. Schiller worked closely with MacIntosh to turn his ideas and innovations into reality. "We made storyboards together of how it all should look, and from those he drew his plans," says Schiller.

A noteworthy example is seen when Eloy serves Adam tea. She makes it with an interesting Rube Goldberg contraption that heats up the water, soaks the teabags in the hot water, and pours the tea into a cup. "He invented that thing," Bill Murray recalls. "It's just extraordinary because it looks like it really works—and I think it did really work. He sort of came up with it out of coconut shells. The level of invention was very high."

As Adam and Eloy embrace, Ted Breughel and his cohorts barge through one of the geodesic dome's panels and pull the two apart. In what is one of the film's funniest moments, Breughel slaps Adam, but quickly apologizes for it. Breughel then gives Adam an angry little speech, with typical 1950s B-movie acting, about the fact that he is on a Consumer Moon and he is not supposed to fool around with the lunar natives. One of Breughel's cohorts then punches Adam and he falls to the ground, at which point he mysteriously falls back to earth. He is suddenly wearing his tuxedo and falls from outer space into an alley next to Carnegie Hall. The film once again turns to black-and-white. Hugo shows up and explains that Adam is now an artist. He points to his name on the poster on the wall, and Adam enters the building, where the same stagehands from the beginning of the film are waiting for him to enter.

Adam is suddenly a brilliant pianist and has a sold-out performance at Carnegie Hall. The audience marvels at his skills as he plays Chopin's 'Polonaise' on the piano. It is just like the concert scene at the opening of the film, only now Adam is no longer sitting behind a player piano. Some familiar faces appear in the audience: Maurice Blaget and the Port Authority Artist Testing Center's nude model, Mara Hofmeier and her *Lifewalk 5000* boyfriend, and Uncle Mort and Aunt Anita.

Meanwhile, a horse-drawn carriage pulls up in front of Carnegie Hall. The carriage driver is played by veteran actor Lawrence Tierney, best known from Robert Wise's *Born to Kill* and years later, Quentin Tarantino's *Reservoir Dogs*. A mysterious woman who later turns out to be Eloy climbs out, wearing the most lavish costume seen in the entire film. "The shape of the hood on her cape came from an eighteenth century traveling bonnet called a Calash, but I did it in metallic futuristic fabric and attached it to this sweeping full-length cape," says costume designer Sheila Kehoe. "Even though it's only on camera briefly, I think it creates just the right effect when she descends from the carriage."

When Adam ends his performance, the audience throws roses at him, but there is something missing. He looks around, and hidden in the balcony he finds his true love: Eloy. The ending is reminiscent of Marcel Carné's film *Les Enfants du Paradis*, and particularly the final scene in which Garance makes a similar entrance and hides in the audience. The film was a favorite of Laila Nabulsi, but Schiller never saw it.

The movie closes with a shot of Hugo, Father Knickerbocker and two other bums warming themselves up by a garbage bin fire outside Carnegie Hall. The story has come full circle.

Chapter 14
Script to Screen

Nothing Lasts Forever provides a satisfying ending, but there are some questions that go unanswered. Why bring people to the moon when they can shop on earth? How can Adam be punched off the moon and fall back to earth? Not everything in the film makes sense, and Schiller owns up to the fact that there are loopholes. But *Nothing Lasts Forever* is not intended to have a coherent script. Schiller admits that this was the first feature script he ever wrote and says that he never read a book about how to structure a screenplay. He did not know how to develop characters and how to put together a solid plot. But that is not always necessary, of course. Schiller's friend Dan Aykroyd, for example, wrote *The Blues Brothers* without reading any books or following any guidelines on how to write a script.

A solid screenplay usually has characters that have to overcome something. Adam Beckett does not overcome anything by his own actions. He is driven to become an artist, but in the end, he is magically turned into an artist because he was kind and generous to homeless people and strangers—which he already was at the beginning of the film. In terms of traditional storytelling, the payback is undeserved. Adam should not have become an artist because he never practiced to be one.

In this regard, *Nothing Lasts Forever* may be seen as a statement against formula. There is nothing conventional about the story arc. At most, it suggests that perhaps there is more to art than practice, hard work, experience and the ability to reflect one's self onto a specific medium. Not everybody can become an artist through practice and hard work. Ultimately, it is more spiritual than that. It's a gift, but nobody knows where it comes from and why certain people have this gift bestowed upon them. Josef Lhevinne, who years earlier recorded the piano rolls that were used for *Nothing Lasts Forever*, practiced hours each day to perfect and maintain the ability to perform complicated compositions like Chopin's 'Polonaise.' Nevertheless, the same success is not guaranteed to anybody else who practices as much as Lhevinne did. In the end, an artist has a gift. Whether it's hereditary, instilled upon birth, given by God or earned in a previous lifetime, this gift is necessary in order to be a true artist.

In *Nothing Lasts Forever*, that gift is visualized by The Gift of Music, a gold lyre.

Rather than earning it by completing a goal or overcoming an obstacle, as conventional storylines might dictate, Adam is given the gift as a result of his kindness.

For a comedic fantasy like *Nothing Lasts Forever*, there is no need for it to completely make sense because it is a collection of interesting, funny and charming ideas and characters. The loopholes in the film are minor flaws that do not harm the picture much. What really matters in the film is its style, its sense of humor, and its breadth of innovation and creativity. But since movie watchers are used to certain formulas, it is only natural that not everybody liked it and MGM had no clue what to do with it.

Co-Producer John Head did not care for it. "It's a fantasy, obviously," he says. "But somehow, in order to make a fantasy work, it has to be complete and have rules, and I just never thought that was successfully done. There were bits where we're still very much in the real world and then times where we weren't. It was all a bit confused. The attempt at this genre didn't work—at least not for me." Head did enjoy Schiller's short films and his Henry Miller documentary. "In my opinion, he's much better at short form than long form," he adds.

One of the flaws of *Nothing Lasts Forever* is its weak central character. Adam is not a fully fleshed-out protagonist. In the beginning of the film, Adam clearly addresses his mission to become an artist. That is his journey, and in the end of the film, he is successful. But a lot is lost in between. The rules of storytelling dictate that the protagonist must overcome a struggle in order to reach his goal. Adam does not overcome any struggle by his own doing. The turning points in his journey are initiated by supporting characters.

Adam takes hardly any actions himself in the film. From the very beginning, Adam travels back to the United States because a Swedish architect tells him to. He does take the initiative to live by himself and declines an offer to go to the Columbia art school. But it is Mara who takes Adam to galleries and concerts and explores his potential artistic abilities. Not Adam. Just moments after meeting Mara, Adam asks if he may tag along with her as she goes to the espresso bar.

Adam's mission in the film is to bring love to the moon. While he does accomplish this, it is again not by his own doing. First of all, Adam is selected for this mission by Father Knickerbocker because of Adam's kindness and generosity towards homeless people and strangers. But this is a quality that he already possesses at the start of the film. It is not a human quality that develops within him as the film progresses. Then, when Adam leaves the Inner Sanctum, he boards a bus by accident. He had no idea that the bus was headed toward the moon. Once he is on the moon, he again has no clue what to do. Eloy tells him that he must escape, which he does. This is the only daring risk taken by Adam—jumping off the tram and hiding behind a crashed Soviet probe. Eloy does the rest of the work: She takes him to her geodesic dome where they sing and kiss until Ted Breughel and his cohorts show up, which they were expecting to happen at any moment. Adam barely attempts to fight back and does not have anything to say back to Brueghel. Breughel hits him and apologizes for it, and then has somebody else knock him out. Moments later, Adam is an artist playing in Carnegie Hall—all without any growth, development or change in his character, and without hard work.

In addition to being a passive protagonist, Adam is also childlike. He is incredibly innocent. Even though he spent a considerable amount of time traveling in Europe, he still has the undying enthusiasm and naïveté of a boy who has experienced little in life. Adam is very respectful of everything and everybody that he comes across. This openness is the only hint of the worldliness he should hold after spending time on his own in Europe.

In the bus to the moon, flight attendant Freida Shimkus gives Adam a Lunartini—a martini with a flashing light in it, as well as a secret ingredient that triggers the passengers into a shopping frenzy. All the elderly passengers are enthralled by the beverage, but Adam is repulsed by the strange taste. He does take the flashing plastic light out of the glass and sticks it in his coat pocket, much like a child who collects any interesting-looking toy they might find.

But Adam seems much more in tune with older generations than he does with his own. Even though he likes Mara, he does not care for his generation's art and the pretentious galleries and happenings that are part of that scene. Adam has more in common with the tastes of older generations, and gets along much better with the elderly. He quickly befriends Hugo, an elderly homeless man, and seems to feel very much at ease with the senior citizens on the bus to the moon. He affectionately talks with them and even dances with an old lady in the Lunarcruiser ballroom while Eddie Fisher performs. The hint of madness in Adam, which Mara mentions she sees in him early on in the film, is very hard to find.

Another flaw in Adam's character is that what lies behind his drive and desire to become an artist is not clearly revealed. From the beginning of the film until moments before the end, Adam wants to be an artist. Not necessarily a pianist, or a writer, or a painter. Just an artist. He does not show any passion for any medium. He does want to be a genuine artist, as demonstrated by the nightmare he has in the beginning, where he is a fake artist. As such, he does not seem to be after the fame and riches associated with being an artist. He has an undying need to be creative, but does not give the impression that he is interested in the craft. It almost seems like a feeling of predestination. Aside from that, it is unknown why Adam wants to be an artist. It could be to escape the daily routine of work and the inherent need for financial stability, which is perhaps why he associates with the homeless people so well. They have no responsibility and in the Inner Sanctum, Father Knickerbocker tells Adam of his potential to bring light and color into the world with his love.

Overall, the unanswered questions and unpolished characters do little to deter from the brilliance of *Nothing Lasts Forever*. Simply put, there is nothing else like it.

One aspect of the film that helps make it fascinating is its lack of a definite time setting. It's anachronistic, and typical of Schiller's brand of time capsule humor. It looks as if it was produced in the 1940s and many of the characters look, dress and speak as if they were living in the 1950s. Even the color scenes are saturated like classic color films, and old stock footage is used effectively, too.

But there are elements of the 1980s present as well. The New York art scene that the film satirizes is that of the early 1980s, when the film was produced. There are also futuristic elements, such as lunar travel, which reference not only the unforeseen future but also the science fiction B-movie phenomenon of the 1950s. The film is an amalgamation of all these different time periods. As a joke, Tom Schiller used to tell people that *Nothing Lasts Forever* was made in the 1950s, but was lost for many years. In his letter to the audience at the first screenings in February and March of 1983, Schiller joked that he made the film in Culver City in 1952, but that the negatives were lost for thirty years. He claimed that he worked as a waiter all those years until the negatives were recovered. Schiller had a vision that his film would be found someday in a vault next to actual films from the 1950s, and that it would confuse the archeologists who find it—much like what happened with the Kamen family in *The Treasure of Morton Kamen*.

Furthermore, people looked differently in the 1940s and 50s from the way older people look today, or in 1983. Rarely do films capture this reality as well as *Nothing Lasts Forever*. There are extras and characters that have one or two lines, and they look exactly like people did in the 40s and 50s. Their facial features are rougher and more contoured and their postures more exaggerated than the way people appear today. Schiller carefully selected these people from cattle calls. Hundreds of people appeared for the casting calls and as they walked by, Schiller picked out the ones that looked right. Almost every film produced in the last two decades but set before 1950 feature ordinary-looking people as minor characters or extras, and this is what makes *Nothing Lasts Forever* appear so authentic—even for a fantasy film.

The film's production was much like a fantasy as well. Aside from the disagreement between Schiller and Michaels early on in the production and a few other problems along the way, the shoot went smoothly. "It was like a dream come true," Schiller remembers. "It was Springtime in New York, it wasn't cold. It was the most wonderful experience I ever had—to be my first film and have a New York crew and all those actors. I had complete freedom."

Bill Murray admired the manner in which Tom Schiller directed. "He wasn't an ordinary guy fluffing his way through, yelling at people and telling them what to do," the actor remembers. "We always used to joke about guys that grew a beard when they directed their first movie, so they looked like they had a little more authority. Tom was serious and really paid attention to the performance you were giving. When he got what he wanted, he would really show that he was pleased. He would either smile or laugh or he would look at you and nod his head very seriously like 'Yes, that's exactly what I want.'"

"He made me feel like he really trusted me and whatever I did was spot on," Lauren Tom remembers of her director. "I've had the experience one other time, with director Mike Figgis, and I think it's a real gift that a director gives an actor. The atmosphere felt safe."

When Tom Schiller started writing *Nothing Lasts Forever* in 1981, he had never written a feature length screenplay before. When he finished his script, it was just sixty pages long, an unusually short page count for a feature film. He practically ignored character and plot development techniques and wrote the film in his own way—which is part of what makes the film so unique.

Like any other film, *Nothing Lasts Forever* went through numerous changes before it started filming. Early drafts of the screenplay and preliminary storyboards show how the story evolved. At first, the film was intended to be much more dream-like, but at the same time grounded in reality. While the screenplay is structured similarly to the finished film and features all of the same characters, the biggest difference is that the story's fantastical elements—Adam's journey into the Inner Sanctum and his trip to the moon—turn out to be dreams. In the final film, Adam does actually venture into the Inner Sanctum and does fly to the moon.

An early draft, dated September 1981, introduces Adam as a twenty year-old "in search of himself and his art." Adam is essentially the same character with the same plight, but he has trouble drawing the line between dream and reality. There are a few minor differences that shape the audience's perception of him, such as the mention that his parents died in a car crash, a bit more background on what he did in Europe, and an early instance where he curses. All of these were changed in the final draft of the screenplay. Also, a newsreel mentioning the 10.3 earthquake that wiped California off the map, a scene that was assembled for the film but ended up on the cutting room floor, is also in the script and the tragic event is referenced on several occasions.

The first major difference is found towards the beginning of the story, after Adam has his first conflict with the Port Authority. Helen Flagella, the official at the Hoboken Manhattan Checkpoint, demands to see Adam's portfolio, which Adam hasn't accumulated yet, so she allows him to enter Manhattan under the condition that Adam take an art test within forty-eight hours. In the film, Adam next appears at his Aunt and Uncle's apartment in Manhattan. In the script, a scene is cut out that would have shown how Adam gets from Hoboken to Manhattan. Since the subway system is shut down, Adam doesn't know what to do. He spots a tugboat that is about to head for Manhattan, and asks the old tugboat captain if he can hitch a ride.

The tugboat captain is a salty old man who has seen the city in its heyday. He is very friendly to Adam and the two have a lengthy exchange about how New York has changed over the last thirty years. The tugboat captain was to be played by Drummond Erskine, who later in the film plays a Lunarcruiser passenger who has had too much to drink. The scene would have helped establish Adam's rapport with the elderly generation. Ultimately, it was too expensive to shoot, so the scene was dropped.

Another notable difference in this and subsequent drafts of the screenplay is an early encounter with Mara. In the film, Adam first meets Mara when she shows up in the Holland Tunnel. He mentions there that he had seen her before at the Port Authority Artist Testing Center. It's a bit of a loophole, because that encounter is not in the film. In the script, the encounter is addressed. In an extension of the art test scene, Mara and Adam meet before Adam takes his test. Mara bursts out of the Testing Center and drops her portfolio filled with erotic portraits. Adam helps her pick up the scattered drawings and the two momentarily look each other in the eye. They have a brief exchange before Mara leaves and Adam takes his test.

The characters of Aunt Anita and Uncle Mort are also more fleshed out in Schiller's early screenplays. In the film, Mort and Anita appear in just two scenes before leaving for Bali, and later make a brief appearance at the final concert. The script contains a number of additional scenes featuring Mort and Anita. In one scene, Anita encourages Adam to take up on Mort's offer to get him into Columbia. She says that Adam's parents wanted him to go to college, but Adam replies that he hates school.

The biggest differences occur after Adam has visited the Inner Sanctum. Adam approaches bums on the street, thinking that they know Hugo and Father Knickerbocker. They give him odd stares and ask him for money, but have no idea what Adam is talking about. Then Adam returns to work, where he is immediately fired by Buck Heller, and later finds himself in Mort's office. As it turns out, Mort is a psychiatrist. Adam tells him the complete story of his journey into the Inner Sanctum, but Mort doesn't believe a word of it. He is certain that Adam was dreaming and gives him some medication, which Adam quickly tosses into a trashcan after leaving Mort's office.

After Adam finds out that Mara has been sleeping with another man, he wanders into a bar. He has a few drinks and begins to chain smoke. A Welsh poet sits next to him, to whom Adam mentions that he needs to get out of town. Adam is then led through the subway and onto a bus by random homeless people. They do not speak to Adam, but their gestures lead Adam into certain directions. One bum motions Adam to a nearby bus and gives him a white disc which all of the Lunarcruiser passengers wear around their necks. Of course, in the finished film, Adam randomly boards a bus after running around the city all night and sneaks onto the aircraft without anybody noticing.

Ted Breughel's part in the film is vastly expanded in the final cut. In the early scripts, Breughel is just one of several flight attendants, while some of those characters have been combined into Breughel's character in the film.

Once Adam is on the moon, there was originally going to be a scene set inside the Copernicus Consumer Zone, but the whole idea was scrapped because it would have been too expensive to build the extensive sets. The inside of the Consumer Zone would have been like a big department store. Fueled by the secret ingredient in their Lunartinis, the Lunarcruiser passengers excitedly push their shopping carts through the aisles and fill them in a frenzy, as if they were competing in a race. Adam also enters the shopping area but decides to only buy an orange. He takes his near-empty shopping cart to the check-out area, where a Lunar native insists that he has to buy more than just an orange. Adam balks at her demand, and she calls up

Ted Breughel to take care of the young under-consumer. Adam makes his escape and encounters Eloy outside, at which point the story momentarily resumes as it does in the finished film, as they flee to Eloy's geodesic dome.

Building a giant Consumer Zone set was clearly not in the budget, so it is understandable that the scene was removed from further drafts. The scene would have helped further define Adam's character. By putting only an orange in his shopping cart, Adam provides an interesting contrast between him and the zealous elderly shoppers. The scene also would have made a statement about consumerism, much like Schiller's teenage film *Supra Market*.

The next big difference between the early screenplays and the final film takes place after Ted Breughel and his cohorts have caught up with Adam inside Eloy's geodesic dome quarters. In the film, Adam is punched in the face and falls down on the ground, at which point he falls back to earth and finds himself in front of Carnegie Hall. In the early draft of the screenplay and the early storyboards, Adam is also punched, but then wakes up in a bed in the New York State Mental Hospital. Uncle Mort and several nurses are there as well, and Mort orders the nurses to inject Adam with medication.

Adam wakes up a day or two later, and Mort explains that Adam was found wandering around in an abandoned New Jersey supermarket. Mort blames it all on a nervous breakdown, which Adam has trouble believing.

In the hospital, Adam meets a wise old man named Oscar—a character clearly based on Oscar Haimo, the noted mixologist who befriended Tom Schiller in the 1970s. While Oscar would have appeared in just one scene, he is an important person in Adam's life because he acts as a mentor. One day, while Adam is sitting outside, a nurse wheels Oscar next to Adam and introduces them to each other. Out of nowhere, Oscar begins to explain that he was a successful gambler in the past, and in 1936 he was head waiter at the New York World's Fair. He then asks Adam why he is in the hospital, to which Adam replies that he has been told that he had a nervous breakdown. Oscar tells him that the doctors have no imagination and are probably wrong. Oscar believes Adam when he tells of his trip to the moon. The old man then gives him some advice on becoming an artist: "Do it! Be it—take the plunge. Nothing lasts forever."

Later, Adam wanders into a hospital room marked 'music room,' where he sits down at a dusty piano. A nurse walks in and tells Adam that he has a visitor—Hugo. Hugo appears to remind Adam that he has been given his art. Adam doesn't understand, until Hugo tell him that he's sitting at it—the piano. Adam begins playing the piano and flawlessly performs Chopin's 'Polonaise.' When he finishes, Hugo has disappeared and a crowd of doctors, nurses and patients have wandered into the room. They break into applause.

The scene would have segued into a montage of whirling headlines and playbills from all over the world, concluding with a newspaper swirl announcing the conclusion of Adam Beckett's world tour at Carnegie Hall.

At Carnegie Hall, Adam is greeted by well-wishers before he finally goes on stage, including Uncle Mort, Aunt Anita and Mara. Just as in the final film,

Adam then has his sold out performance and finds Eloy in the audience, who arrived in a horse-drawn carriage.

Even though the early drafts and storyboard outlines of *Nothing Lasts Forever* conclude that Adam's dreams did actually happen, they are much more grounded in reality than the final cut of the film. In the actual film, there is less ambiguity about whether what Adam has gone through was a dream or reality.

The final cut of *Nothing Lasts Forever* runs a mere eighty-three minutes, including its end credits, which is short for a feature film. Nevertheless, since so much happens in the film, it does not tend to give the sensation that time is passing by very fast. Certain elements that were scrapped in pre-production—such as Adam's encounter with the tugboat captain and his additional discussions with Uncle Mort and Aunt Anita— might have helped expand Adam's character, but would have made the film too long.

TOM SCHILLER

June 9, 1982

ZACH-

    Just a quick note to thank you for your
work in NOTHING. Despite momentary difficulties,
I enjoyed working with you and particularly enjoyed
sharing your sense of humor about the whole thing.
That, above all, is your most important asset regarding
the film- and that is ultimately what makes you succeed.
I feel we really both laughed the hardest at things which
only we could percieve- (Burt Wood, John Garson, etc,
etc.) The million and one tiny funny things which make
this up.

    I hope the film is a smash and that thousands of
girls all over the world cream in their jeans over you
in it.

    Good luck with whatever is next. And, who knows=
perhaps we might make another one together! (ADAM GOES
TO MEXICO CITY?)

                        Bravo, Beckett!

                        Tom.

Chapter 15
Out With the Old,
In With the New

While principal photography on *Nothing Lasts Forever* went well, post-production was not always as pleasant. Tom Schiller worked closely with composer Howard Shore on the score from the very beginning, even co-writing lyrics to some of the music. Shore was a childhood friend of Lorne Michaels and was the musical director for *Saturday Night Live* since its inception. He had composed a few movie scores at this point, including several films for David Cronenberg, and years later won three Academy Awards for his work on the *Lord of the Rings* films. Shore put in a lot of effort and composed a wonderful score for *Nothing Lasts Forever*.

Shore was on the set regularly, which is highly unusual for a film composer. Production designer John Starke, who has worked on many films over the

Howard Shore, Lorne Michaels, Tom Schiller and Cheryl Hardwick have dinner at Hawaii Kai after recording the *Nothing Lasts Forever* score.

145

years, had never seen that before and has never seen it since. Shore and Schiller seemed to get along well at the time—they had known each other for years and were happy to collaborate on a feature-length movie. But as the shooting progressed, things slowly began to sour.

Schiller wanted to bring in his own old records and use some of those to augment Shore's score. At the time, he actually preferred his scratch-track. "Howard had done a bunch of movies," recalls Lorne Michaels, "whereas Tom was much more used to needle-drop, which would be a little bit problematic on a feature."

"I think Howard just felt that he'd been cast aside after putting in a lot of work with the music and working with Tom really closely," says John Head. "And then Tom decided to do it his own way, and Howard didn't really fit in with that. He was excluded."

Lorne Michaels felt torn as well. Howard Shore was his childhood friend, but he had also been Schiller's friend for many years now. In the end, it was MGM who made a decision.

"It was very tense and uncomfortable," Schiller says. "It's because I was pig-headed about keeping my original scratch track, and I also didn't have the foresight to make the leap of trust that the music he was writing was actually great, which it was. And I blame myself for that."

The final cut of the film contains Howard Shore's original score. The music is reminiscent of classic themes of 40s and 50s musicals. It sounds epic and adventurous, but also romantic. Shore has composed some wonderful film scores over the last twenty years, and his work on *Nothing Lasts Forever* is among his best. Had the film been released, the soundtrack would have, too. The end credits even state: "Soundtrack album available on Warner Bros. Records."

Schiller has come to love Howard Shore's score over the years, especially in seeing the film at a special theatrical screening with a sold-out audience twenty years later.

Nothing Lasts Forever was a disappointing experience for Lorne Michaels not only because it was never released, but also because of the way he was treated by MGM. Even though he was not hands-on involved with the production, he was supposed to be the mediator between MGM and Schiller. "I was the protector," says Michaels. "I ran interference, until Tom sort of developed his own relationship with the studio. I think they were more comfortable dealing with him than they were with me. I was more questioning, and I think he was more trusting." As a result, Michaels became marginalized.

Freddie Fields was running the studio at the time, and he himself was a movie producer, which Lorne Michaels believes is the reason behind the studio-director relationship. Instead of talking to the producer, the studio began to talk with the director directly.

The studio wanted Schiller to make some changes to *Nothing Lasts For-*

ever, which Michaels claims he would not have allowed that easily. "I wanted it to be treated in a different way," says Michaels. "But it was Tom's first film and I think he was trying to do what it was they wanted.

"There had been a group of people that had been around Tom that had worked with him on the show, [or] that had known him since California," Michaels adds. "Howard being one of them, myself being one of them, and John Head being another one of them. I think there was the feeling that, with the studio's—for a lack of a better word—encouragement, that they wanted to do the picture that Tom wanted to do. It put me in a very awkward position since they were looking at me to be the one who sort of guaranteed or looked after it." Even though Michaels was cut out of the equation after Freddie Fields started dealing directly with Schiller, there was still the sense that MGM was holding Michaels responsible for the picture.

Both Schiller and Michaels had their own cut of the film. Both were very similar, only with minor differences like the Movietone newsreel footage of a California earthquake and Adam's vow to become an artist missing from Michaels' cut. The changes bothered Schiller at the time, but they no longer bother him as much today. Another difference in Michaels' cut that Schiller believes benefited the film is that Michaels added shots of Father Knickerbocker looking at Adam and Eloy through his magical screen in the Inner Sanctum while Adam and Eloy were in the geodesic dome. These cutaways provided an excellent way to break away from the action.

When the executives at MGM screened *Nothing Lasts Forever*, they told Tom Schiller that it was an 'art film.' Schiller was ecstatic. To him, that was the greatest compliment he could possibly receive. But Lorne Michaels realized that this was bad news.

"When Freddie Fields declared it an art film, that was not a good thing," says Michaels. "My suggestion to MGM was that you could make a Tom Schiller picture and as long as the budget parameters were fixed and he was left alone, that you would get something that was original, funny and brilliant—but would be for a special audience, and would have to be handled in a certain kind of way. They had now put enough money into it that they were expecting, with Bill Murray and Dan Aykroyd, that they were going to get a version of *Stripes*.

"For me, what I loved about *Nothing Lasts Forever* is what I loved about his films for *Saturday Night Live*," Michaels adds. "It's just Tom's vision of things. I thought it was charming and original, but it strained to be a commercial picture, which was a burden that was put on him—I thought unnecessarily. I think it was judged in a different way."

Because MGM was in deep financial trouble, they had to be careful about where to put their resources. In the end, the studio decided that it would be impossible to risk marketing a black-and-white art film. MGM was blind-sided by the fact that they weren't getting the '*Saturday Night Live* movie' they were expecting.

In early 1983, *Nothing Lasts Forever* was completed and the studio was not happy with it. They were staggered. While some executives at MGM liked the film, such as Senior Vice President of Production Management George Justin, nobody at MGM had any clue what to do with it. This was not a commercial motion picture. It was an art film. Freddie Fields was not happy with Lorne Michaels and company, with whom he recently had a falling-out. The fate of *Nothing Lasts Forever* remained undecided. It was shelved indefinitely. Next on the agenda: *Nineteen Eighty-Five*.

Lorne Michaels, Jim Downey, Tom Davis and Al Franken went to a meeting with Freddie Fields to discuss the *Nineteen Eighty-Five* screenplay, which had just been finished after well over a year of writing. Michaels and company had not received any response to the project from MGM as of late. The meeting took place at Broadway Video. Michaels, Franken, Davis and Downey were there, as were Freddie Fields and one of his associates, and perhaps one or two other people. The three writers began to read their comedy screenplay from beginning to end. Since it can take hours to read a script, this is a very uncommon process. Moreover, the script to *Nineteen Eighty-Five* was 142 pages—more than twice as long as Tom Schiller's *Nothing Lasts Forever* screenplay.

"An entire feature length film was read aloud, with directions," Tom Davis recalls. "Not one laugh came from Freddie Fields. Not one." It was an awkward situation, stretched out over hours. Fields was silent. Franken, Davis and Downey should have stopped after about ten minutes. Ten minutes would have probably been sufficient, but they kept going.

"We decided, if we were going down, we were going down swinging," says Davis. "And so we read the whole fucking thing, which is ridiculous. Everybody had to sit through it. We had taken two years to write it because we were idiots."

When they reached the last page, Fields stood up and said that he had to make a few phone calls. He left the room, and *Nineteen Eighty-Five* became a moot point. Lorne Michaels' contract dissolved soon after.

"Schiller got his film made, which was genius," Davis adds. "It will be appreciated and it's going to be very popular in the future, but it's better than the bitter wind that blew out the candle on my deal. I just squandered precious time."

Shortly after *Nothing Lasts Forever* was completed, Lorne Michaels held a screening of the finished film in his private screening room at Broadway Video. Many of his high-profile friends filled up the thirty-odd seats in The Broadway Screening Room. Paul Simon, who had been one of Michaels' closest friends for many years, was there. Mike Nichols, the Academy Award-winning director who directed the filmed version of the *Gilda Live* Broadway production for Michaels, was there. Louis Malle, the legendary French New Wave director who was developing a film for John Belushi at the time of his death, was there with his wife, actress Candice Bergen. Lillian Ross, a writer for *The New Yorker* whom Schiller admired was also there to see the film. It was a who's who of powerful players that

Michaels wanted to show his film to. Schiller had known Paul Simon for several years, and Louis Malle and Mike Nichols were two wonderful directors that he admired very much. Their approval would have meant the world to him. Instead, the screening turned out to be a disappointment.

Michaels sat with his friends in the front rows of the screening room while Schiller had to sit towards the back. Schiller felt left out, as if he was sitting in Tourist Class. Adding to that, the sound was turned up way too high. Schiller was too nervous to ask for it to be turned down, so the volume remained at that level for all eighty-three minutes. It grated on Schiller's nerves. John Starke was in attendance as well, as were a number of others who were involved in the making of the film. To them, the screening was not so catastrophic. They laughed at the jokes, but Lorne Michaels and his friends remained silent.

"When you do a comedy and you're involved with it as closely as we all were, you think some funny things are funnier than they actually are," says Starke. "That's just the nature of the beast. They become inside jokes, so there was some silence in parts that we thought were particularly funny."

When the film ended, Lorne Michaels and his guests passed Schiller as they walked out in the midst of absolute silence.

"Cut it to the bone," was all that Louis Malle had to say to Schiller as he passed by.

When Mike Nichols walked by, he turned around and looked Schiller in the eye. "Good for you!" he exclaimed on his way out of the room.

Candice Bergen told him that he made "a beautiful, beautiful film," which Schiller appreciated. But it was the only direct, unambiguous comment that he received.

"They just didn't get it," Laila Nabulsi recalls, "and Tom was really upset about it."

A few days later, Schiller called up Lillian Ross, the *New Yorker* writer who was doing a story on Lorne Michaels. It was clear to him at the screening that she did not like the film, so he wanted to find out exactly why. She confirmed Schiller's suspicions that she disliked the film, and was frank in her explanation of the reasons why. Schiller was crushed. "I don't know how some people could manage getting a bad review without it hurting their feelings," he says, "but these things really hurt mine."

Most studio films go through a preview process to monitor audience response. *Nothing Lasts Forever* had not had any preview screenings. This was the first time that a crowd gathered to see the film projected, so it was the first time that Schiller saw how an audience reacted to his film.

"Nothing would have delighted me more than everybody rising to their feet and applauding at the end, but it's not what happened," Lorne Michaels recalls of the screening. "They were all friends of mine at that time, and I think everybody was incredibly supportive of what I was doing and what Tom was doing. But I think that it was probably the beginning of the air coming out of the balloon. There was so much hype coming from the studio to Tom about it being a work of genius—all straight Hollywood stuff. And I think this was a New York screening. This was not a Hollywood screening. And also, that would be a very tough room, with Mike Nichols and Louis Malle."

The most painful aspect for Tom Schiller was the fact that the film was invited to play at the prestigious Directors' Fortnight at the Cannes Film Festival, but MGM did not allow it to appear.

Schiller heard that there was a gentleman in town from the Cannes Film Festival who was looking for films to be screened at the popular festival.

"Somehow I heard that there was a man in town who was looking for films for Cannes," Schiller recalls. "So I sent over a print of the film to this guy and I got a phone call from him. He said 'Messieur, you have created a *chef d'oeuvre*—a masterpiece. Please meet me at the Algonquin hotel.' So I meet this guy at the Algonquin hotel and he orders champagne and says 'You will be the sensation of the Cannes Directors' Fortnight.'"

The Frenchman was Pierre-Henri Deleau, co-founder of the Directors' Fortnight (the out-of-competition director showcase) and at that time the General Delegate of the Cannes Film Festival. "I fell in love with this film—the story, its humor, and its style," Deleau recalls more than twenty years later. "I think it certainly would have been a great success, because this film has a unique tone."

"I was the most excited I'd ever been," says Schiller. "To have a French guy like my movie was the ultimate praise for me. That a European would get it."

"It seems a perfect example of humor to me, and especially nonsense humor," Deleau adds. "It reminds me of the work of the Surrealists—unclassifiable and personal. Quite the way I like it." Schiller called Freddie Fields and full of excitement told the MGM president the wonderful news: *Nothing Lasts Forever* was invited to play at Cannes. Sadly, the excitement did not last very long.

"He said 'You can't send it to Cannes. You'd get hurt,'" Schiller recalls. "I said 'What? Give me an example of a film that was ever hurt at Cannes.' He said 'Baby, I can give you a list of fifty on your desk by tomorrow.'"

Nothing showed up on Schiller's desk the next morning. Nor did anything show up in the days and weeks that followed. Fields had given him a bad excuse and failed to back it up.

"Studios sometimes refuse," says Deleau, "because they are afraid of the international critics which can stop the success of a film if they don't like it." For *Nothing Lasts Forever*, MGM had already decided that they were not going to release it. Since MGM was unable to market the film, they didn't want anything to do with it.

"That was the most heartbreaking thing, because that was my dream," Schiller says. "To be recognized in the European market as an interesting American director."

Pierre-Henri Deleau loved the film so much that he invited it to play at Cannes two years in a row. Both years, MGM did not let it go, and did not give Schiller a good explanation of why not. "Today, I still remain convinced," Deleau says, "even if I did not see it again for a long time, that this film did not become old-fashioned and is part of the great succession of films crushed by the business industry."

"I think Tom was led to believe by the studio that they loved the picture and that they would support the picture," says Lorne Michaels. "And then when they didn't, I think he was astonished, because I think there had been nothing in what they had said to him beforehand that would have led him to believe it."

There are many theories about why *Nothing Lasts Forever* was not released. Technically, the film was released, but nobody who worked on the film refers to it as such. *Nothing Lasts Forever* had a short test release in Seattle in 1984. A few different stories float around—some are apocryphal, and some are true...but they do not provide a solid explanation.

The story that MGM (and later Turner Entertainment, which purchased *Nothing Lasts Forever* as part of a package of hundreds of titles from the MGM library a few years later) gave Schiller cited music rights as a reason for not releasing the film. Many films use popular music which needs to be cleared for theatrical, home video and television distribution. *Nothing Lasts Forever* did not contain any songs that would have proved challenging or unusually expensive to clear, so this is likely a blanket statement that the studios gave Schiller.

Bill Murray likes to tell a story about Lorne Michaels in a limousine. He does not remember where the story originates, and even admits that he is unsure of its validity. But that has not stopped him from telling it. "Supposedly, Lorne said something about the movie studio that was releasing the film (MGM) in the limousine on the way home from a World Series game or something," Murray says. "He didn't know that one of the people in the car was with the studio. I think they made a decision then and there to never release the movie. That's the story. True or false, it's a good story."

"Not true," says Lorne Michaels. There was indeed a snafu between him and MGM, but it had no bearing on the release of *Nothing Lasts Forever*. Michaels was already off the picture by this time. "What happened was, they made a deal with Tom for his next picture, but no one told me. I called up and went 'Well, wait a minute...You're talking to Tom.' They wanted him to make some changes, and I didn't want to make the changes. They talked about his being under contract at MGM. In a sense, I became marginalized. That's when I had my disagreement with the studio and that's when it got dark and murky."

Another story that has circulated claims that Lorne Michaels himself made the choice not to release it, following the screening he held at Broadway Video. Like Bill Murray's limousine story, this is untrue. "At that point, MGM was no longer talking to me," Michaels says. "It's the only thing in my life and in my career that I was, in a sense, taken off. Suddenly it was Tom and the studio, and Tom made decisions that he made. And then when we were all so far gone by that point, because we had been eliminated, and the picture then didn't get released, there was nothing that could be done."

"In the middle of the whole process, MGM thought they had Woody Allen on their hands," says Lorne Michaels' agent, Bernie Brillstein. "They thought they had a big star, and they sort of eliminated Lorne from the entire process. We didn't know about it until Lorne had no more input, and then we found out that MGM was making an overall deal with Tom."

Schiller has no recollection of any discussions of follow-up projects with MGM. He believes that if such talks took place, they were merely comments made in passing. For example, Boaty Boatwright once told Schiller that she thought he would get a deal for another movie. Regardless of whether MGM did or did not talk to Schiller about being under contract, when *Nothing Lasts Forever* was finished, so was Schiller in MGM's books. No movie contract ever materialized. "I would have jumped at the chance to make a second motion picture, but in reality I was barely speaking to MGM. I think I had only one or two meetings with Freddie Fields. I know the studio was going through a lot of changes, and I never quite understood the relationships between Lorne and Freddie Fields.

"I think they were just trying to fulfill Lorne's contract with the cheapest movie possible," Schiller adds. "When they found out it wasn't a yuck-yuck *SNL* movie but a weird 'art' film, everyone wanted to wash their hands of it."

"What unhappiness I have about it is just that the potential didn't get reached, and that I couldn't protect it," says Michaels. "That was taken away from me by the studio, which saw that if they dealt with Tom directly, they thought that they could get what they wanted. And then when they got what they wanted, they didn't like it. I have enormous regret that I was not able to be there for the picture at the end. But that's just the way it worked out."

"I regret that all of us were so inexperienced with working in the studio system," says Tom Schiller. "I now understand Lorne's situation as producer on the picture, and how his hands were tied. One thing I liked about him as a producer was the way he ran interference between me and the corporation I happened to be working for. He created an environment where I could enjoy maximum creative freedom. But I suppose it got botched up with *Nothing Lasts Forever*, one of his first major studio productions. I think now he'd do better."

Lorne Michaels used the difficulties surrounding *Nothing Lasts Forever* as a learning experience. "I had better experiences later on," he says. "When I went in to do *Wayne's World*, I had a meeting with the man who was then running Paramount, Frank Mancuso. I said 'This is what I want to do, and at this budget level, will I be left alone?' And that was the agreement."

The real reason why *Nothing Lasts Forever* went unreleased is a combination of factors: MGM had limited funds, MGM did not like the movie, Murray and Aykroyd's names were not allowed to be used in publicity, the movie was an art film, and MGM had no clue what to do with it.

Hardly any low-profile MGM and United Artists films were released in 1983. *Eureka*, a Nicolas Roeg film starring Gene Hackman and Rutger Hauer, was also shot in 1982 but had not yet seen the light of day. Neither had *House of God*, a medical comedy based on Samuel Shem's novel of the same name that had been sitting on the shelves even longer. *House of God* was written and directed by Donald Wrye (*Ice Castles*) and starred Tim Matheson and onetime *Saturday Night Live* regulars Joe Piscopo, Gilbert Gottfried and George Coe. MGM's income was mostly limited to the *James Bond* and *Rocky* franchises, so they could only use their slim marketing budget for surefire hits. They could not afford to risk those dollars on art-house films. Because there had never been anything like it before and MGM had no clue what to do with it, *Nothing Lasts Forever* was shelved indefinitely.

In his book *Fade Out: The Calamitous Final Days of MGM*, former MGM Senior Vice President Peter Bart recalls a 1983 screening of *Nothing Lasts Forever* for newly-appointed CEO Frank Yablans. Boaty Boatwright also remembers the screening. Production head Freddie Fields had recently been demoted. Yablans had to sit through an assortment of the studio's recently completed films, and *Nothing Lasts Forever* was one of them. He didn't even finish watching the film. While *Nothing Lasts Forever* probably had its supporters and detractors at MGM, Yablans' dislike of the film makes it no surprise that the studio put so little stock into the film upon completion. MGM went through a series of regime changes in the early 1980s. The studio was a revolving door—executives and production heads departed as fast as they had arrived—and with Lorne Michaels removed from the film, there was nobody there to really champion *Nothing Lasts Forever*.

In the summer of 1984, MGM finally found a window of opportunity. On June 8th, two films were released to theaters nationwide: *Ghostbusters* and *Gremlins*. *Ghostbusters* starred Dan Aykroyd and Bill Murray, and *Gremlins* starred Zach Galligan. Despite competing against each other, the films were instant smash hits. *Ghostbusters* made over a half billion dollars worldwide, and *Gremlins* grossed a couple hundred million as well. They were two of the biggest moneymakers of 1984. *Nothing Lasts Forever* featured three stars from these films, so MGM saw a fine opportunity to finally release the film.

After MGM and United Artists officially merged in 1983, they formed a separate banner under which they released foreign and independent films. *Nothing Lasts Forever* was put into this category, as was *Eureka*. They would finally make it to select art-house theaters in the summer of 1984, but with barely any publicity or promotion. They were unceremoniously dumped into the marketplace, as if they never had a chance to begin with.

Eureka was fortunate enough to make it to Los Angeles. *House of God* never played anywhere at all. *Nothing Lasts Forever* was sent to one theater in Seattle. Intended as a test release, it is tough to tell the extent of the future plans MGM/UA Classics had for the film. They had no idea what to do with the film, so a test run seemed like something worth trying with the hope that they could launch it into art house theaters across the country shortly thereafter. But why start in Seattle? Simply put, Seattle was the perfect sample of the United States movie-going audience. Seattle was seen as a microcosmic version of the United States. Had *Nothing Lasts Forever* been a mainstream film, Seattle would have been the perfect place to test it. But MGM, which was now presided over by a new regime of executives, failed to take note of Freddie Fields' accurate realization almost two years before: *Nothing Lasts Forever* was an art film. As such, Seattle was not the best place to test market the film for a potential art house release.

MGM even produced a trailer, although where it played (and if it played anywhere at all) is unknown, as is the point in time at which it was assembled. The trailer follows Adam through an ordinary day, complete with narration. It starts off with Adam's art test, then moves on to a cup of coffee with Mara, working in the Holland Tunnel, watching a movie on the miniature television set, and finally, a bus trip to the moon. The title is shown and the narrator announces: "from Lorne Michaels and Tom Schiller of *Saturday Night Live*," and rattles off a list of the film's wide range of stars—with two major omissions.

MGM/UA Classics came across a problem: Dan Aykroyd and Bill Murray's names were not allowed to be used in the selling of the film. They were not seen or mentioned at all in the *Nothing Lasts Forever* trailer. On the *Nothing Lasts Forever* poster, created for the 1984 would-be art house release, Dan Aykroyd's name is listed among the cameos, but Bill Murray is not listed at all. Since Murray is the villain and appears in a third of the entire film, he should have been the fourth-billed actor—after Zach Galligan, Lauren Tom and Apollonia Van Ravenstein. Sadly, this was not part of Murray's contract. He was paid scale for his week on the set, and although he loved the script, he appeared in the film as a favor to Tom Schiller. Murray had the exact same deal on *Tootsie*—he was in the film, but his name could not be used for publicity.

It was understandable that Murray was not given fourth billing in 1982. Schiller did not want his film to be too commercial, and it would only mislead Bill Murray fans into seeing a film that was unlike the comedian's other films. MGM had faced a similar problem when releasing 1981's *Pennies from Heaven*, a dramatic musical set during the depression. Steve Martin was the star of the film, a remake of Dennis Potter's British mini-series. Audiences were expecting the same zany Steve Martin that they came to know so well in *The Jerk* and on *Saturday Night Live*. The film was previewed at a university, where everyone waiting in line was ready to watch what they thought would be another crazy Steve Martin comedy. *Pennies from Heaven* is the farthest from it. It was poorly received by the preview audience, and the expensive film was a financial failure.

MGM did not want to short-sell its audiences again. *Saturday Night Live* fans were not necessarily the target audience for *Nothing Lasts Forever*. Who the target audience was—that was the big question. It was impossible to market. But should Murray have made an exception two years later? The film had been shelved for almost two years. The odds that it would be released in any fashion were still slim. Bill Murray's name on the marquee might have gotten the film

Tom Schiller's choice for the theatrical poster.

released, but Murray had to worry about his track record. He could not afford to mislead his audience, especially in anticipation of his dramatic acting debut, *The Razor's Edge*, scheduled for release in the Fall.

Even with Murray's name attached, would that have saved the film? It probably would have led to a launch in Los Angeles and New York, where it undoubtedly would have garnered a cult following. Whether it would have recouped its three million dollar investment is anyone's guess.

MGM/UA's official *Nothing Lasts Forever* poster.

MGM did not invest a lot of money and effort in the Seattle release. The film played at one theater for two weeks—the newspaper ads specified that it was a two-week limited engagement. Schiller tried to make sure that the film was adequately promoted. To do this, he enlisted the help of two *Saturday Night Live* fans with whom he had struck up a correspondence: Jackie Schmidt [neé Angvall] and Leslie McCutcheon. The two high school students wrote to Tom Schiller in December of 1983. Schiller responded a month later and regularly corresponded with the avid fans.

When MGM/UA Classics decided to test *Nothing Lasts Forever* in Seattle, Schiller contacted his Seattle fans and asked them to help promote it. Schiller had already mentioned his film in one of his letters: "*Nothing Lasts Forever* is my suppressed classic—accepted at Cannes but heretofore unreleased. Pray for me and it."

In the Summer of 1984, McCutcheon received a phone call from Schiller, who informed her that *Nothing Lasts Forever* would be making its premiere run at the Crest Cinema in Seattle on Wednesday, August 29. The theater, located approximately ten miles north of downtown Seattle, was known for playing obscure and foreign films, although during *Nothing Lasts Forever*'s run, it shared the marquee with *The Karate Kid*, *Star Trek III*, and *The Neverending Story*. "Tom wrote on the outside of one envelope: 'World Premiere—MGM's *Nothing Lasts Forever*, Seattle Aug 29, 1984...watch for it,'" Jackie Schmidt remembers. "What I recall is him asking us to promote it for him by putting up flyers all over the city. We happily obliged. We were inspired in a big way because we thought he was coming to town."

A week later, a heavy box filled with flyers from MGM made its way to McCutcheon's doorstep. The girls, plus McCutcheon's thirteen year-old sister, enthusiastically set about displaying the flyers around town. "We started on the small island where we lived, about fifteen miles east of Seattle, placing them with great care in mailboxes and tacking them on the message board at the local grocery store," McCutcheon recalls. "It didn't take long to exhaust the realms of the community, though this was hardly a setback considering the conventional, somewhat reserved population was overall unlikely to appreciate anything more quirky than *Family Ties*."

The girls next moved on to more diverse areas—Capitol Hill and the University District—whose inhabitants would be more likely to appreciate a film as offbeat as *Nothing Lasts Forever*. "We left piles of the multi-colored flyers in as many stores as we could talk into cooperating," McCutcheon recalls, "and didn't leave a lamp post, community bulletin board, phone booth, lavatory stall door, windshield or mail slot unflyered."

The girls were ecstatic to be able to help their famous pen pal, but received disappointing news a few days before the date of the premiere. Schiller intended to come to Seattle, but had to bow out due to a personal emergency. The girls were crushed. "In the end, despite the despair suffered at the last-minute turn of events, we thoroughly enjoyed the experience and were deeply honored to have been part of the film, however minimally," McCutcheon adds. "We were still thrilled to in a sense 'represent' him in our limited little teen-age sort of way at the premiere."

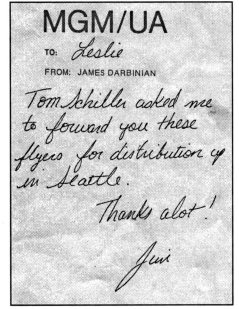

MGM/UA

TO: Leslie

FROM: JAMES DARBINIAN

Tom Schiller asked me to forward you these flyers for distribution in Seattle.

Thanks alot!

Jim

Photo by Jackie Schmidt and Leslie McCutcheon.

Shade Rupe, a high school friend of Schmidt and McCutcheon's, was introduced to Tom Schiller by the pair during their crusade to publicize *Nothing
Lasts Forever*. Intrigued by their commitment to the film's success and aware of
Schiller's unique and imaginative work for *Saturday Night Live*, Rupe also made
the trip to the Crest and became an instant convert. On a film outing to the
Pike Place Cinema in downtown Seattle, Rupe noticed a couple of movie-re-
lated food items in the glass concessions case: Sitting beside a 'Plate o' Shrimp'
from *Repo Man* was an enormous coffee cup with a small card reading 'Triple
Espresso,' clearly a nod to the coffee bar scene in *Nothing Lasts Forever*.

Variety and several Seattle newspapers reviewed the film. Jim Emerson of *The
Seattle Times*, in his August 30, 1984 review, called the film "quirky and just a bit
jerky" and argued that the film "gets a little tedious as it strings one precious conceit
after another." At least *Variety* praised Zach Galligan's performance, and pointed out
that the film has "surely one of the oddest love stories extant." Other than that, the
trade paper found the film to be a bit too long, even at just eighty-three minutes,
though not unpleasant. William Arnold of the *Seattle Post-Intelligencer* had no trouble
admitting that *Nothing Lasts Forever* did not work for him at all, calling the film
"even too weird for the cultists of the midnight movie circuit." Nevertheless, he
closes his August 29, 1984 review with the caution that he might be completely
wrong. "The movie is so consistently weird and so utterly meaningless that I hereby
leave open the possibility that I may have missed it completely and that time and the
French critics will find it to be a masterpiece—the ultimate expression of '80s-style
cultural confusion and the *Citizen Kane* of bizarre sci-fi comedy. In which case I take
back all the bad things I had to say about it."

The reaction to the film's two-week engagement was mixed. The Seattle audiences did not seem to get the film and the turnout was a disappointment. The film

did not perform well enough to warrant an expansion to other territories. It is also possible that MGM dumped the film at the Crest for its limited premiere engagement as a way of fulfilling a contractual obligation to give the film a theatrical release, with little intention of monitoring the film's prospects for a further release.

Nothing Lasts Forever had a few art house and midnight screenings in New York a year later. Haoui Montag and Stephen Saban of *Details Magazine* were very generous in their praise and support of the film. Montag called it a "delightfully conceived and executed film [that] has been lost to us for years. One of the more refreshing cinematic experiences in recent memory, it is destined to be the cult hit of the year." Saban wrote: "What do you do eventually with a brilliantly eccentric comedy whose basic plot concerns the lunar romance between an Earth boy and a moon maiden? Show it at midnight." That's exactly what happened to *Nothing Lasts Forever*. It played regularly at the Eighth Street Playhouse in Greenwich Village, until the theater received a cease-and-desist letter from MGM. It was never explained to Schiller why MGM suddenly did not allow for the film to be screened anymore. The film also played at a science fiction convention, the National Academy of Science Fiction, Horror and Fantasy Films, in July of 1987.

Later on, *Nothing Lasts Forever* did have a minor release on television outside of the United States. It has aired in countries including Germany, the Netherlands, Italy and Argentina. In some countries, the film has been dubbed. In Italy, the opening and closing titles were translated as well, but with a humorous misspelling: Lorne Michaels is credited as Horne Michaels.

Almost every year, Tom Schiller gets a residual check of about five or six dollars, reassuring him that his film is at least seen somewhere. But *Nothing Lasts Forever* has never been broadcast on television in the United States.

The so-called 'release' of *Nothing Lasts Forever* was a disappointment to everyone involved, but especially Tom Schiller. "What could his reaction be but the reaction that all of us shared? They just didn't know what they were doing," says Dan Aykroyd of MGM's decision not to expand the film. "There was just no boldness there and no faith in what it could have been."

"I think Tom is a genuine artist," says Lorne Michaels, "and I think if he had made *Nothing Lasts Forever* for a place that would have just appreciated it and him as an artist and given it the possibility of being the first feature film from a very talented filmmaker—and it had been done in the proper scale and without the kind of pressure and craziness that enveloped it—I think it would have been a successful thing."

Schiller says that he could spend hours trying to think of what might have happened, but that won't help anybody. He takes satisfaction with the fact that some people have seen his would-be cult film, and that many of them enjoyed it.

"The most important part of the story," Michaels adds, "is that Tom got to make the picture that he wanted to make."

Chapter 16
Comedy Experiments

After the saddening experience that was *Nothing Lasts Forever*, Schiller was hired as a writer for the HBO comedy series *Not Necessarily the News*. The program was much like *Saturday Night Live's Weekend Update* segment, but also contained a few sketches. Schiller only worked there for a few months. He also made three short films with comedienne Joy Behar for Lorne Michaels' short-lived primetime sketch comedy series *The New Show* in 1984. Titled *Here's Joy*, the films followed Behar in her journey to become a comic. In the first film, she makes the giant leap of leaving her home in Brooklyn and saying goodbye to all her family to pursue a career in show business. A five-minute drive over the Brooklyn Bridge later, and she has arrived in New York City. In another entry, Behar is in a nightclub and is poisoned so that she can be used as an usher at Radio City Music Hall. The three shorts were done on video, and Behar sometimes played them at stand-up comedy appearances as well.

Also in 1984, Schiller collaborated with legendary independent filmmaker Robert Downey Sr. (*Putney Swope, Greaser's Palace*) on a half-hour pilot for NBC. Downey sought out Schiller for the project, which was called *Film Boat*. It consisted almost entirely of old public domain stock footage. Schiller, who was the only person to appear in the program, played the captain of the Film Boat. He more or less served as a bookend for all the clips that were shown. In the pilot episode, which was the only episode that was produced, they showed part of an old film in which Dustin Hoffman appeared and scenes from 1930s anti-drug propaganda films like *Reefer Madness*. Schiller loved working with Downey on the project, but it was simply too weird for NBC. The pilot was not accepted.

Schiller also worked on two screenplays shortly after *Nothing Lasts Forever*. He co-wrote *Horny Devil* with Lauren Versel Bresnan for Bill Murray. It was a back-in-time story along the lines of *It's a Wonderful Life* in which Murray's character gets to experience what effect he has had on people in the past and present. Murray personally commissioned Schiller to write the script, but nothing happened to it. Murray took a vacation after 1984's colossal hit *Ghostbusters* and the critical and financial disappointment *The Razor's Edge*. Aside from a brief appearance in *Little Shop of*

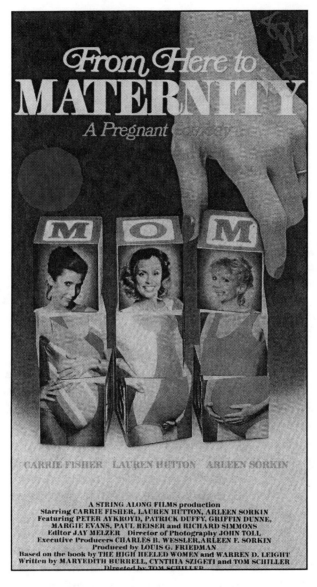

Horrors in 1986, Murray made no films for four years. He lived in Paris and studied at the Sorbonne, and did not make his comeback until 1988 with *Scrooged*—a modern adaptation of *A Christmas Carol* that also found Murray looking into the past, present and future. Schiller's other screenplay was *Safari* for Art Linson, the producer of films like *Carwash*, *Where the Buffalo Roam* (which Linson also directed) and *Fast Times at Ridgemont High*. Co-written by Sandy Krinski, a veteran sitcom writer of shows like *Alice* and *Three's Company*, *Safari* was about yuppies who start a hotel in Africa. Neither of the scripts were produced. "My heart wasn't in those as much as it was in *Nothing Lasts Forever*," Schiller recalls.

In the mid-eighties, the premium cable network Cinemax started a project called *Cinemax Comedy Experiment*. Each week there would be a new thirty-minute special. They usually had a small budget and were shot on videotape. The specials varied from Chris Elliott's *FDR—A One Man Show*, which was a recorded stage production, to *Your New American Actress Friend* with Sandra Bernhard, and Firesign Theatre's *Eat or Be Eaten*. The program sometimes allowed comics to try their hand at directing. Eugene Levy made his directorial debut with *Autobiographies: The Enigma of Bobby Bittman*, which he also wrote and starred in. Levy also appeared alongside many of his *SCTV* cast mates in the two-parter *The Canadian Conspiracy*. *Saturday Night Live*'s Gary Weis directed *Action Family*, in which Chris Elliott played a private detective. Each episode was completely different, and there was no link between the shows, other than that they were intended to be funny and experimental. Tom Schiller contributed two *Cinemax Comedy Experiments*.

Schiller's first was 1986's *From Here to Maternity*, a 25-minute comedy that is a parody of the classic *From Here to Eternity* in name only. It stars Carrie Fisher, Lauren Hutton, Arleen Sorkin, Paul Reiser and Peter Aykroyd. The film is a comedy for pregnant women and focuses on three women (Fisher, Hutton and Sorkin) who are going through labor. It was later released on home video.

The film is based on a book of the same name, written by The High Heeled Women—Tracey Berg, Cassandra Danz, Mary Fulham and Arleen Sorkin— and Warren D. Leight, while the screenplay was written by Maryedith Burrell, Cynthia Szigeti and Tom Schiller.

Carrie Fisher plays Veronica, a successful businesswoman who is constantly reminded of her biological clock. She is single but desperately wants to have a child. She wanders into a Maternity Mission, a church for women who are juggling successful careers but want to have children. Here Veronica meets Caroline (Lauren Hutton) and Judy (Arleen Sorkin). Judy hasn't had sex with her husband in ages and Caroline has no husband at all. At the end of the meeting at the Maternity Mission, the three women commit to having a child as soon as possible and try to figure out a way to get pregnant.

Caroline, a piano teacher, holds a cocktail party for pianists, but nobody seems interesting to her. All her potential suitors aren't right, or they are distracted by her loud biological clock, which can be heard ticking at all times. She quickly ends up drunk and doesn't wake up until the party is over. She meets Marco (Paul Reiser), the driver who is supposed to take her home. The two end up spending the night together.

Veronica goes to The Stork Club, which looks like an elegant restaurant. At her table, she is given a menu from which to choose her match. After a short wait, a doctor (played by Griffin Dunne) comes to the table to artificially in-seminate her while a blindfolded violinist provides some romantic music.

Meanwhile, Judy has to convince her husband Jack (Peter Aykroyd) to have a child with her, but all he does is sit in front of the television until Judy informs him of the tax advantages of having a child.

Content with their pregnancies, the three friends now have to prepare for delivery. They all go to an expectant parent exercise class with instructor Richard Simmons, who prepares them for the process of childbirth. Veronica's experience is compared to a business merger, while Judy turns into a B-movie monster. The actual childbirths are hectic, but the three women make it and can put their journeys 'from here to maternity' behind them.

The film has plenty of Schiller's trademark style and humor, usually evident in the transitions. The film opens with black-and-white footage of an old-fashioned ambulance driving through heavy traffic, for example, and there are additional cutaways to stock footage throughout the film.

The great thing about *From Here to Maternity* is that it never forgets its purpose. The film opens with the text: "To all women everywhere who are beginning to feel the vague stirrings of motherhood this story is affectionately dedicated." Almost every joke deals with the natural but sometimes confusing experiences that expecting couples go through. The film has a very specific audience and will probably not appeal as much to everybody else.

Two years later, Schiller directed another *Cinemax Comedy Experiment* entitled *Flapjack Floozie*, starring Teri Garr. Schiller co-wrote *Flapjack Floozie* with Sandy Krinski, with whom he earlier collaborated on *Safari*. Schiller does not consider this to be one of his greatest works, and he is within reason for thinking so. For a variety of reasons, the film does not work. Set in the 1930s, Teri Garr plays Helen Eagles, a successful actress who is addicted to pancakes. *Flapjack Floozie* has the same old-fashioned look and feel of many of Schiller's films, except the entire film is in color—which detracts from the overall product. The film is a mixture of Billy Wilder's *The Lost Weekend* and 1934's *Imitation of Life*, a racial drama about a woman who starts a successful pancake mix business with her former maid, which turns into a flapjack empire. *Flapjack Floozie* deals with Teri Garr's pancake addiction in the same manner in which Billy Wilder presented Ray Milland's alcoholism in *The Lost Weekend*. Plus, the film has a similar melodramatic, rags-to-riches tone as *Imitation of Life*.

Schiller asked his long-time friend Teri Garr to appear as the title character. Garr was reluctant at first, but eventually agreed. "He said he had a funny idea and asked me if I wanted to do it. I didn't really want to," Garr recalls. "At first I said 'No,' but then it's hard to say 'No' to Tom."

The film starts off with Eagles addressing the viewer. Garr is elegantly dressed up as an old lady and thanks SchillerVision for bringing her story of pancake addiction to the screen. The film then flashes back to Bill's Diner in the Bowery in 1948. Bill the owner and cook tells the new waitress (played by *Saturday Night Live*'s Laraine Newman) about former actress Helen Eagles, who stumbles into the diner at the same time each day to slurp down a stack of pancakes. Bill then proceeds to tell the story of Eagles' life.

As Bill says, Helen Eagles was born on the road, in a saloon in Montana. Her parents were part of The Flying Eagles, a dance troop. As soon as Helen was born, she was a part of the act. At this point, it becomes very obvious that there was little to no budget for *Flapjack Floozie*. There are hardly any sets. Bill's Diner is simply a grill on a black, empty stage with some tables around it. There are no walls. But it's not just Bill's Diner that is like this. All of the so-called sets are in fact the same empty stage with some props set up. Sometimes the stage has upright panels that are painted with cartoonish backgrounds that the characters walk in front of. As a result, the whole production has the atmosphere of a stage play.

Helen ate pancakes twice each day as she toured the country with her successful act. Despite eating so many pancakes, she does not gain a single pound. Finally, the addiction becomes too much and Helen fires her parents and her maid, Jenny. Helen meets Rudy 'Diamonds' Callucci (Peter Aykroyd), a gangster who showers her with beautiful jewelry and opens a club for her—Helen Eagles' Club Copacapancake. Callucci hopes that the club will steal away all the business from Al Capone's speakeasies. Helen falls in love with Callucci, but it's short-lived. On the day of the opening of Club Copacapancake, after Helen's first performance, Capone's thugs pay Callucci a visit. For a long period of time, the thugs shoot at Callucci. Peter Aykroyd dances around as he is shot with machineguns. He should be falling down, but the lead being pumped into his body at a constant rate keeps him upright. It lasts so long that it becomes very funny—one of the few highlights of the film.

Her new boyfriend's death sends Helen Eagles deeper into her pancake addiction. She loses the club and all her money, and now lives on the streets, selling her body for pancakes. Thankfully, her former maid Jenny finds her wandering on the street and promises to save her. She brings Helen to The International House of Psychiatry.

Helen is strapped into a straightjacket while Dr. Kipper, played by British actor John Standing (*The Elephant Man*, *Mrs. Dalloway*), tries to cure her of her addiction with a variety of tests, ranging from ice baths to shock treatment. Despite being much older than Helen, Dr. Kipper soon falls in love with his patient. When she claims to be cured, he blindly believes her and lets her go. Helen quickly regains her status as a Hollywood star, but immediately relapses.

While traveling in an airplane, she takes her luggage into the bathroom while everyone is asleep. With a miniature stove, she prepares a pancake. Helen tosses her pancake into the air with her frying pan in order to flip it over, but it sticks to the ceiling. It quickly falls down and lands on top of her head, searing her face and throat. Helen Eagles now comes into Bill's Diner each day dressed in a black veil. Bill continues telling his new waitress the story and says that Dr. Kipper felt so bad about misdiagnosing Helen that he left psychiatry and dedicated his life to curing pancake burns.

Just moments later, Dr. Kipper conveniently walks into the diner and tells Helen that he believes he has found the cure. After extensive surgery, Helen's face

There was Show Business
in her blood but syrup in her veins.

TERI GARR
in
"FLAPJACK FLOOZIE"
in
SCHILLERVISION

looks as good as new and she has finally kicked the flapjack addiction. She then breaks out in song and dance and is quickly joined by the entire hospital staff.

Flapjack Floozie is typical of Schiller's humor and style, but it does not work because it is too long and the jokes are few and far between. The concept is not interesting enough to sustain a thirty-minute film. Another major problem is its small budget. Whereas low budgets can occasionally make films entertaining, there is no humor derived from the inexpensive sets in *Flapjack Floozie*. The sets might have looked better in black-and-white, but in color they look corny.

Schiller does a lot with very little, but it's not enough to make the film entertaining. *Flapjack Floozie* might have worked better if it was twenty minutes shorter and in black-and-white. At its current length, it's probably better when accompanied by an introduction by *Bad Theater*'s Leonard Pinth-Garnell.

Throughout the years, even when not working, Schiller often kept himself busy behind the camera. "Ever since I was 16, I pretty much always carried a camera around," says Schiller. "First super8 film, then super8 sound, and then video. I'd always do something, just to keep sharp." He made funny short films with cast members at *Saturday Night Live* or other friends. It was a way to be creative, have fun, and pass time all at once.

"I used to always make impromptu short films at parties," Schiller says. "One of my things was to just take people and have them say a line, and edit in the camera. Then at the end of the party, I'd plug it in and we'd all watch it."

One day, Schiller made a short video with Tim Robbins and Laila Nabulsi. It was around Halloween-time and the three were hanging out together, with Robbins dressed up as a bunny. David Cronenberg's film *The Fly* had come out not long before, so they used some of the visuals in that film as an inspiration. The result was both humorous and surreal. In one of the more memorable scenes, Tim Robbins stands in front of a bathroom mirror, dressed in bunny-outfit, while milk oozes out of his mouth.

These videos were usually intended only for those who made the film, and were not supposed to be seen by anybody else. "I call them disposable movies," Schiller says. "They're just sketches that you throw away."

In 1988, Schiller directed an episode of the television series *Baby Boom*. Following the success of the 1987 Diane Keaton feature comedy, the film's creators, Charles Shyer and Nancy Meyers, attempted to bring the story of a successful New York businesswoman who inherits a baby to the small screen. The sitcom featured the same premise, only now J.C. Wiatt was played by Kate Jackson—fresh off her four-year run on *Scarecrow and Mrs. King*—instead of Diane Keaton. Sam Wannamaker reprised his role from the film, as did the twin actors who played the baby. Comic Joy Behar, whom Schiller had worked with in the past, was a regular as well. The producers insisted on bringing some interesting directors on board. One of them was actress Mary Kay Place, one was film/television/novel writer Robert Klane, and another was Tom Schiller.

Schiller directed the third episode, entitled *The Center*. In the episode, J.C. Wiatt takes her new baby to a training course which promises that the baby will become more intelligent. It was a standard modern sitcom, which Schiller did not care for. Despite some minor conflicts, the episode came out fine, but Schiller was left with another bad Hollywood experience. *Baby Boom* was canceled after fourteen episodes.

Schiller's Reel	Airdate	Host
Love Is a Dream	December 17, 1988	Melanie Griffith
Broadway Story - Opening Night	March 25, 1989	Mary Tyler Moore
Broadway Story - Daisy's Big Break	April 15, 1989	Dolly Parton
Broadway Story - Phibes Infernal Machine	Unaired, 1989	-
Broadway Story - Olive of Death	Unaired, 1989	-
Falling In Love	October 28, 1989	James Woods
Dieter In Space	December 16, 1989	Andie MacDowell
Hooked On Sushi	February 24, 1990	Fred Savage
Acting Is My Life	Unaired, 1990	-
The Land Before Television	Unaired, 1990	-
The Vision of Van Gogh	October 20, 1990	George Steinbrenner

SchillerVision	Airdate	Host
SchillerVision #1	November 17, 1990	Dennis Hopper
SchillerVision Theater Christmas Special	December 15, 1990	Dennis Quaid
The Story of Television: The Producer	Unaired, 1991	-
Shirley, I Love You	Unaired, 1991	-
Our Noisy Noisy World	Unaired, 1991	-
SchillerVisions: Arcocentesis	Unaired, 1991	-
SchillerVisions: Hidden Camera Commercials	November 16, 1991	Linda Hamilton
SchillerVisions: Exercise Machine Craze	Unaired, 1991	-
SchillerVisions: Thje ATM Story	Unaired, 1991	-
Million Dollar Zombie	March 21, 1990	Mary Stuart Masterson

Schiller's Reel	Airdate	Host
Civil Rights	Unaired, 1992	-
New York's Strangest & Most Bizarre People: Shorty, the Guy Who Can't Cross the Street	Unaired, 1992	-
Big Girl Goes To Town	Unaired, 1993	-
Dieter's Dream	March 20, 1993	Miranda Richardson
While the City Sweeps	April 17, 1993	Kirstie Alley
Criminal Encounter	May 15, 1993	Kevin Kline
Will Work For Food	November 13, 1993	Rosie O'Donnell
New York's Strangest & Most Bizarre People: Tortoise Man	Unaired, 1993	-
The Violin	Unaired, 1993	-
Laura	Unaired, 1993	-

Chapter 17
One More Saturday Night

Saturday Night Live, in the meantime, had resumed its position as a late night institution after a few troublesome years. In the early 1980s, the show was on the brink of cancellation but was saved in large part by the presence of up-and-coming comic Eddie Murphy. When Murphy left in 1984, the cast was replaced with a group of established performers including Billy Crystal, Christopher Guest and Martin Short. However, they agreed to appear on the show for only one year. The next year, *Saturday Night Live* would have to start over again from scratch. NBC was once again ready to cancel the show, but Lorne Michaels was unable to let his creation die and returned to the show in 1985. He has been the executive producer ever since.

Saturday Night Live was still a showcase of outstanding short films, but the show no longer had a resident filmmaker. After Schiller left in 1980, no new filmmaker was brought on to replace him. Instead, the show used different film-makers each week to provide these short films.

Future Academy Award-winning director Jonathan Demme (*Melvin and Howard, The Silence of the Lambs, Philadelphia*) contributed a spoof of the *Gidget* films entitled *Gidget Goes to Hell*. Cuban-born director Leon Ichaso (*Sugar Hill, Piñero*) directed Gilbert Gottfried as a New York City bullfighter in *Pepe Gonzalez*. Actor/director Bill Paxton directed and appeared in *Fish Heads*, a unique music video for the unique song by Bill Mumy's band Barnes & Barnes. Randal Kleiser (*Grease, The Blue Lagoon*) directed *Foot Fetish*. Yoko Ono made *Seasons of Glass*, a tribute to John Lennon. *Hot Dogs for Gauguin*, a 1972 award-winning student film from director Martin Brest (*Beverly Hills Cop, Scent of a Woman*) starring Danny DeVito, was also shown. Andy Warhol appeared in three oddball video segments entitled *Andy Warhol's TV*. In short, *Saturday Night Live* was a show-case for short films made by talented up-and-coming directors.

The 1983-84 and 1984-85 seasons in particular included a large amount of filmed and pre-taped material. As *Saturday Night Live*'s latest break-out star in the early 1980s, Eddie Murphy quickly became a movie star, appearing in hits like *48 Hours* and *Beverly Hills Cop*. For his fourth and final season, Murphy negotiated for less appearances on the show. His contract stipulated that he appear in just ten of that season's nineteen live shows, and that he had to pre-tape ten additional appearances for some of the episodes in which he would not appear live. Pre-tapes are bits of video footage that are mixed in with the live show because they would not be feasible to perform live, but in this case, they were done so that Murphy did not have to be in New York every week. This allowed Murphy to further pursue his successful movie career.

The formula seemed to work, so the next season producer Dick Ebersol delegated a significant amount of the airtime to short films and pre-tapes. Bob Tischler was the producer of these segments, using directors such as Claude Kerven and occasionally a staff writer like Andy Breckman. Sometimes part of a sketch would be performed live, while the rest was pre-taped. As a result, the dynamic of the show changed. But that's not to say that the pre-tapes were not funny. One of the most famous of these bits featured Martin Short and Harry Shearer as male synchronized swimmers. Other films and pre-tapes were not nearly as memorable, but each week they amounted to well over a third of the entire program's running time. At one point, the show even added a recurring cartoon. *Tippi the Turtle*, an adult cartoon by Jack Zander, showed a turtle smoking cigarettes and involving himself in other adult acts. The cartoon never caught on and was dropped after three appearances.

When Lorne Michaels returned the next year with a new cast, he put the *Live* back in *Saturday Night Live*. Pre-tapes and short films were once again limited to just a few per episode, but there was still no resident filmmaker. Just like Ebersol, Michaels relied on visiting filmmakers rather than having one film director on staff. John Head was in charge of commissioning the films, although he did license one film that was already completed, *The Hustler of Money* starring future cast member Ben Stiller. But the majority of the films were commissioned. John Head's friend William Wegman, who appeared with his dog Man Ray in one of Gary Weis' early shorts as well as two 1981 shorts, directed 1986's *Dog Baseball*, about a baseball game with dogs. In 1986, Tim Robbins wrote and directed the short film *Bob Roberts*, about a rightwing folksinger. Laila Nabulsi, an associate producer on *Saturday Night Live* the year before, produced the short. In 1992, after Robbins had become a well-known actor, he spun off the character into a feature-length film of the same title. Also in 1986, Jim Jarmusch made his popular short film *Coffee and Cigarettes*, starring Roberto Benigni and Steven Wright. Jarmusch made numerous other *Coffee and Cigarettes* shorts, albeit not for the show. All were featured in the 2003 feature film compilation of the same title, alongside new short films with stars like Bill Murray and Taylor Mead.

Other short films that John Head commissioned include *Hollywood Mom* starring Tracy Ullman, Spike Lee's *Horn of Plenty*, and Todd Solondz' *How I Became a Leading Artistic Figure in New York City's East Village Cultural Landscape*. Sadly, not many of the short films were aired during the live broadcasts, although some were later re-inserted into reruns.

In 1988, Lorne Michaels called Tom Schiller and asked him to come back to the show to direct more short films. Schiller anxiously signed on, though in retrospect he blames his return on "a morbid fascination with reliving the past." He just wanted to have another chance to make short films again.

Schiller's friendship with Lorne Michaels continued as usual. Starting in 1984 with *The New Show,* for which Schiller directed the Joy Behar shorts, Michaels and Schiller resumed their collaboration as if their disagreement on the set of *Nothing Lasts Forever* never happened. Moreover, the subject of *Nothing Lasts Forever* was never brought up. It was in the past and both had put it behind them.

When Tom Schiller returned to *Saturday Night Live* in 1988, the focus of his films changed. Whereas the films he made between 1977 and 1980 were highly creative short films on a variety of topics that reflected his way of looking at things, the films he made between 1988 and 1994 were more like miniature movies. The focus shifted from nothing in particular to recreating classic film genres. With a few exceptions, all of the films he made during this era attempted to reconstruct old filmmaking styles, ranging from colorful Hollywood musicals, B-grade horror films and 1950s television variety specials, to public television documentaries and silent films. Using black-and-white was no longer an aesthetic choice but a tool used to parody dead genres.

A lot had changed at *Saturday Night Live* when Schiller returned. Obviously, none of the original cast members were with the show, but some of the writers had returned in the mid-80s. Herb Sargent, already a veteran writer when he joined *Saturday Night Live* in 1975, was still roaming the halls. The three *Nineteen Eighty-Five* survivors—Jim Downey, Al Franken and Tom Davis— were all there, although Davis describes himself as "a wounded elephant heading towards the graveyard" during those years. And, of course, Lorne Michaels was there, as was director Dave Wilson and many of the original technical crew.

The biggest difference was that Schiller no longer had the budget to shoot all of his films on actual film stock like he did in the 1970s. Instead of it being a compromise, Schiller saw it as an interesting challenge. Thankfully, video had come a long way in the last decade, so Schiller used editing effects to make his video productions look like old film reels. While his budgets went down (in relative terms) his set design became more lavish. For his classic era films, he mostly used actual locations, but for his new productions he had sets built in the studio.

The toughest challenge was getting the material on the air. Schiller was initially brought back as both a filmmaker and a writer, but stopped writing after two seasons because hardly any of his sketches got on the air. Schiller doesn't even remember what writing he contributed to the show during those years. Added to that was the fact that there were now approximately twenty writers on the show instead of ten. There was a lot more competition to get a sketch on the air.

"He wrote plenty of stuff," says Tom Davis. "Very few of them got on and that was a very depressing thing for him, as it is for any writer. You really don't remember much stuff that doesn't get on. There's a great heap behind every one of us—things that never got produced—and that does sort of compost down into some dark organic comic soil and you can't remember it. That's the nature of memory."

Schiller had the same problem with his films, which were his main focus. In the 1970s, he made seventeen films, of which thirteen made it to air. Of the twenty-nine short films he directed between 1988 and 1994, only fifteen were broadcast. There were even two instances where Schiller didn't have a single film on for almost a year: *The SchillerVision Theatre Christmas Spectacular* aired in December of 1990, while his next film, *Hidden Camera Commercials*, didn't run until November of 1991. Even worse than that was the length of time between *Million Dollar Zombie*, which aired on March 21st, 1992, and *Dieter's Dream*, which aired on March 20th, 1993. During those long periods, Schiller made numerous other films, but either Lorne Michaels did not care for them, the dress rehearsal audience did not like them, or they just did not fit in the schedule.

Schiller's first new film was his best of this era. *Love is a Dream* is a touching romantic musical without a single laugh, yet it marks one of the greatest moments in *Saturday Night Live* history.

Love is a Dream premiered during the December 17, 1988 episode hosted by Melanie Griffith. Once again, the film looks as if it was made in a different time period. It's a musical, using the theme from *The Emperor Waltz*, Billy Wilder's 1948 film starring Bing Crosby. The song is also called 'Emperor Waltz,' and is sung by Crosby at the very end of that film. It was originally composed by Johann Strauß in the nineteenth century as 'Kaiser Walzer' ('The Emperor's Waltz'), but Johnny Burke wrote the lyrics specifically for Crosby in the film.

Love is a Dream begins in black-and-white in front of a New York City bank. Cast member Jan Hooks, convincingly made up to look like an old lady, walks in and is let into the bank deposit area by an old security guard. Using her key, she opens her deposit box, brings it to a nearby table and sits down. The box contains a tiara and a pearl necklace. She places the tiara on her head and the camera moves upward to reveal Phil Hartman, dressed as a prince, standing behind her.

The movie turns from black-and-white into color, and Hartman begins to sing—lip-synching to Bing Crosby. Jan Hooks is suddenly young as well, and the two parade down an elegant flight of stairs and dance in a ballroom while singing together. The song originally had no female vocals, so Schiller modified the music to allow for it—writing lyrics for what was originally a musical interlude. The color segment looks exactly like a classic 1940s musical, and despite featuring the recognizable faces of Phil Hartman and Jan Hooks, it could easily be mistaken as such.

The ballroom dancing scenes were modeled after the very last scene of *The Emperor Waltz*, in which Bing Crosby sings the title theme while dancing with Joan Fontaine. In the scene, Fontaine also wears a tiara and has a dress that looks a lot like the one that Jan Hooks is wearing. Phil Hartman is also dressed similarly to Bing Crosby. The main difference between *The Emperor Waltz* and

Phil Hartman and Jan Hooks. Courtesy Neal Marshad Productions.

Love is a Dream is that the ballroom is much bigger and filled with dozens of dressed-up couples in *The Emperor Waltz*. In *Love is a Dream*, the ballroom is very small and Hartman and Hooks are the only ones dancing, with several violinists playing on the sides.

At the end of the film, Jan Hooks sits down and takes off her tiara and necklace. The film reverts to black-and-white, and Hooks is once again an old lady. As she exits the bank deposit area, she blows a kiss to the security guard, who is revealed to be none other than Phil Hartman, now made up to look like an old man.

Love is a Dream has no punch line. There is not a single laugh in the film, and it was not intended to be funny. It is simply a charming and sweet film. "I had that idea when I was in Junior High or something—that a woman would go and try on a tiara, but then the person who gave it to her would appear with her in the safety deposit box area and take her on a little fantasy dance," Schiller says. "And then the guy that was holding the box was the guy that she was dancing with. It was just intended to be sort of dream-like." Perhaps it serves as the best example of what Tom Schiller contributed to *Saturday Night Live* through some of his films: It helped give the show a heart.

Like *La Dolce Gilda* and *Don't Look Back in Anger* before it, *Love is a Dream* also has an air of sadness looming over it following the death of one of its stars, Phil Hartman. On September 26, 1999, at the *Saturday Night Live* 25th anniversary special, the cast members of the 1986 through 1990 seasons reunited to honor their cast mate Phil Hartman, who died tragically at the age of forty-nine just a year earlier. Jon Lovitz and Jan Hooks stood in front of Dennis Miller, Mike Myers, Kevin Nealon, Victoria Jackson and Nora Dunn. The only cast member missing was Dana Carvey, who was unable to attend the event due to a personal health scare. As Lovitz and Hooks were ready to speak, many of them attempted to smile as they fought back tears.

Jon Lovitz said that in the eight years that Phil spent on the show, he worked with over twenty-five cast members. Lovitz was in tears and had a tough time saying his two lines of dialogue. Then Jan Hooks took over and introduced their tribute to Phil Hartman. "The following is a film that Phil and I did together in our third season. This is for you, Phil. We love you so much." It was the most emotional moment of the night.

Love is a Dream followed in its entirety, a decision made by Lorne Michaels. "Just as I thought Tom's film with Belushi dancing on the graves was a wonder-

Tom Schiller, Phil Hartman, Neal Marshad and Jan Hooks.
Photos courtesy Neal Marshad Productions.

ful moment for John and captured a part that was loveable about John, and *La Dolce Gilda* did with Gilda, I thought this captured the elegance of Phil," Michaels says. "And it was a pure Tom vision." The film did not represent Phil Hartman's comedic genius, nor did it show even a hint of how funny he was capable of being. But on this night, it was the perfect way to remember Phil Hartman.

Of all the *Saturday Night Live* cast members that Schiller worked with between 1988 and 1994, Phil Hartman was the one with whom he enjoyed

Phil Hartman, Jan Hooks and Neal Marshad. Photos courtesy Neal Marshad Productions.

working most. It comes as no surprise that Hartman appears in more of Schiller's short films than anyone else.

"I approach Phil's extant performances with a certain reserve, and seeing him on-screen almost always makes me sad," says Phil Hartman's older brother, John Hartmann. "I did not see many *Saturday Night Live* episodes in their original airing, and although Phil's presence there was always a source of pride for our family, it wasn't until the one-hour versions hit the cable that I became fully aware of the depth and quality of his work. It's clear to me now that the 'genius' appellation, so often tagged on him, was very definitely deserved.

"Tom Schiller is a lover of movies and their history. His creative collaborations with Phil are singular highlights in both careers," Hartmann adds. "For me, *Love is a Dream* represents the most formidable picture of who Phil really was and warmly demonstrates his true affection for his longtime theatrical mate, the wonderful Jan Hooks, who portrayed his love interest dozens of times. She played Cinnamon to his Sandy and they were ever united in their love and art."

"Copying the right style is the joke for Tom, so I thought it was absolutely perfect," says Mike Myers. "The essence of Phil was his ability to cop a style. It requires a tremendous instrument to have the versatility to be able to recreate so many styles, and that was Phil Hartman."

Phil Hartman, Tom Schiller and Jan Hooks.

Neal Marshad, Tom Schiller and Phil Hartman.

"Phil pops up in my life somewhere almost every day," says Hartmann. "Sometimes it's hard to watch, but when it's Tom's work I always smile at what clearly demonstrates Phil's sweet heart and his warm, loving way. We will forever bear the weight of his absence."

Tom Schiller followed *Love is a Dream* with the ambitious four-part serial *Broadway Story*, which was intended to air over four separate episodes of *Saturday Night Live*. Each entry lasted four and a half minutes. *Broadway Story*—"A tale of the great white way and the glamorous men and women who live it," as Schiller explains in his narration—was presented by SchillerVision in association with General Electric (the parent company of NBC). In traditional Schiller fashion, it captures the look of 1930s movies that went behind the scenes of Broadway—films like 1936's *The Great Ziegfeld*, 1941's *Ziegfeld Girl* and the *Broadway Melody* series that started in 1929. However, actual serials in those days were mostly capers, adventure stories and thrill pictures with cliffhanger endings that enticed the viewers to return for the next episode.

For *Broadway Story*, Schiller utilized the entire cast of the 1988-1989 *Saturday Night Live* season. The opening of each episode introduced the cast, but Schiller gave them typical 1930s stage names. The cast is as follows:

Gaspard LeGrand (Jon Lovitz) as Lionel Belmont, the good-hearted
  Broadway theatre owner.
Alfred and Vivianne Funt (Jan Hooks and Phil Hartman) as Mr.
  and Mrs. First Nighter, wealthy New York theatre patrons.
Fifi D'Ouberville (Nora Dunn) as Pola Bordoni, the traitorous
  star of Belmont's hit show.
Ralph Creamer (Dennis Miller) as Tristan Phibes, the sometimes-
  masked, villainous mogul who has a competing theater across
  from the Belmont Theatre and tries to sabotage his competitor's
  operations.
Mickey Pivnic (Dana Carvey) and Boris Lehmann (Kevin Nealon)
  as Johnny Venus and Vic, two of Tristan Phibes' thugs.
Pap Whitman (A. Whitney Brown) and Timmy Jones (Mike Myers)
  as "Pops" and Jimmy, a stagehand and his newsie son.
And Margaret Pischmonger (Victoria Jackson) as Broadway Daisy,
  a cigarette lady at the Belmont Theatre who dreams of becoming a Broadway star.

One of Lorne Michaels' rules at *Saturday Night Live* is not to use funny names. There have been a few characters with silly names over the years, like Roseanne Roseannadanna, but Michaels' overall philosophy is not to use bad puns for character names. Schiller uses funny character names in many of his films, and *Broadway Story* is no exception, but he never borders on turning the names into a joke.

Broadway Story's first entry, *Opening Night*, begins with Mr. and Mrs. First Nighter deciding whether to attend the premiere of the new Belmont show or the new Phibes show, since both premiere on the same night. They decide to first go to the Belmont show and then cross the street to the Phibes show during intermission.

Just before the show starts, Belmont's star Pola Bordoni calls up Tristan Phibes and they agree to let her be kidnapped. Phibes is an evil theater owner who wears a black veil in front of his face whenever he is in the company of others. Dennis Miller was not happy with the idea. His voice was also changed to sound deeper, which Miller was unhappy with as well. He complained to Schiller that not even his own mother would recognize him, but agreed to do it anyway.

In the second episode, *Daisy's Big Break*, Phibes' henchmen Johnny Venus and Vic sneak into the Belmont Theatre in nurse uniforms to supposedly take Pola Bordoni—who happily conspires in her own kidnapping plot—to the hospital. When Pola Bordoni doesn't show up on the stage, Belmont panics. Mr. and Mrs. First Nighter grow impatient and consider withdrawing their funding of the theater. When Belmont finally finds out that Bordoni is leaving for the hospital, he sends Broadway Daisy to the stage. She begins to dance to the orchestra music and the crowd immediately falls in love with her.

Victoria Jackson

Jon Lovitz

The newspaper runs a story about Broadway's newest star and how Broadway Daisy is even bigger than Pola Bordoni. Phibes and Bordoni are unhappy with the news and plot their next scheme: calling the police and claiming that there is an indecent show going on at the Belmont. The police quickly rush to the theatre and pull Daisy off the stage.

The third episode, *Phibes Infernal Machine*, starts with Tristan Phibes using his Theatre Lighting System—which doubles as an infernal machine—to destroy the Belmont Theatre. While the police raid is going on at the Belmont, Phibes pushes the 'Destroy Belmont' button and the building collapses. The entire area is reduced to a pile of rubble and crowds run out fearing for their lives.

Belmont crawls up out of a pile of bricks. Everyone has survived except for Pap Whitman—who only made one short appearance in the entire piece. Jimmy, Belmont and the First Nighters vow to get rid of Tristan Phibes once and for all. Jimmy quickly brings in a contraption he invented to kill subway rats. By putting a miniature explosive in an olive, Jimmy is able to remotely launch an explosion. But somebody has to plant the explosive.

Mrs. First Nighter volunteers her services at the start of the fourth episode, *Olive of Death*. Jimmy agrees to detonate the bomb at midnight, so she has several minutes left. She is able to make her way into the Phibes Theatre dressing room and drops the olive in Phibes' martini so that they can celebrate the destruction of the Belmont Theatre. But Pola Bordoni is under the impression that First Nighter is trying to woo him, and knocks her out with a punch. She then pours the martini over her head and puts the olive in First Nighter's mouth.

When the clock strikes midnight, Jimmy launches his remote detonation. With a moment to spare, Mrs. First Nighter awakens and quickly tosses the olive in Pola Bordoni's direction. Bordoni is laughing like an evil scientist, so the olive drops right into her wide-open mouth. She explodes and the Phibes Theatre crumbles to the ground.

Belmont, Daisy, Jimmy and the First Nighters celebrate their victory over Phibes while they are on a train to Hollywood. Jimmy announces that he and Daisy will soon marry, and Mr. First Nighter says that he will buy them all a Hollywood movie studio so that Belmont can make moving pictures. At the moment he says 'Hollywood' the film turns from black-and-white to color and they all begin to cheer and wave at the camera.

As the train rides away, a superimposed text promises a sequel, *Hollywood Story*, with the same cast. Unfortunately, there never was a *Hollywood Story*, and the third and fourth episodes of *Broadway Story* were never even aired. The third episode was later re-inserted into an episode for cable re-runs, but the fourth has never been broadcast.

The *Broadway Story* episodes look amazingly authentic, thanks in part to the super8 sound film that Schiller shot them on. Schiller accurately recreates the film look of 1930s films. The film is scratchy, during certain portions the dubbing is off, and there are frames missing. As a result, it looks like an old, neglected and unrestored film reel that was found in a vault.

Chapter 18
Television Take-offs

Unlike the initial seventeen *Schiller's Reels*, which have much less of a common thread, the short films made by Tom Schiller between 1988 and 1994 can be categorized into three groups. Nearly half of the films were take-offs of television, such as funny documentaries and short television specials. Examples are *The Vision of Van Gogh*, a PBS-like documentary involving the famous impressionist's eyesight; *While the City Sweeps*, a television show for and by nightshift workers; and *SchillerVisions*, a Swedish documentary series about cultural oddities. Other films were genre-oriented. Schiller made a few horror shorts (such as *Hooked on Sushi* and *Million Dollar Zombie*), a few fairy tales (including *The Land Before Television*), and even a funny science fiction film (*Dieter in Space*). Arguably, the most memorable shorts are the ones in which Schiller recreates the film look of classic Hollywood. In addition to *Love is a Dream* and the *Broadway Story* series, Schiller also imitated old-fashioned Hollywood films with *The Violin* and *Laura*, among others.

The first of Schiller's television take-offs that was broadcast is *SchillerVision Theatre*. *SchillerVision Theatre* was not like any of his previous *Schiller's Reels* and it did not bear the *Schiller's Reel* logo at the beginning.

SchillerVision Theatre is a variety special, which normally would have run a full hour on 1950s primetime television, but is obnoxiously condensed into three minutes. The show is modeled after 1950s variety specials, complete with corporate sponsors like the Dynamic Car Corporation and Man-Bra. Host Trevor Duncan (played by Schiller) introduces the feature presentation, *Sudden Pressure*, a drama about a feeling that, according to Duncan, all men and women experience at some point in their lives. In the film, a man hurries through the city, running down busy sidewalks and crossing heavy traffic. It is clearly stock footage from either the NBC archives or the public domain. Duncan quickly interrupts the film with a fake commercial for Man-Bra, which offers support for the brawny man. It predated by several years a famous *Seinfeld* episode in which Manzere, also a bra for men, was introduced.

Sudden Pressure then resumes. The man is still running through the streets until he finally reaches a door. The film utilizes original material instead of stock footage, although it is not easy to notice because it is seamlessly blended in. The man opens the door and the camera pans upward to reveal a 'Gentlemen' sign on the door. It's a clever reference to Schiller's very first film *The Door*, which had the exact same plot.

After the film ends, Duncan previews next week's show, in which they will screen another film. A full trailer for the film is shown, using stock footage of color civil war films. The film is a cross-over spoof of *Gandhi* and *Gone with the Wind* called *Gandhi with the Windy*. The trailer promises romance and epic battle scenes, in "a beloved tale of War, Love and Peace." The soundtrack is an Indian variation of the *Gone with the Wind* theme. The funniest bit from the trailer is a clip of Gandhi— played by Schiller himself—telling Scarlett O'Hara in a thick East-Indian accent:

Tom Schiller as Gandhi.

"Frankly, my dear, I am not giving one damn." He then stumbles off into the distance, dressed in white cloth and leaning on a walking stick. Finally, Trevor Duncan concludes the broadcast and the 1950s NBC station ID is shown.

The second and last *SchillerVision Theatre* aired on December 15, 1990, right in time for the holidays. Entitled *The SchillerVision Theatre Christmas Spectacular*, it was also hosted by Trevor Duncan. It is again a program of at least one hour that is condensed into a few minutes. The opening crawl promises such guest stars as Burl Ives, Little Mary Toonis, Reverend Fulton Sheen, the SchillerVision Holiday Singers, Guy Lombardo and his Orchestra, and Abel Johnson live from Times Square. None of them actually appear, except for Abel Johnson, played by Schiller himself, and the SchillerVision Holiday Singers. The sponsors this time include Electro-Shave Razors, the Streamliner Limited railroad transport company (New York to Los Angeles in only four days), and De Longeur cigarettes (longer cigarettes for a sophisticated smoke).

Trevor Duncan introduces the evening's feature presentation: *The Story of Christmas* starring Burl Ives. Of course, *The Story of Christmas* starring Burl Ives does not exist. Schiller once again shows public domain footage, this time of Santa Claus in his sled and climbing up chimneys.

An inside joke in *The Story of Christmas* is that it is produced by Victor de Cordova—the same name used for the producer of *Sudden Pressure*, and adapted from Charles Dickens' story by Jerome Belt, also the writer of *Sudden Pressure*. Both are made-up names that Schiller has used frequently in his works. But *The Story of Christmas* hasn't even gotten through its opening credits when Trevor Duncan interrupts the film for a word from the sponsors. The first commercial is for Klinger 100% Human Hair Yarmulkes.

When *The Story of Christmas* resumes moments later, it has already ended with a shot of Santa Claus wishing everybody a Merry Christmas. The next

Tom Schiller as Abel Johnson.

commercial is for McGinty Blended Scotch Whiskey for hard-working shopping mall Santas. The commercial shows Santa Claus with a little person on his
lap, played by *Twin Peaks* actor Michael J. Anderson, who also takes a sip of the
whiskey. Anderson had already made his debut on *Twin Peaks* when he appeared
in this film. Schiller says that he cast him because he showed up a day early for
his audition and did not want to turn him away. Anderson was a good sport and
Schiller liked working with him so much that he used him again in a later film.

Next, Trevor Duncan introduces Abel Johnson, who is standing by live at
Times Square where they are about to ring in the New Year—1953. As Johnson
awaits the Ball drop, the New Year's Eve Ball tumbles off of the One Times Square
building. Just as it is about to plunge into the crowd below, the ball swerves upward and flies down Broadway and into the NBC Studio, where it shrinks and
becomes a sing-a-long ball that highlights the text at the bottom of the screen.

Trevor Duncan and the SchillerVision Holiday Singers then proceed to sing
'Auld Lang Syne' while the New Year's Eve Ball highlights the words so viewers at
home can sing along. Finally, while the Holiday Singers are still singing, Trevor
Duncan wishes his viewers a good night and tells them to tune in next time. It
once again closes with a vintage NBC station ID.

The *SchillerVision Theatre* bits were Schiller's favorite bits of all his contributions to *Saturday Night Live* between 1988 and 1994 because they were modeled after television programs that he grew up with in the 1950s. Of all of Schiller's
films, these are the two most nostalgic.

Schiller's nostalgia, his yearning for simpler times, is apparent in many of
his films, but none so strongly as the two *SchillerVision Theatre* shorts. As quick
and obnoxious as they may appear, they capture the spirit of classic television by

Tom Schiller as Trevor Duncan.

Tom Schiller and Michael J. Anderson.

packing hours worth of entertainment into three-minute clips. Even though both *SchillerVision Theatre* shorts made it to air, they were not popular enough to warrant further installments.

After both *SchillerVision* shorts aired in 1990, Schiller retired the *Schiller's Reel* logo and now labeled all of his short films *SchillerVision. Schiller's Reel* had been a staple for years but starting with the two *SchillerVision Theatre* shorts, everything became *SchillerVision*. There is no real difference between *Schiller's Reel* and *SchillerVision*, despite the fact that many of the *SchillerVision* segments were more like pre-taped sketches rather than actual short films. Sadly, only four of the ten *SchillerVision* segments made it to air.

In 1991, Tom Schiller starred in four *SchillerVision* shorts as Swedish television host Knorben Knussen. Knussen hosts the program *SchillerVisions*, which

Tom Schiller and Chris Farley

can be compared to American programs like *Hard Copy* and *RealTV*. In each episode, Knussen introduces video clips of American trends and speaks via live satellite with experts, witnesses or victims.

Hidden Camera Commercials became an instant classic due to Chris Farley's over-the-top performance as the victim of a hidden camera commercial experiment. Knussen shows a clip from a commercial for a popular Colombian coffee brand in which a gentleman sitting in a restaurant is told that the coffee he is drinking is not what he ordered, but instead a different brand of Colombian

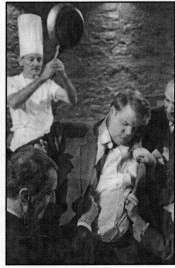

decaffeinated coffee crystals. The gentleman is delighted and enjoys the coffee. But Knussen explains that to achieve such a result, 264 takes had to be recorded with other customers to get the desired spontaneous result. Knussen introduces subject #65, where everything went wrong.

In the same restaurant, Chris Farley and his wife are drinking coffee. The waiter walks over and politely tells him that he is not drinking the coffee that he ordered, but instead the Colombian decaffeinated coffee crystals. Chris Farley is courteous and smiling, but asks the waiter to repeat himself. Then the smile fades quickly and Farley is outraged.

"Why you son of a bitch!" the formerly polite customer says. Farley is now steaming with anger and pushes his table over. He begins attacking his waiter. "You lied to me!" he screams as he punches him in the face. He picks up cream pies from the dessert table and throws them at an elderly couple. He takes dishes and throws them to the floor, all the while screaming. His wife is at his feet, crying. He has become a madman, at one point even laughing as he swears to God that he will avenge what has just been done to him.

The camera frantically zooms in and out to give it a cinematic feel, as does the dramatic music. In total, four people try to hold Farley down, until finally the chef hits him on the head with a frying pan and he slowly plunges to the ground.

Next, Knorben Knussen speaks live via satellite with the hidden camera commercial victim and asks how he feels. Farley, who now wears a neck brace and has bandage swathed around his head, ingenuously answers: "Angry."

Hidden Camera Commercials marks one of Chris Farley's greatest performances on *Saturday Night Live*. His ability to transform from a sweet, kind
gentleman into a maniac is simply brilliant. Many sketches have allowed Farley
to go crazy, but probably none as destructive as *Hidden Camera Commercials*. It
was appropriately included in *The Best of Chris Farley*, a television special and
home video release that was put together after Farley's death in 1997.

"It's the real man in the real-life situation taken to the absurd, and shot
well with a classy, beautifully covered, lit and edited style," describes Dan Aykroyd,
a fan of the piece. *Hidden Camera Commercials* was by far the best of the
SchillerVisions films with Knorben Knussen. As such, it was also the only one
that made it to air.

The Vision of Van Gogh offers a curious take on the works of Vincent van
Gogh. It suggests that Van Gogh's impressionist painting style was not due to
his innovation, but actually a result of poor eye sight. Schiller himself, complete
with red hair and a red beard, plays Vincent van Gogh. The resemblance is far
from striking, but the point is driven across—he's supposed to be Van Gogh.
The film features voice-overs from Vincent and his brother Theo, reading from
their well-documented correspondence.

Vincent is outside, baking in the sun while at work on his famous *Auvers-
sur-Oise* (*Wheat Field with Crows*—his very last painting). In his letter to Theo,
which is read while Vincent is shown painting, he asks his brother why he isn't
selling any of his paintings. Furthermore, he complains about his failing vision
and his inability to see what he paints. In his reply, which is read immediately
thereafter, Theo says that nobody in Paris likes the paintings. The film cuts away
to footage of French aristocrats—elegantly dressed old ladies and men with wiry
mustaches—balking at his works. But Theo adds that his optometrist friend might
have the solution. He believes that Vincent may be suffering from astigmatism, so
Theo sends along a pair of glasses.

Ironically, a similar fate befell one of van Gogh's contemporaries, Claude
Monet. Monet suffered from diminishing eyesight, but he continued to paint as
he saw the world. As he became older and his vision weakened, his works became vaguer and blurrier. Of course, Van Gogh was an impressionist and his
style was intentionally rough. His broad strokes were symbolic of the emotions
he tried to convey through his works.

Vincent tries on the glasses and a new world opens up to him. Suddenly he
sees everything clearly and now is able to paint in photo-realism. No more rough
brushstrokes. He paints a number of inane portraits, and the same posh French-
men who were disgusted by his previous works are now amazed. Vincent's new
paintings look exactly like photographs, but with Van Gogh's trademark signature
'Vincent' scribbled at the bottom. Among his new, critically acclaimed paintings
are a portrait of a pig and various renderings of chimpanzees in human clothing.

In terms of style, *The Vision of Van Gogh* is reminiscent of PBS documentaries about painters—complete with re-enactments, renaissance music and dramatic narration by actors like Donald Sutherland. Schiller has again successfully recreated a genre.

The Vision of Van Gogh has an intelligent premise with a juvenile, slapstick punch line—the contrast of which adds to the genius of this short. In a way, the film symbolizes the direction that *Saturday Night Live* took in the early 1990s and how Schiller began to figure outside of the equation. While it once had an intellectual edge, the show's sense of humor changed to appeal to the changing times and its changing audience. This was around the time that recurring sketches like *The Gap Girls* became popular. Schiller started to fit in less. As a result, his contributions to the show changed as well.

While the City Sweeps is one of Schiller's weaker entries. While it's mildly amusing, its concept is not trademark Schiller. Arguably, it could have even been done as a live sketch. Taking its title from Fritz Lang's 1956 film *While the City Sleeps*, the film is set in a luxurious office lobby in the nonexistent Avcom building. The evening is about to start and everybody is preparing to leave the building, except for the security guards and the cleaning crews who are starting their workdays. Rob Schneider plays Carlos, the security guard sitting at the lobby desk. He yawningly examines the security monitors while signing out the departing workers. Kevin Nealon plays an office worker who signs out and tells Carlos that he is lucky not to have to sit in an empty office all day. As soon as Nealon has left the building, Carlos gets ready for show time.

An old janitor played by Tim Meadows drops his mop and sits down behind the security desk, where he puts on a headset. One of the cameras is pointed at Carlos, who announces that *Security Camera Spectacular* is about to begin. *Security Camera Spectacular* is a variety show broadcast via closed circuit security monitors to nightshift workers throughout the Manhattan area. The evening's entertainment includes Los Cleaning Ladies, a group of dancing cleaning ladies (including Melanie Hutsell), from the 19th floor; Cam McCullough and The Maintenance Men (led by Chris Farley), who sing 'Roll Out the Barrel' from the 48th floor; *The Sonya Grabinski Show*, a talk show in which Sonya (Julia Sweeney) discusses going through other people's garbage with a panel of guests (including Adam Sandler) from the 50th floor; and the comedy of Amos and Smokey, an old elevator operator (Chris Rock) and his ventriloquist dummy, from the service elevator. The show even has corporate sponsors—janitorial products like Sani-Flush and Plastex wet floor signs.

The programming lasts the entire night. When the sun comes up, Carlos wishes all of his viewers a fond farewell, and everybody goes back to work as if nothing happened.

While the City Sweeps is an amusing short that manages to use most of the *Saturday Night Live* cast. As a pre-taped sketch, it's wonderful. It combines many funny elements and characters with nightshift humor. But as a *Schiller's Reel* short film, it's not in the same league as many of Schiller's other works. In terms of style, it's lacking. Had it not been for Schiller's creative use of music in the opening and closing of the film, it could have just as well been done as a live sketch. Particularly the end, when Schiller presents a montage of *Security Camera Spectacular* programming set to dramatic music, makes the film slightly more than just a pre-tape.

Criminal Encounter aired a few weeks later. Rob Schneider plays Pedro, a Spanish immigrant who is brought to a prison conference room to be reunited with Harley (played by Chris Farley), the tough inmate who shot and robbed him. Presiding over the reunion is Morley Frugen, played by Tom Schiller, who sits the two men at a table. Pedro explains that he came to America wanting to be a dancer, but because Harley shot him in his leg, his dreams were shattered. Harley gives a list of reasons why he did it: his parents abused him, drugs, unemployment, he had a lot of laundry to do that night…Finally, Frugen asks the criminal and the victim to dance together. The two reluctantly slow-dance as the film draws to a close. A title card explains that Pedro later stabbed Harley and is now serving five years.

Of all of Schiller's short films, *Criminal Encounter* is his least favorite because he felt it did not really belong to him. Another writer on the show came up with it and wrote the script, and it lasted a little too long for Schiller's tastes. Schiller doesn't generally have a problem working with other people's ideas and scripts, but he did not care for *Criminal Encounter*.

Of the thirty-one short films that Schiller directed between 1988 and 1994, only fifteen made it to the final broadcasts. Some of the sixteen omitted films were classics, while others were weak and understandably cut after dress rehearsal. The first films to be cut were *Broadway Story* volumes three and four. The third episode was eventually inserted into the sixty-minute cable version of the *Saturday Night Live* episode hosted by Demi Moore. It was a strange place to put it, because that episode originally aired before the shows hosted by Mary Tyler Moore and Dolly Parton, in which the first two *Broadway Story* serials appeared. Moreover, the fourth and final *Broadway Story* was never aired at all, which means that nobody found out how the serial came to an end.

The first stand-alone short that did not make it into the show was a terrific film entitled *Acting is my Life*, starring Nora Dunn. Dunn really shines in this film as Genevieve, an ostentatious actress who is preparing for what appears to be an important role. The film is shot documentary-style and follows Dunn as she goes through the motions of readying herself for her next job, including vocal exercises.

Tom Schiller, who also narrates, plays the mild-mannered director, Jerry Belt,[17] who tries to get Genevieve through her scenes at a soundstage for what appears to be voice-over work. But when it comes time to record, Genevieve freezes.

She is unable to say her lines and motions to Belt that she will not proceed. Belt offers her a cup of water, but she immediately spits it out, notifying him that she only drinks Alpine Springs. During her tantrum, she also demands that the air conditioning be shut off, and then vigilantly insists that her acting teacher Len Lester be brought to the studio to help her through her breakdown.

Lester is played by Schiller favorite John Garson. Once he finally arrives, the portly gentleman gives Genevieve a few words of advice in a thick accent. Finally, she is able to read her line: "I'm sorry, the number you have reached is not in service at this time." Everyone in the studio cheers and Genevieve is given a bouquet of flowers.

Acting is my Life is simple in terms of its concept, punch line and execution. What ultimately makes the film is Nora Dunn's performance. She creates a great character who switches from jovial to a diva in a moment's notice. Dunn memorably played smarmy, smug characters on *Saturday Night Live*. She was typecast. *Acting is my Life* gives her the opportunity to be a pleasant, genuinely likeable person, albeit overly gregarious. It's a showcase for her versatility, and she makes it seem effortless.

John Garson, who is a great fit in all of Schiller's projects that he appeared in, is also outstanding as the buoyant acting coach. Garson walked around with a cane and his lines are tough to comprehend underneath his thick accent and congested voice, but all to the benefit of the character. Sadly, his declining health is noticeable. Garson passed away shortly after the film's completion.

Nevertheless, *Acting is my Life* did not air. Arguably, one of the problems is its length. At four minutes, it is one of Schiller's longer pieces. Even though the pacing is solid, it has enough material that it could have done without.

Of the *SchillerVisions* series, in which Schiller played Swedish television host Knorben Knussen, only *Hidden Camera Commercials* made it to air. There were three other entries that did not.

In *Arcocentesis*, Knussen talks via live satellite to scientist Helmut Klaus (also played by Schiller), who is in a spa in Germany. Klaus devised the theory of Arcocentesis, that man can create energy and live off his own waste matter. He argues—all the while smoking a cigarette in a hot tub—that man lives to create energy. Since human waste is a form of energy, he claims that man can create its own energy cycle instead of working hard to make a living in order to support his use of energy.

Arcocentesis is bathroom humor that tries to be intelligent. While there are some funny moments, in the end it is still bathroom humor. While Schiller's Helmut Klaus character is an excellent impression of a perverted, middle-aged German man, not all of his jokes are funny. After Schiller completed *Arcocentesis*, he was called into the NBC censors office. The tape was played and the people in the office laughed, but they explained that it was not suitable for television. In all the years that Schiller worked on the show, this was the only time that he had to deal with the censors.

In *Exercise Machine Craze*, Knorben Knussen delves into the American exercise machine trend and examines whether exercise machines ordered from television infomercials work. *SchillerVisions* conducted their own experiment with the Exer Glider, an elliptical exercise machine. The test rabbit is Roland Meyer, an 'Average American' played by Chris Farley. At the start of the experiment, Meyer is 220 pounds. Nothing happened after the first two weeks of using the machine, but in the third week, he gained one pound and developed a bigger chest. Weeks later, Meyer has big breasts, long hair and a much higher voice. He has become a woman. Knussen speaks to Meyer via live satellite and asks how he/she feels about the experiment. Farley is now fully dressed like a woman and responds, just as in *Hidden Camera Commercials*: "Angry."

Exercise Machine Craze follows the same formula as *Hidden Camera Commercials* but is not nearly as funny. It had a brilliant concept and even allowed for Schiller's trademark stylishness, but the idea behind *Exercise Machine Craze* is too far out. Why would a man turn into a woman by using an exercise machine? The suggestion is perhaps that most men who use exercise machines use it to become muscled and look manly. In that regard, it's an interesting parable, but it does not translate into funny television.

In the final *SchillerVisions* episode, *The ATM Story*, Knussen traces the past, present and future of the ATM, upon which Americans have become so dependent. David Spade stars as man through the ages, as Knussen introduces the various incarnations of the ATM machine throughout history. Knussen starts off with the Stone Age ATM, a cartoonish look at the year 3000 BC. A caveman approaches a big rock and slides a stone tablet into a slot, grunts, and pounds the rock with his wooden club until little pebbles of currency come out at the bottom. Knussen then flashes forward to 1933, where David Spade uses an ATM machine at the bank. But, as Knussen describes, the 1930s ATMs were not time-efficient because on the other side of the wall, a grouchy old man (played by Dana Carvey) has to look up everybody's account in the book, verify the balance, mark down the withdrawal, and slide a bill through the slot.

Knussen then discusses the modern ATM, which still is not perfect. The respective clip shows Spade at an ATM that is out-of-order, with four people in line in front of him frozen and covered in cobwebs. Finally, Knussen moves on to the ATM of the future and speaks to Arthur Saliva, President of the American Electronic Bankers Association (played by Schiller himself) who promises even more uses for ATMs in the future. The next few clips show these potential uses: Chris Farley pushes a button for pizza, and immediately a pizza slides out of a large slot; an ATM minister pronounces Tim Meadows and Ellen Cleghorne husband and wife; another ATM serves hot coffee. The next clip finds David Spade punching an ATM button that is labeled 'Get Laid.' The ATM machine is a sliding door into a bordello. The final clip finds Spade the next day at the ATM confessional, which claims that he is spiritually bankrupt and shall be banished to hell. The screen fills up with flames and Knorben Knussen wishes his audience goodnight.

The ATM Story is much more amusing than both of the other unaired *SchillerVisions*. It's among Schiller's most clever pieces that would have appealed to *Saturday Night Live*'s new audience. Additionally, it's the perfect vehicle for David Spade, whose wisecracking but wimpy young character is symbolic of the upper-class Manhattan youths who become reliant on ATM machines as a never-ending well of funds. *Saturday Night Live* made a mistake by not airing *The ATM Story*.

Hidden Camera Commercials, Exercise Machine Craze and *The ATM Story* allowed Schiller to present an outsider's view of American trends. He offered the idea that for every hidden camera commercial on television, there must be hundreds of filmed attempts that did not turn out as well. He presented the opposite results of the use of an exercise machine. And he humorously looked into the future of convenience services like the ATM and suggested what else might become automated in the future. *Arcocentesis*, on the other hand, examines asinine German scientific experiments—which pop up regularly in the news in Western Europe—from a Swedish perspective. The Swedish perspective is unnecessary, so perhaps that is one of the reasons why that film does not work.

Schiller himself is the lead in the unaired short *The Story of Television: The Producer*. It is much like the two *SchillerVision Theatre* specials, which did make it to air. *The Story of Television* comes complete with a corporate sponsor: Sagon ('No Gas' spelled backwards, as the commercial's jingle explains), which is promoted throughout the four-minute short. The film starts out with vintage interviews with RCA televisionaries General David Sarnoff and Dr. Vladimir Zworykin. The footage is real. Zworykin is considered to be the father of television, and both he and Sarnoff were television pioneers. Why this footage is in *The Story of Television: The Producer* is unknown. It has very little to do with the rest of the piece.

The centerpiece of the film is a live interview with successful producer Hal Shimkus. Schiller plays Shimkus as a pompous television veteran who sits on top of a late night talk show desk and hurries through the questions. Shimkus, wearing sunglasses and smoking a cigarette, gives quick answers and tells the interviewer that he needs to be in a meeting shortly, so he needs to hurry up with the questions. One of the more humorous questions is about Shimkus' television background. Shimkus enthusiastically explains that he grew up in local television and worked on *The Jerome Sheldman Show*, a local cable program from 1962. As Shimkus continues talking about that show, a bad public domain video clip is shown. In the clip, a man dressed as a clown dances around a piano…badly. Shimkus then cuts off the interview and explains that he needs to get back to work.

One way of perceiving *The Story of Television* is as a joke on smug television producer types. Hal Shimkus is an amalgamation of various television producers, especially Gary Morton, Lucille Ball's second husband. As a whole, *The Story of Television: The Producer* is not very cohesive. In the *SchillerVision Theatre* films, Schiller at least tied all the various bits together in an amusing manner. In *The Story of Television*, the three main ingredients are footage of television pioneers Sarnoff and Zworykin, the Sagon commercials, and the interview with Hal Shimkus. They do not blend together well. It also lacks the zing of *SchillerVision Theatre*. The film is slow-paced and misses the consistency of Schiller's better works.

In 1992's *Civil Rights*, Tim Meadows plays a man who was present at several major civil rights rallies in the 1960s. A television-style documentary, the film was originally Meadows' idea, so he and Schiller collaborated on it. The film begins in a church where Tim Meadows discusses how his father was involved in the civil rights movement, and how proud he is of him. His father was no Malcolm X or a Martin Luther King, but he spoke up and made his voice heard. It then shows clips of the marches, the speeches, and his father standing in the crowds, occasionally speaking out. The film seamlessly mixes archival footage with new footage of Tim Meadows, playing his own father. But while Malcolm X and Martin Luther King speak about equality, all Meadows' character can think of is food. He asks the leaders: "To march is all well and good, but what I want to know is, will there be sandwiches when we're through?"

He is initially booed by the other audience members and marchers, but at the other marches he attends, nobody seems to mind that he is eating turkey legs, sandwiches and corn-on-the-cob. While other marchers hold signs that say 'End Segregation Now!' or 'Freedom in 1963, Promised in 1863,' Meadows' sign reads 'Cut Beef Prices!' At the end of the film, in the church, Tim Meadows expresses his gratitude for his father's courage, and says that he misses him.

Saturday Night Live writer and producer Jim Downey feared that the film might be considered racist, and it did not air. While at times the film walks the line of the offensive, it is a thoughtful tribute to the civil rights movement. The inserts of Meadows chomping down on a turkey leg (and throwing it behind him when he finishes it, quickly moving on to a second piece) are funny, but not disrespectful to the content of the speeches by Malcolm X and Martin Luther King. Meadows is attentive and carefully listens to what they have to say—it's just that he got hungry each time there was a march.

On the other hand, Downey's concern at the time does not seem completely unreasonable. Had it been aired, the film might have offended some viewers who took it too seriously. It takes just a few upset viewers and a handful of complaints to lead to a story in the newspaper. Granted, *Saturday Night Live* has run a handful of other sketches over the past thirty years that could be considered much more offensive than *Civil Rights*.

In terms of Schiller's direction, *Civil Rights* again demonstrates his ability to recreate the visual style of old film and blend it with actual footage from the 1960s. While the overall film is very funny and Meadows is excellent in playing his own father, *Civil Rights* is also touching.

Just like with *SchillerVisions*, Schiller also created what would have been a recurring bit, *New York's Strangest and Most Bizarre People*, in 1992. There were only two entries, neither of which made it to the live show. Both opened with the same photo collage of peculiar human beings, such as one of the microcephalics from *Freaks*, a clown, and an old man who can swallow his own face. *Saturday Night Live's* announcer Don Pardo narrated the intros.

Adam Sandler played the title character in the first film, *Shorty: The Guy Who Can't Cross the Street*. The black-and-white film consists of Sandler playing an awkward man who is afraid to cross the street. Each time he tries to walk, a car honks its horn and Shorty quickly jumps back onto the curb. After a while, people on the other side of the street encourage Shorty to cross. When he finally does, the people on the other side of the street assault him.

Shorty is relatively funny because of Adam Sandler's spastic performance, and the punch line, in which he is pummeled for no apparent reason, is also amusing. Plus, at two minutes, the length was just right. Again, it's another film that should have been aired.

The second entry was not nearly as funny, and it's just as well that it never made it to air. Chris Farley stars as *Tortoise Man: The Person Who is a Car*. The film begins with some back story, told by Don Pardo. Pardo explains that twenty-nine years ago, a woman gave birth to a baby boy in the back of a 1957 Lamborghini I-7, one of the smallest cars. The unibrowed Staten Islander raised her son inside the car exclusively on fast food. Years later, the boy has become a man—played by Chris Farley. Tortoise Man, as he is called, lives in the same car by himself. Due to his obesity, he is unable to leave his car—man and machine have become one. He continues to eat only fast food, but is frustrated and sad when children mock him for being an automobile. The film closes with Farley dreaming of one day being able to free himself from his metal encasement with the jaws of life. Until that time, Pardo says, Tortoise Man continues to be one of *New York's Strangest and Most Bizarre People*.

Chapter 19
Once Upon a Time

In 1989, Mike Myers created the recurring character Dieter, the peculiar host of the German talk show *Sprockets*. In most *Sprockets* sketches, Dieter interviewed a guest and then asked them to dance to Kraftwerk music or to touch his pet monkey, which usually sat on a pedestal beside him. *Sprockets* had already become a popular recurring sketch, and within a year of making his first appearance, Mike Myers and Tom Schiller built a short film around Dieter. Previously, *Schiller's Reel* films had been original ideas that did not feature existing *Saturday Night Live* characters. The retro-futuristic holiday-themed short *Dieter in Space* was the first to use an existing character from the show. It aired on December 16, 1989.

Dieter in Space is one of just a few of Schiller's short films that the director did not completely write himself. Schiller and Myers shaped and sculpted the film together. Myers joined the cast as a midseason addition in January of 1989, shortly after Schiller returned to the show. He watched *Saturday Night Live* as a child and wanted to be on the show since he was eleven, so he was familiar with *Schiller's Reel*. Myers did not have an office for the first year and a half that he was on the show, so Schiller often let him hang around. Schiller showed old movies and played old phonographs, and let Myers play on his piano. To Myers, Schiller represented everything that he imagined being a cool artist in New York would be like.

Myers claims that he is not one to do a lot of research, preferring instead to go by 'fuzzy memories.' For the *Austin Powers* films, he used his own vague recollections of the sixties culture in Great Britain. With the *Sprockets* sketches, the same rings true and Myers looked at what little he knew about the German art scene. "In Tom I saw a fellow lover of all things strange and Euro," Myers recalls. "He had all this great footage from German science fiction, and it all got incorporated."

While the Dieter sketches normally involved Mike Myers' spandex-clad character as the host of his own talk show, *Dieter in Space* only uses the character and some of his trademarks. Like many of Schiller's other films, it looks like an old film. Specifically, Schiller was recreating the old newsreel look of the 1930s combined with Nazi propaganda. Schiller also cleverly used some terrific stock footage from a German science fiction film.

The film begins with Schiller himself as a reporter for German television, announcing that Dieter, the host of the popular television show *Sprockets*, will launch a monkey into space. Dieter, his monkey Klaus, *Sprockets* fan club president Greta Hornaday, and Dr. Möbius (played by Schiller regular John Garson) arrive at Bahnhof Flughafen, which is filled with thousands of spectators for their press conference and the launch of the spaceship. The spaceship is a cross between a zeppelin and a rocket, and the crowd scenes are stock footage of what looks like a Hitler march. Dieter and his crew gather inside the spaceship and answer questions via a live video feed.

Working with the monkey was fun, but as is often the case with animals, it's not always easy. Despite being dressed in a little space suit, the monkey had a predilection for masturbation, at times making it tough to get a shot in.

One journalist asks Dieter why he is sending a monkey into space. Without a moment to think, Dieter replies: "Because art is dead." The footage of the journalists is also stock footage that has been dubbed with Schiller's English dialogue. After a few questions, Dieter and his crew get ready to leave the ship and say goodbye to the monkey. The monkey shakes everybody's hands, but then accidentally pulls a lever to launch the rocket. Dr. Möbius screams and the rocket takes off with everyone inside.

The rocket launch is from the 1939 German film *Weltraumschiff 1 startet*, directed by Anton Kutter. It shows the vertical launch of a zeppelin-like spaceship off of a ramp. The special effects were groundbreaking for 1939.[18] Schiller uses the footage of the rocket being launched on a ramp over and over so that it looks as if the rocket glides over miles of ramp before it blasts into the air. But Schiller does it so much that it becomes obvious, making it even funnier. Schiller even inserts a quick glimpse of the evil scientist from *The Enigma of Dr. Schiller* as the rocket shoots into space. It is totally random and even though its appearance in *Dieter in Space* makes no sense, it does fit the expressionist style and mood of the film.

Once the ship is in outer space, the press regains contact with Dieter and his crew. Half-floating due to the lack of gravity, Dieter admits that he is doomed, but that he is enjoying it. He begins singing 'Auld Lang Syne,' and his crew quickly joins in. Finally, Dieter wishes everybody watching a Merry Christmas and a Happy New Year.

Dieter in Space proved that Tom Schiller could make a wonderful *Schiller's Reel* built around a character he did not create, that was just as artful and stylish as any of his other films. He made only one other short with an existing character—*Dieter's Dream*, also with the *Sprockets* host—three years later.

Dieter's Dream did not bear the *Schiller's Reel* logo, let alone any logo at all. The film was a mixture of pre-taped material and the live in-studio broadcast. It aired during the March 20, 1993 episode hosted by Miranda Richardson. Richardson also appears in *Dieter's Dream*, so it was taped in the week prior to the live broadcast. The film begins with a close-up of Dieter sitting in the *Saturday Night Live* audience. He slowly falls asleep and begins to dream.

The film turns to scratchy black-and-white film stock and an obese old man in diapers announces the title of the film. Dieter leaps into the air, much like Marcello Mastroianni does in the famous opening to Fellini's *8 ½*. Dieter hovers through the street until an old-fashioned limousine pulls up. A window rolls down and Miranda Richardson, dressed in leather, tells Dieter that he is having a dream. Another window rolls down and Dieter's mother also tells him that he is having a dream. A third window rolls down, and sportscaster Marv Albert (playing himself) tells Dieter the same thing. Dieter enters the car, which is driven by a deer, and Richardson asks Dieter if he would like a Fresca. Two other characters are also inside: Susan the She-Male (a recurring *Sprockets* character played by Phil Hartman), and the diapered old man from the beginning of the film.

The film also features Dieter ice skating in the nude, and in one of the film's funniest bits, Dieter and Richardson spoof *Silhouette Syllables* from the 1970s children's show *The Electric Company*. Richardson claims that she is a whore and then claims to be a nun. Then, her silhouette appears on the left side of the screen, in front of a white background, and says 'whore.' Dieter's silhouette appears on the right side and he says 'nun.' The words appear on the screen and join together to form a new word: 'whorenun.' Dieter's dream ends when he finds out that his monkey Klaus has been turned into a pair of underwear, which he is wearing himself.

Dieter's Dream is Schiller at his most surreal. It gave him and Mike Myers an opportunity to have fun with German pseudo-realism and even insert an homage to Fellini. The film was such a success that it was included in *The Best of Mike Myers*, a collection of Myers' funniest bits from his seven-year stint on *Saturday Night Live*.

Hooked on Sushi has a similar feel to the many Chinatown detective stories and mysteries from the 1930s—such as the Charlie Chan series and its imitations. But it is also a disturbing horror story. Kevin Nealon plays a *film noir* protagonist—complete with classic *film noir* narration—who stops for lunch at Futaba, a sushi restaurant. Of course, Futaba is also the name that Schiller gave to John Belushi's Samurai character as well as the hip gallery in *Nothing Lasts Forever*. The film was shot at Zutto Restaurant on Hudson Street in Tribeca, which is right across the street from the bank used in *Love is a Dream*.

Nealon, dressed in the typical *film noir* raincoat, walks into Futaba because everything else in the area is closed. He is the only customer. Stan Egi, Michi Kobi and Peter Yoshida play the chef and the servers. Nealon decides to order the Sushi special, and as soon as he does, the 'Open' sign hanging in the window is secretly turned over by one of the employees. Nealon's narration ends after he places his order.

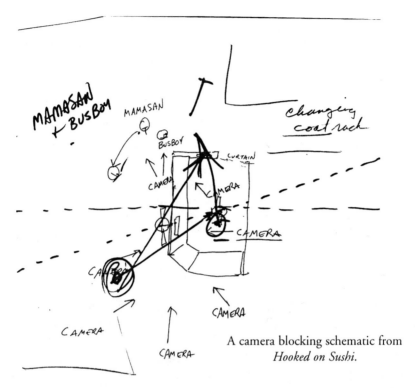

A camera blocking schematic from
Hooked on Sushi.

Nealon is served three pieces of sushi. He tries the first one, which tastes fine. But unbeknownst to Nealon, the chef puts a fishhook in the second piece. Nealon hesitates before biting into the second piece—as if he senses that something is afoot. But he puts it in his mouth anyway, and suddenly one of the servers in the back room of the restaurant starts reeling him in with his fishing rod. The chef and the other server eagerly cheer him on. Nealon struggles, but is dragged over the counter and into the back room, at which point the chef approaches him with a chopping knife. The 'Closed' sign in the window is turned over again, and moments later a selection of eyes and fingers are put on display in the counter vitrine. A new customer walks in and is welcomed by the crew, just like Nealon was at the beginning of the film.

Like Peter Aykroyd in *Java Junkie*, Kevin Nealon is a good fit for the emblematic *film noir* hero. He has the right facial features, but most importantly, the right voice. Based on appearance alone, he gives the impression that he is a detective even though there's no mention of it.

Nealon's character is essentially a fish. On the one hand he is a weak, innocent victim. He is non-threatening and doesn't catch on to anything. But on the other hand, he actually gets reeled in and chopped up like an actual fish at the end of the film. It's an interesting analogy.

Hooked on Sushi is as amusing and stylish as any *Schiller's Reel*. Schiller again recreates a long-gone genre, but it distinguishes itself because it's Schiller's most disturbing piece—let alone one of *Saturday Night Live*'s most disturbing bits. The show has broadcast sketches in which limbs are cut off, but it's always done in a comedic manner, in which part of the humor stems from the fact that it doesn't look real. But *Hooked on Sushi* will make even the least squeamish person feel queasy. Its mere suggestion of a big fishhook in someone's mouth is painful.

In addition to both *SchillerVision Theatre* shorts and *Hidden Camera Commercials*, the only other *SchillerVision* film that aired was *Million Dollar Zombie*, starring Victoria Jackson, Chris Farley and Phil Hartman.

Million Dollar Zombie is shot in the style of a black-and-white horror film from the sixties. Shot on 16mm film, in its opening scenes it admirably recreates the low budget, non-Hollywood film look of movies like *Night of the Living Dead* or *Carnival of Souls*—which were independently shot in Pennsylvania, Utah and Kansas. In *Million Dollar Zombie*, Victoria Jackson plays the wife of Chris Farley, an unemployed, alcoholic redneck who complains that she spends too much of his money. After Farley decides to go for a drink one night, Jackson receives a letter in the mail from Ed McMahon and the Publishers Clearing House. The letter says that she has won a million dollars, so she drives to the return address on the envelope to claim her prize.

At the Publishers Clearing House, an old and spooky wooden manor, a mysterious diminutive man (played by Michael J. Anderson) opens the door and leads her to a guest room where Mr. McMahon will see her shortly. Jackson anxiously waits for McMahon until she looks out of the window and sees robed, hooded zombies chanting "We are winners."

She then overhears Ed McMahon talking in the room below her, and finds a door in the floor hidden underneath the rug. It leads to the Publishers Clearing House dungeon, which she enters with a flashlight in her hands. After walking down the cobwebbed stairwell, two zombies stop her and chain her to a wall. Ed McMahon, played by Phil Hartman, appears in his *Tonight Show* outfit with a microphone stand. He uses the microphone to hypnotize her and repeats "You may already be a winner" until she falls asleep.

Victoria Jackson was uncomfortable about being chained to the wall with her shirt open, revealing her bra. "I thought it was extremely risqué," she recalls. "It was pretty sexual to me, to be in bondage with my bra showing."

Suddenly, Chris Farley and two other hillbillies appear out of nowhere. McMahon takes the microphone off the stand to reveal a stiletto at the edge, which he uses to attack Farley. But Farley has the perfect weapon to stop him: a cross with a photograph of Jay Leno in the middle. McMahon falls to the ground and Farley uses the microphone stiletto to kill him. As he dies, McMahon yells out his trademark "Heyo!" and his body dissolves into a pile of money—one million dollars. Chris Farley explains to Victoria Jackson that he used her as bait so that he could get to McMahon—it was a plan all along. They lovingly reunite and the million dollars is divided among the hillbillies and zombies in the room.

Farley and Jackson make a cute backwoods couple, especially at the end. Schiller made a great decision at the moment when the two embrace after he has defeated the evil Ed McMahon. They look like they are about to kiss each other, but at the last moment decide to hug and smile into the camera. It's a charming and unexpected little moment that probably wouldn't have worked with any of the other cast members.

"I was just standing there like 'What? What's going on here? Where's the joke?'" Jackson remembers. "I still don't know what the plot was of that one."

Farley and Jackson capture the essence of sixties B-grade, non-Hollywood acting in the opening scene where they argue over the bills. They give the idea that they are acting in a film for the very first time, which adds to the home-made feel of the genre it is attempting to spoof. Jackson again provides a great example of this acting when she is in the guest room waiting for Ed McMahon. She acts like a first-time actress as she talks to herself about how excited she is to be a millionairess. But as the film becomes more cartoonish, so do the performances—in particular Chris Farley's when he barges in to the rescue.

Phil Hartman does a brilliant Ed McMahon impression, which he had performed on the show many times before. "The Ed impression was born on *Saturday Night Live* as a reflection of Dana Carvey's brilliant impression of Johnny Carson," says John Hartmann.

Schiller retired the *SchillerVision* banner in early 1992. All of the following shorts resumed under the name *Schiller's Reel*.

Schiller again plays the lead in *Shirley, I Love You*. Another of Schiller's less consistent works, *Shirley, I Love You* simply does not seem to gel. Schiller plays Max 'Tightwad' Shimkus, a grey old man who stumbles through the Bury Yourself Budget Cemetery to visit the grave of his wife Shirley. He starts talking to his dead wife and tells her how much he loves her and misses her. Shirley, played by Palm Springs journalist Gloria Greer, starts talking to him from beyond the grave. A hand reaches out of the grave and grabs him by the throat, nearly choking him to death.

Shimkus is then jolted awake from his nightmare. Relieved, he stumbles out of bed to look at himself in the mirror, only to find Shirley staring right at him.

The film switches over to a local television news segment, in which the anchor reports that Shimkus died of a heart attack in his bathroom, with the words 'Shirley, I Love You' scribbled on the mirror. The film ends with a shot of Shirley waving goodbye to the camera while a creepy *Twilight Zone*-like tune plays in the background.

While Schiller is very funny as Max Shimkus, and the idea of a Budget Cemetery is amusing in itself, the apparition of Gloria Greer seems out of place. Schiller could have done something funnier with the concept. Schiller should be credited, though, for its intrinsic Palm Springs look. The oversaturated colors add to the temperature of the film, which gives the film a dizzying, sunstroke atmosphere.

Dana Carvey is the star of *The Land Before Television*, a short film that is presented as a fairy tale. After each *Saturday Night Live* show, Carvey is followed by mobs of fans who want his autograph and ask him to recite his most famous lines. Carvey blames this on television, and wishes that he lived in a far-off place where there was no television. His wish comes true and with a poof, Carvey dissolves into thin air. He flies to a faraway dream land, a small area with blue skies, white clouds and green grass. An old man dressed in green greets him and tells him that he has arrived in the Land Before Television. The old man turns out to be Peter Pan, stuck in the Land Before Television for eighty-five years. He introduces Carvey to Thumbelina, an old lady who dances around with a bottle of liquor in her hand, and a toy soldier, an old man sitting around on a chair. Carvey thinks it's wonderful that there is no television, but Peter Pan tells him that everybody is bored out of their minds. Worst of all, there are no residuals.

Pan then introduces Carvey to Hans Christian Andersen, the renowned nineteenth century author of dozens of fables and fairy tales. Andersen, played

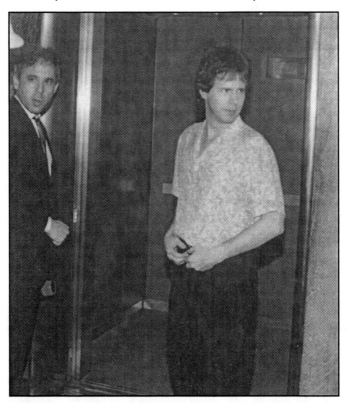

Tom Schiller and Dana Carvey. Courtesy Neal Marshad Productions.

Drummond Erskine, Dana Carvey, Tom Schiller, Elaine Swann, Kuno Sponholz,
Frank O'Brien and Neal Marshad. Courtesy Neal Marshad Productions.

by Schiller's friend and *Nothing Lasts Forever* Lunarcruiser Drummond Erskine,
reads stories out of a book. After listening to Andersen for a while, Carvey
becomes bored. He gathers all four citizens of the Land Before Television and
shares his revelation—that television provides millions of people with wholesome entertainment, and that he is destined to be on television. He wishes that
he could return, and Peter Pan tells him that he had that power all along. Pan
gives him a remote control and Carvey is transported back to the NBC Studios
lobby. A technician recognizes him and asks for his autograph. Grateful to be
recognized, Carvey gladly agrees to sign an autograph.

Despite a major flaw, *The Land Before Television* is an enjoyable short. Dana
Carvey is likeable as the hounded celebrity who wishes that he was never famous,
and it's a good concept that should have worked. The main problem is the set of the
Land Before Television. The Land Before Television is supposed to look like an old-
fashioned fantasy land. It should have been like Peter Pan's Neverland, or at least the
Austrian Alps where Julie Andrews sings 'The Sound of Music.' It should have looked
natural—an area not yet polluted by television, let alone popular culture. Schiller's
Land Before Television looks too plastic. He shot it in a small studio, which is all too
obvious. It looks very confined, but worst of all, it looks extremely cheap. Rather
than looking like a dreamland, the Land Before Television is a small room with a
green mat, cardboard trees, plastic clouds and blue wallpaper.

Aside from the inexpensive set design, the film works well as a fairy tale
take-off. The gentle storybook narration almost turns the film into a four-minute
episode of *Shelley Duvall's Faerie Tale Theatre,* and Dana Carvey has the appropriate childlike demeanor to play someone who would fly off to an imaginary

land where there is no television.

Our Noisy, Noisy World stars cast member Julia Sweeney and Stephen Hibbert[19] as a married couple who lead a very loud life. From the moment they wake up in the morning and the alarm clock rings, to shaving, to using a hairdryer, to making breakfast for their two children, they are rarely able to understand each other due to the deafening noise coming from their environment. Hibbert works at an airport and Sweeney works in a loud pet store all day. When they come home, they find their children running around playing cowboys and Indians with the television turned up high.

The couple rushes out the door for some peace and quiet. They drive out and stall their car by a train track, anticipating a moment of peace so that they can understand each other without having to scream. Hibbert wants to tell Sweeney something, but just as he is ready to speak, a train passes and he has to wait. Once the train has passed, a car behind them starts honking. Hibbert finally gives up trying to say something, so he kisses her.

At just two minutes, *Our Noisy, Noisy World* is short and sweet. Despite having the feel of a fairy tale, it's one of Schiller's most modern films—there's an electric razor, the children eat Major Crunch cereal (Cap'n Crunch with a black mustache), Hibbert uses a coffee grinder, Sweeney uses a blender, and so on. All are unusual in a Schiller film. It's a sweet but goofy commentary on how loud modern family life is despite all these technical advances that are supposed to make life easier, but how little it matters at the end of the day.

Melanie Hutsell is the star of *Big Girl Goes to Town*, a spoof of the *Godzilla* movie series. Hutsell is a gap-toothed teenager who lives with her parents in a lighthouse in the Bay of Fundy, Canada. She gets a letter—a very small one— from her pen pal in New York City, inviting her to visit. Hutsell argues that she is a big girl now, so her parents let her go. She leaves in a rowboat, but first her parents give her some money—which is very small.

As she arrives, Schiller utilizes stock footage of old-fashioned New York. Everybody runs away from Hutsell, and she quickly realizes that she is a giant. She starts looking for her pen pal Tony while New Yorkers flee their cars and run for cover. A squad of policemen starts firing at her. Hutsell is scared off and returns home. The film closes with Hutsell at home with her parents again, happy to be back.

Big Girl Goes to Town has a good concept, but Hutsell cannot carry a film of this length by herself. At four-and-a-half minutes, it's way too long. While the black-and-white stock footage of the New York harbor circa 1950 is interesting and blends in reasonably well with the rest of the film, the special effects don't look nearly as good and give the short film a distinct 'video' look.

Chapter 20
Hollywood's Golden Age

Falling in Love is a romantic musical in the vein of *Love is a Dream*, but not nearly as memorable. In a high-rise, Victoria Jackson and Jon Lovitz play a reunited couple at an elegant party who sing Vaughn Monroe's 'Falling In Love.'

They take a break from singing to drink champagne and discuss their situation by the piano. It appears that they had split up, but now they agree to fall in love all over again. They leave their champagne by the piano and walk over to the balcony where they continue to sing.

The wind outside starts to blow very hard and Lovitz's tie blows over his face. The couple doesn't mind and enthusiastically continues singing about how happy they are to fall in love again. Soon, the wind blows too hard and they tumble off of the balcony together. The party guests panic and rush to the balcony to see when they hit the ground, while the pianist quickly downs both champagne glasses without anyone noticing. They are at least one hundred floors up. Lovitz and Jackson scream and their fall lasts a full ten seconds.

Jon Lovitz and Victoria Jackson. Courtesy Neal Marshad Productions.

When they finally hit the ground hundreds of feet below, they are unscathed and still standing upright. They immediately continue finishing the song while behind them a police officer makes sure that they are alright.

The film is sweet and charming, but does not rank among Schiller's best. It doesn't have the same production values as *Love is a Dream*—the most obvious comparison. *Falling in Love* takes place in what is supposed to be a luxurious New York apartment, but it looks too empty and doesn't have the gaudy feel of a classic Hollywood musical set. Making the room white and empty was probably done on purpose to make the small set look bigger, but as a result, it does not look flashy and chic like the ballroom in *Love is a Dream*. It clearly shows that Tom Schiller was working with a smaller budget.

Also, Lovitz and the singing voice to which he lip-synchs are not a good match. The voice is too deep for Lovitz's rascally voice, but it is easy to get used to after a few moments. Victoria Jackson, on the other hand, is a better fit. Dressed in a chic outfit, she is able to capture the essence of a glamorous Broadway songstress despite being one of *Saturday Night Live*'s most eccentric and playful cast members.

Unfortunately, the film resorts to a simple gag that is not very funny within the context of a romantic musical. While the idea behind the film—a couple singing 'Falling in Love' and actually falling off a balcony—is amusing, the fact that Lovitz and Jackson fall for ten seconds and aren't hurt doesn't fit with the overall feel of the film up until that moment.

Nevertheless, it's a charming film and Victoria Jackson had the time of her life. "I was raised on 30s and 40s songs because we did not have a TV and my dad used to play them on the piano," Jackson recalls. "I remember that that was a very magical shoot, and the only thing that I didn't like was that I was overweight at the time, and I was kind of mad at myself. I was afraid that Tom was going to fire me from it, and I think he might have said something about the women in the 40s having curvy bodies like that."

Even though Schiller does not appear in the film, it did not mean that he did not have to perform. "He was playing the part, too, even though he was behind the camera," says Jackson. "Tom would walk around the set with the attitude of the directors of the thirties. In my mind it seemed like he had an ascot on. It felt like I was in a thirties movie, and it felt like we were black-and-white, even though we weren't when we were shooting it."

While not the last to be produced, the final *Schiller's Reel* to air on *Saturday Night Live* was broadcast on November 13, 1993. In *Will Work For Food*, a starring vehicle for Norm MacDonald, Schiller uses no dialogue at all. It is a silent black-and-white film in the moody, dramatic vein of Charles Chaplin's *The Kid*, and does an admirable job of matching the look and feel of a film made before 1929, the year that the talking picture took America by storm. Despite having been shot on video, the soundtrack is filled with scratches and many frames are skipped, as often is the case with neglected silent film reels. The acting is also more theatrical than any of Schiller's shorts. Schiller used music from Chaplin's *Limelight*, which further helps turn Norm MacDonald into a character much like The Tramp.

MacDonald plays a homeless man who wakes from a night spent under a bridge. At a nearby burning trashcan, another homeless person (played by Bernie Friedman) tries to warm himself. MacDonald walks over and trades his blanket for Friedman's 'Will Work For Food' sign and walks along the street. An old man played by Tom Schiller picks him up in his car and takes him to his apartment. Norm MacDonald is hungry and looks forward to the meal he believes he is about to be served. Instead, Schiller sits him at a table and puts him to work. Schiller brings over a towering stack of papers, each of which MacDonald needs to stamp.

Next, Schiller has MacDonald shine his shoes—all six pairs. Then he has to do the bookkeeping, and the ironing, and the dusting, and the vacuuming. Then he has to fix the old man's broken watches, clean his dentures, and sit at a typewriter to type out letters. MacDonald's final task is to build a ship-in-bottle model.

Once the ship has been erected, MacDonald has done enough work and Schiller ceremoniously brings out his meal. The old man comes out of the kitchen dressed in a chef's uniform and rolls the meal out on a cart. He lifts up the metal cover, and the seemingly luxurious dinner turns out to be a lousy hot dog on a dry bun.

The old man drops MacDonald off at the bridge and MacDonald steps out of the car disappointed, shaking his fist at the old man as the car leaves. Once he returns to the burning trash can where Bernie Friedman is warming himself, he takes the hot dog out of his pocket and gives it to his homeless friend. Friedman does not want to impose, but MacDonald insists that he take it, and then looks on with satisfaction as his hungry friend enjoys the wiener.

Because the characters do not speak, they have to communicate their feelings via exaggerated facial expressions. Norm MacDonald is excellent, and *Will Work For Food* is perhaps the most in-character part he has ever played on *Saturday Night Live*. He even looks genuinely starved and weather-beaten. His calm demeanor shows MacDonald's potential as a dramatic actor, and it's no surprise that Milos Forman put him in his last two films, *The People vs. Larry Flynt* and *Man on the Moon*.

While Schiller's second term at *Saturday Night Live* was not as solid and consistent as his first, he started and ended with brilliant, heartfelt films. *Love is a Dream*, his first short film to be aired, provided one of *Saturday Night Live's* most memorable and touching moments. Unlike *Love is a Dream*, *Will Work For Food* does have its share of laughs, but its cumulative effect is warm and genuine. Sadly, *Will Work For Food* is mostly forgotten. It aired at a time when it was completely out of tune with the rest of the show. Despite running during an episode featuring James Taylor as the musical guest, it was sandwiched between a sketch in which David Spade played Dick Clark's secretary, and another sketch about teenage girls having a party. 'Out of place' is putting it lightly.

In *Will Work For Food*, Norm MacDonald is given a hot dog for a long day of hard work. It is comparable to the respect and recognition that Tom Schiller received on the show. Half of his films were never shown, and when they were, they were dumped towards the end.

One of Schiller's most interesting contributions is *The Violin*, a black-and-white gem starring Tim Meadows as a homeless man who loiters in front of Juilliard. A young student played by Sarah Silverman walks by with a violin case. Meadows yanks it out of her hands and runs off. He takes the piece to a pawn shop, where he is a regular. Schiller and Julia Sweeney play the Schmidts, an elderly couple who run the store. Mr. Schmidt explains that his wife was a violin teacher before they left Germany. Meadows loves the sound of the instrument and decides that he wants to learn how to play it so that he has something to do in between robberies. Mrs. Schmidt offers to teach him if he continues to bring in stolen goods.

Over the next few months, Meadows brings in plenty of merchandise while Mrs. Schmidt teaches him how to play the violin. Meadows practices hard and becomes an excellent violinist. He is eventually invited to play at Carnegie Hall, where he is a finalist in the Urban Violinist Awards. Phil Hartman—complete with a fancy mustache and blond hair—presents the award. It is the same gold lyre that Adam Beckett is given in the Inner Sanctum in *Nothing Lasts Forever*—The Gift of Music. Schiller kept the prop from the making of the film and re-used it in *The Violin*.

Hartman proudly announces the winner and Meadows rushes to the stage to accept his award. In his speech, he thanks his mother (played by Ellen Cleghorne, seen in the audience) and the Schmidts. He then sends a message to hopeful young artists and explains how he made it to Carnegie Hall: "Not by begging, cheating or stealing, but practice, practice, practice."

The Violin is one of Schiller's best short films of the second era at *Saturday Night Live*. It can be argued that it is a response to *Nothing Lasts Forever*. In *Nothing Lasts Forever*, Adam Beckett is given The Gift of Music simply for being kind, which as established earlier, goes against the rules of storytelling and the development of a character. Adam did not become a pianist by practice, but just by being a nice person. *The Violin* is a clever retort, albeit twelve years after the fact. Meadows becomes a violinist by begging, cheating and stealing, in addition to practice. Some people become artists by stealing ideas, whereas Adam Beckett became an artist for being a wholesome, ambitious young man. Schiller took a lot of heat from MGM and got a poor response at the preview screening at Broadway Video, yet *Nothing Lasts Forever* is one of the most creative and original films ever made. Most other films are different versions of the same story and follow formulas that have been repeated thousands of times over. This is not generally considered stealing, but films that follow a formula do borrow something from existing works. *The Violin* presents the other side of the coin of *Nothing Lasts Forever.* A man who cheats and steals his way into becoming a musician and receives the same applause at Carnegie Hall, only to deny how he truly became an artist.

Nevertheless, Schiller insists that *The Violin* was not made in response to *Nothing Lasts Forever.* He says that it is simply a similar story told in a shorter form.

Schiller directed his final film for *Saturday Night Live* in 1994. The black-and-white musical *Laura* stars Melanie Hutsell as the title character, a coat room clerk at an elegant New York restaurant. Ellen Cleghorne plays Betty, who works in the coat room with her. Laura says that she's desperate: She has no man, no money and no clothes. Suddenly, someone drops off a dashing fur cape. Laura obnoxiously puts it on and tells Betty that if she had a cape like that, she'd surely be able to find true love. She runs out of the restaurant with the cape on, but the moment she steps outside, a carriage rides through a puddle along the sidewalk, splashing mud all over the cape. A handsome gentleman played by Phil Hartman steps out of the carriage and apologizes for the mess. He insists that Laura join him in his horse-drawn carriage and take the cape to a nearby 24-hour cleaner. On the way, Hartman serenades Laura and the film turns from black-and-white into color. It's a beautiful moment, reminiscent of *Love is a Dream,* but it doesn't last long.

Laura awakens at the desk of the coat room moments later. The film has returned to black-and-white. A gentleman, which turns out to be Phil Hartman, is there to pick up his wife's cape—the same one that Laura had dreamed of wearing. Hartman and Hutsell look each other in the eyes as if they already know each other. Hartman thanks Laura and leaves, and Laura goes back to sleep, now with a big smile on her face.

As was the case with *Love is a Dream,* there is nothing funny about *Laura.* There are no jokes and there is no punch line. It's simply a warm, beautiful little musical. Phil Hartman is as charming as ever, and while Melanie Hutsell's character is a little too stubborn to make this film as good as *Love is a Dream,* showing the film would have been a terrific way to close Schiller's career at *Saturday Night Live.*

Chapter 21
Pre-Tape Delegation

During the last few years of his tenure at *Saturday Night Live*, Schiller was relegated more and more to doing pre-tapes. Directing pre-tapes was not always as exciting as directing his own short films, but he enjoyed doing them nonetheless. It even took some of the pressure off having to come up with new film ideas. For example, in the October 2, 1993 episode, host Shannen Doherty discussed her recent marriage in her opening monologue, and then introduced a few video clips of the ceremony—obviously not the actual wedding, but a humorous recreation with actors. The joke was that the clips showed Doherty getting into fights with everybody at her own wedding, playing off her tabloid reputation of being a troublemaker in those days. Schiller was assigned to direct the video clips of the wedding during the week leading up to October 2nd.

One of Schiller's more famous pre-tapes aired a week earlier, on September 25, 1993. Charles Barkley was the host, and Jay Mohr came up with the idea of having Barkley play basketball against Barney, the purple dinosaur that was quickly becoming a children's television phenomenon. The taped segment was part of the monologue, so Schiller was assigned to shoot it during the week leading up the broadcast. In the bit, which immediately became a classic, Barkley plays very rough with Barney—pushing him over and knocking him with his elbows. It kept Schiller busy in between the short films—which were becoming few and far between—but it was not as much of a creative outlet.

There were some pre-tapes that did allow Schiller to be creative—particularly for Mike Myers' recurring *Sprockets* sketches. When Kyle McLachlan hosted on September 29, 1990, he played Karl-Heinz Schelkar, host of *Germany's Most Disturbing Home Videos*, a new segment on *Sprockets*. He introduces four clips, each of which is in black-and-white. In the first clip, a fat old man runs around a lawn sprinkler in a big diaper. The second clip shows a man handing out flyers on the street and being kicked in the testicles by a complete stranger. In the third clip, the dead body of a homeless man is found in the woods. The corpse is turned over to reveal that the man's face is covered with ants. The final clip takes place in a gallery in Hanover, where a man's trousers fall down while he is looking at a painting. While the clips are all disturbing, the third clip of the ant-covered human cadaver in the woods was the most horrific to watch. Nevertheless, the winning clip is Trouser Gallery, sent in by a couple from Münster. They win a 1990 Chevrolet Geo and 10,000 marks.

Mike Myers was amazed at how Schiller was able to film what he had written for him. He was surprised that he could find a heavy actor willing to wear a diaper and run around a sprinkler in Central Park. Myers was equally disturbed and amused by the shot of the homeless corpse covered with ants.

When Woody Harrelson hosted *Saturday Night Live* on May 16, 1992, he played a German filmmaker on *Sprockets*. Schiller was assigned to direct the bizarre film clip that Woody Harrelson's character Gregor Voss was to have directed. The black-and-white film, entitled *Love Werks*, is a nonsensical mixture of German minimalism and neo-expressionism, much like the overall tone of Dieter's show. The film shows Voss looking into the camera and then stiffly looking away in various directions, interspersed with clips of a rooster, a depressed elderly gentleman, a fat man dressed in a cupid's outfit, and a fist squeezing a raw egg to pieces. Part of the appeal of the *Sprockets* sketches is that Dieter is so pretentious that he is funny. This is exactly the case with the clip from *Love Werks* and the entries from *Germany's Most Disturbing Home Videos*. It is also remarkable that these pre-tapes were conceived and executed all within a few days. Sketch ideas are usually submitted on the Tuesday before the live show, so Schiller did not have a lot of time to shoot these pieces.

Another pre-tape highlight is *Happy Fun Ball*, a fake commercial written by Jack Handey, for a simple plastic toy ball that carries dozens of warnings for possible side-effects. The commercial lasts one-and-a-half minutes, of which just twenty seconds are dedicated to the actual toy. The rest of the commercial is a frozen screen with scrolling text read by Phil Hartman. The warnings start off innocently, cautioning pregnant women, the elderly and children under the age of ten not to play with the ball too long, and that it may accelerate to dangerous speeds. But it quickly becomes more serious, as Hartman describes that Happy Fun Ball may cause itching, dizziness, slurred speech and heart palpitations, and has many other dangerous side-effects. The commercial is humorous in its foresight, because in the years following its debut, advertisements for prescription medicine have turned into similar commercials with endless notifications of possible side-effects.

But other pre-tape assignments seem like mundane tasks, such as the opening credits for *Blossom* in which the cast members dance around on a stage, or the opening theme to *The Mimic* in which Alec Baldwin acts like a goofy secret service agent. Schiller is a talented filmmaker and deserved better than being relegated to sequences such as these, but he did not complain. For example, he really liked the challenge of accurately recreating the *Blossom* opening theme with the *Saturday Night Live* cast members.

Budget cuts finally forced Michaels to drop Schiller and other writers in 1994. At first, Schiller was very unhappy to be let go, but has since seen it as a blessing in disguise. "I think the glorious years were the first five years of that show, from '75 to '80," Schiller says. "If I had never gone back, it would have been fine. When I did come back, there was a rich vein that I had for a couple of years there, with Phil Hartman and that crew."

In 1993 and 1994, the show was different from the way it used to be. It was still a solid show, but it had evolved to match the changing times and the changing audiences. The series tends to fluctuate like that. Instead of Phil Hartman, Julia Sweeney and Dennis Miller, performers now included Rob Schneider, Chris Farley and Adam Sandler. It became more sophomoric. "The whole thrust of the show was skewing younger and younger. And I think I was becoming more antiquated like a relic of the past, like at a college where the old professors occupy their chairs collecting cobwebs," Schiller recalls. "I don't think I was in tune with the new thrust of the show, and that's why I probably should have left a couple years earlier."

Tom Schiller's contribution to *Saturday Night Live* is immeasurable, but he has not been a part of the show for over a decade. Occasionally, some of the ten original writers are brought back for a week to write some new material for the show. Tom Davis, for example, regularly returns to contribute a few new sketches. Schiller has never returned for such a stint. In 2001, when John Goodman hosted the show and Dan Aykroyd made a number of special appearances, a new *Bad Theatre* sketch with Leonard Pinth-Garnell was written. Schiller, who had written all of the previous *Bad Theatre* sketches, was not asked to write the new one, and did not find out about its existence until long after it aired. When Dan Aykroyd hosted *Saturday Night Live* in May of 2003, the first-time host thought of a concept that Schiller could be involved with. It would have been a pre-taped on-the-street segment. Schiller was contacted by *Saturday Night Live* during the week leading up to the broadcast, and was excited to work on the bit. Unfortunately, the proposed segment was scrapped before anything was planned.

Today, Schiller watches the show sparingly. "I think it's a staple of American television viewing, like *The Tonight Show*," he says. "I think that it's almost indestructible. It will probably go on forever, and it will always have its ups and downs. There will always be funny things in it and there will always be unfunny things in it, but you can never recapture the excitement of the first couple of years I was lucky enough to have been part of."

Chapter 22
Schiller Goes Commercial

In the decade he spent at *Saturday Night Live*, Tom Schiller won three Emmy awards and numerous Writers Guild awards. But it was not until after he left the show that he received the greatest awards and accolades—for his work as a director of television commercials. Schiller has directed over a hundred commercials since 1995 and has earned many awards, including a Gold Lion and two Bronze Lions at the Cannes Lion International Advertising Awards, five Clio awards, as well as various other awards.

Even while at *Saturday Night Live*, Schiller was involved with other film and video projects. He worked on a documentary for music group Steely Dan in 1995. A friend of frontman Donald Fagen, Schiller was hired to shoot the band in concert. Schiller amassed hours of footage, but it was never cut together. He also directed *The Sweet Smell of Safe Sex*, a short comedy about someone who takes an AIDS test, for Comedy Central. For MTV, he directed *This is Ray*, a half-hour pilot that was done in the style of 1950s educational films. Schiller liked it, but the cable network didn't go for it. For HBO, he made a promo called *HBO Sequels You'll Never See*, and for Nick-at-Nite he directed *Milkman*, also a promo.

In 1995, shortly after being let go from *Saturday Night Live*, Schiller directed his first commercial. Schiller had always thought about doing commercials, but did not seriously consider it until Gary Weis and another friend, Larry Williams, began doing them. Schiller had known Weis from the beach in Los Angeles since he was fifteen and always admired him, and Larry Williams was also a fixture in the early 1970s Chateau Marmont days alongside Schiller, Lorne Michaels, John Head, Gary Weis and a group of other young artists, writers and television people. When Weis and Williams proved successful at making ads, Schiller figured that if they could do it, so could he.

"Ads are sort of like condensed short films, and they're challenging in that you have to tell a story in fifteen or thirty seconds," Schiller says. He looked around for a production company and quickly found one. Typically, the production company sends out a reel of some of Schiller's commercials to a potential client. They examine it and try to see if it matches what they are looking to produce—be it a certain style, tone or sense of humor. Several directors are usually auditioned, and once the director is chosen, they begin work.

The biggest difference between directing short films and commercials is that Schiller doesn't write his own scripts. "It's not as free, and you have to please a client," Schiller admits. "So it's more of a collaboration with the writer and the art director." Nevertheless, Schiller does often get to expand upon the scripts and concepts that he is given. Given his background, he is usually hired for funny spots. Once he tried to do a dramatic spot but it came out funny.

Some of Schiller's favorite commercials include a series of six that he did for Budweiser entitled *Real Men of Genius*. Usually, comedy is fairly restrained and funny commercials only require small sets. With its large outdoor sets and lavish art direction, *Real Men of Genius* was clearly an exception. The commercials salute random and obscure people, such as nudist colony activity coordinators and men who wear really bad toupees. Singer David Bickler of the 1980s rock band Survivor humorously belted out the lyrics. The commercials were completed a few years ago but were initially called *Real American Heroes*. Before they were set to air, the events of September 11 unfolded and they were shelved. Eventually they aired in Great Britain and later on in the United States as well, but it was changed to *Real Men of Genius*.

Schiller is always involved in the casting of the actors. When auditioning, he uses the opportunity to rehearse with the actors, to see what does and does not work. Regardless of Schiller's choice of performers, the client always makes the final decision, but usually they go along with Schiller's casting choices. Schiller then works with the actors for about two days.

Furthermore, Schiller is also involved in finding locations, choosing his crew, and picking out the wardrobe. He works closely with the ad agency's creative team and often tries to make their ideas even funnier by expanding on them. The shoot itself usually takes up one to four days, sometimes with a budget as high as one million dollars.

One of Schiller's specialties at *Saturday Night Live* was to copy old-fashioned film styles and genres. With commercials, Schiller is often brought aboard for that very reason. His acclaimed commercial for Courtyard by Marriott has the look and sound of a videotaped hotel reception speech. It looks like C-SPAN programming, and that is exactly what Schiller wanted to recreate. In the commercial, someone introduces the keynote speaker, who is sitting at the podium table. Everyone applauds, including the keynote speaker, who has apparently forgotten that he has to go up to the stage. Finally, someone next to him whispers in his ear that he is supposed to go up, and he rushes to the stage. The commercial closes with the text: "Never underestimate the importance of a good night's rest."

Some of Schiller's other commercials include a Heineken commercial featuring John Travolta, which was done as a tie-in to the film *Swordfish*; a Kellogg's spot with William Shatner, humorously emphasizing the kitsch factor of some-one like Shatner pushing a breakfast cereal; and a Metamucil commercial in which someone pours the fiber drink into the Old Faithful Geyser at Yellowstone.

Schiller was teamed up with comedian and *The Daily Show* correspondent Ed Helms for a series of four commercials for another beer company. Helms played an independent filmmaker in the vein of Michael Moore who digs into the company to find out why its beer tastes colder than other beers. In one of the spots, Helms quizzes a barman and offers far-fetched conspiracy theories. In another spot, he visits a laboratory and asks scientists if the brewery gathered all the ice from the ice age and used it in its brewing process to make the beer taste cooler. In the final commercial, Helms actually visits the brewery in Colorado and heckles the tour guide.

Helms enjoyed making the commercials and working with Schiller, but thinks that he and his director could have made them much funnier had they been given the chance. As is the case with many multi-million dollar ad campaigns, the bureaucratic process makes it tough to make last-minute changes to scripts that have already gone through the many expensive, time-consuming stages of legal and corporate scrutiny.

"There were definitely little moments of sort of fun explorations," Helms says. "I love to improvise. I love to do like twenty takes and do every one differently, and I know that Tom is into that, too." Schiller and Helms did not have enough freedom to let the creative juices flow as much as they wanted, but still managed to produce a series of entertaining spots. Unfortunately, due to political reasons, the ads were never shown.

Schiller always has fun when he is working, and making this series of commercials was no exception. For example, at the beginning of the shooting day he took out a Mr. Microphone toy—an old 1980s children's cassette player with a microphone attached. He played a tape of old movie trailer music and then used the microphone to make a welcome announcement for everybody on the set. "He runs the set as kind of a showman," says Helms. "It keeps everyone entertained and motivated and happy to be there. It gets everybody on his side really quickly. He kind of wins you over."

Schiller loves directing commercials. Having already done about fifty short films, he sees commercials as miniaturized films and is fascinated by the concept of going even shorter. With well over a hundred commercials under his belt, the challenge to pack as much humor as possible into fifteen or thirty seconds is part of what keeps Schiller going.

Since Schiller left *Saturday Night Live*, short films have mostly been replaced by cartoons. In 1993 and 1994, *Beavis and Butthead* creator Mike Judge contributed a total of three *Office Space* cartoons featuring the character Milton. Though short-lived, it eventually spawned the cult classic feature film of the same name. In 1994, *Kids in the Hall* veteran Bruce McCulloch wrote and directed a few non-animated short films, which he starred in himself. Two of them, *Stalking* and *Snowbird*, made it on the air. A third, *Vacation*, didn't make it, although it was later inserted into a rerun as a way of replacing a copyright-infringing sketch written by Jay Mohr.

McCulloch's tenure was short-lived and instead of showing short films, Lorne Michaels opted for cartoons again. Long-time writer and one-time cast member Robert Smigel wrote a series of cartoons entitled *TV Funhouse*. With recurring episodes like *The Ambiguously Gay Duo*, *Fun with Real Audio* and *The X-Presidents*, *TV Funhouse* was an enormous hit. Smigel's cartoons have run regularly on the show since 1996.

Between 2000 and 2002, staff writer Adam McKay contributed a number of short films, usually featuring cast members and occasionally a guest actor. Ben Stiller and Will Ferrell appeared in *The Heat is On*; Steve Buscemi sat behind the counter at a pawn shop in *Stavenhagens Pawnshop*; Molly Shannon and McKay himself played dognappers in *Five Finger Discount*; and an unknown actor starred in *Neil Armstrong: The Ohio Years*, about the famous astronaut's post-lunar retirement. Willem Dafoe, Andy Richter and Will Ferrell starred in the office comedy *The Procedure*, but it did not air as part of the original broadcast. It was later inserted into a cable re-run, just like Bruce McCulloch's *Vacation*.

McKay made a total of eight short films, and while most of them were good, they often felt like an odd match with the rest of the show. The problem was not that the short films had changed, but that the show itself did not lend itself to live-action shorts anymore. This was the same problem that Tom Schiller faced towards the end of his second stay at *Saturday Night Live*. While at one time the short film provided a much-needed breakaway from the stage, this is now no longer necessary. The pacing of the show has evolved so much that there is no need for short films to provide a break.

Sketches don't run as long as they used to, either. As a whole, the show has become tighter. Robert Smigel's cartoons work because they are fast-paced. The action is quicker and the jokes are jam-packed. Live-action shorts, on the other hand, are more traditional in that they need a beginning, a middle and an end. If anything, a short film on today's *Saturday Night Live* only slows it down.

Furthermore, *Saturday Night Live* is one of the few true variety programs of its kind. In the 1970s, there were dozens of other variety shows with sketch comedy and music and a live audience atmosphere. *Saturday Night Live*'s short films were unique because they added a cinematic quality that helped set it apart from the rest. Today, the excitement of live sketch comedy is unique to NBC on Saturday nights so the live action short is no longer needed for that unique sense of variety.

Saturday Night Live provided a showcase for short films in the 1970s and 1980s. Talented directors were brought on to contribute shorts. Today, with the independent film scene more popular than ever and several cable channels dedicated to showing both short films and full-length independent features, that outlet is redundant.

But most importantly, the short films were once a regular part of the show. There was at least one short each week. It was an expected ingredient—comedy, music, fake commercials, a monologue and a short film. Today's *Saturday Night Live* viewers are no longer used to it, so when a new live-action short film is unexpectedly broadcast, they will naturally be averted. Lorne Michaels would have to experiment with his formula to accommodate short films again, but with the program being the well-oiled machine that it is, why bother?

Michaels claims that he has not given up on short films, and gave it another try during the season finale of the twenty-ninth season. Towards the end of the show—as Tom Schiller knows, the typical slot for the live action short—Michaels fit in writer T. Sean Shannon's *The Adventures of Harold*, a short film about a balding Junior High School student. "I'd written a screenplay that Lorne loved, based on Harold," says Shannon. "It's one of these screenplays everyone loves, but no one wants to make. So we were trying to get it off the ground by doing a *Harold* short."

Shannon shot the short with a 24p digital video camera but gave it an intentionally washed-out film look. He believes that *The Adventures of Harold* was somewhat compromised by less-than-satisfactory make-up effects. Unable to convince the young actor who played Harold to shave his head, a bald wig was used instead. Shannon was unhappy with it and had to digitally remove the plastic wrinkles and wig lines in post-production. As a result, plans for a second *Harold* short, which was supposed to be shot at the same time, were scrapped. Nevertheless, the one film that was completed is amusing, and Shannon hopes to revisit the character in the future.

T. Sean Shannon also directed *Bear City*, a series of short films that ran during the show's thirtieth season. Fred Willard narrated the shorts, which feature actors in bear suits. Shot in Los Angeles in the summer of 2004, the *Bear City* films envision a world in which bears take over the roles of humans. For example, one of the shorts shows two bears arguing after being in a car accident.

With T. Sean Shannon as a resident filmmaker, hopefully Michaels will stick to his guns and really commit to making the live action short film a regular part of *Saturday Night Live* again.

"To me, that was always a fun thing, when a film came up," T. Sean Shannon says. "TV is changing so much that everything is *now, now, hurry, hurry, hurry, where's the pay-off, right now*. I think that's the nature of TV now—the shorter attention span, the hundred more channels you can turn to. There's so many alternatives that now it has to conform more to the viewer than it did before. I think the kids these days can't sit around and just dig on something on some other level.

"It shouldn't be just a bunch of gags—it's more of a tone," Shannon adds. "The more rope they're given, they have a little slack to just be, if not necessarily laugh-out-loud funny, really interesting and cool."

"In the early days it was like there was a love of cinema," Tom Schiller says. "On a live comedy show, it was really neat to see something that was done on film. I love just the idea of short films. It's a noble thing to do—to direct and write. I think it's very important. Maybe the audience was different in the early days, but I think people do still appreciate film."

"Jonathan Demme made a short film. Mike Judge made a short film. Tons of people over the years…" says Lorne Michaels. "Steven Spielberg even made one. We didn't run it, but he made one. Albert Brooks made some interesting ones, Gary Weis obviously made some interesting ones. Tom's I think were the most impressive ones that were ever on the show.

"It was the sort of thing that I was interested in," Michaels adds, reflecting on the role of the short film on *Saturday Night Live*. "I think Tom's were a large part of the fabric of what that 70s show was, in the same way that Andy Kaufman was. I think Tom is a genuine artist."

As for feature films, Tom Schiller is unsure if he will ever make another. If there were no rules of structure or formula to abide by, he would love to write and direct again, but the general attitude in Hollywood tends not to allow for that. In an interview with film critic Jim Emerson of *The Seattle Times* in 1984, when *Nothing Lasts Forever* had its test release in Seattle, Schiller said that he'd like to "do five features before death." Today, Schiller feels completely at ease in directing commercials. He is grateful that he had the chance to make *Nothing Lasts Forever*, but is content if no further opportunity to make a film ever pops up.

Schiller is still hopeful that one day his feature film, which he loves as much as he does a firstborn child, will be released in some fashion. He considers it a secret success because it has been seen on television around the world, but *Nothing Lasts Forever* deserves to be seen by more people. Lauren Tom, Dan Aykroyd and Bill Murray share his hopefulness. "Tom gave me my first chance in the movies and I thought it was really going to take me somewhere fast," says Lauren Tom. "Alas, it didn't, so that was pretty disappointing. But I'm ever hopeful. You never know."

Nothing Lasts Forever is currently owned by Turner Entertainment. Turner bought-out the film, as well as hundreds of other titles in the MGM library when MGM went through its many financial predicaments. Turner Entertainment is owned by Warner Brothers, which also handles Turner's DVD releases. Warner Brothers has released excellent special edition DVDs of many films with outstanding film transfers. But the studio has such an enormous library of titles. It would take an awful long time to get to a film as unknown as *Nothing Lasts Forever*.

Additionally, Warner Brothers has a policy not to license their films to other home video companies, while some of the other studios often license video rights to companies like Anchor Bay Entertainment and Rhino Home Video. Therefore, perhaps the only hope for the film to see the light of day is to convince the studio to release it on DVD themselves. Both Dan Aykroyd and Bill Murray stated that they would participate in the special feature content.

"It suffers from a gross underexposure," says Aykroyd. "They should look into a DVD package, because with the right publicity you can get it to people in their homes directly like that."

Bill Murray believes that it should also be seen in theaters, where it looks best. "It just needs to be seen," he says. "I always thought that this was a movie that would be discovered sometime. It should be on a midnight movie list on television so people can see it. But it's a film and it should also be in art houses and in college tours. There should be more prints struck of it."

In April 2004, Bill Murray and Tom Schiller introduced *Nothing Lasts Forever* in front of a sold-out crowd at the Brooklyn Academy of Music as part of a Bill Murray retrospective. The special screening marked the first time that the film had been projected in front of an audience in over fifteen years. In his introduction and the question-and-answer session that followed, Murray praised the film for its brilliant script and the director for his creativity. The crowd loved the film, laughing at all the right moments. Schiller likened it to a can of laughter being opened after being sealed shut for all those years. A month later, the film returned for another screening, this time introduced by Schiller and Zach Galligan.

"Someone has to sort of champion it," Murray adds. "There has to be some kind of creativity out there in merchandising and distribution, and it could be part of something like that. It's the kind of movie where people would be taken by it if they saw it."

"I still hold out hope that it will be released somehow," Schiller says. "Even if by jungle telegraph." Until that happens, Tom Schiller's forgotten masterpiece will remain an overlooked treasure, buried deeply in the Turner archives where it has patiently waited for twenty years.

Zach Galligan and Tom Schiller at a screening of *Nothing Lasts Forever*—May 2004.

"Tom always made a point of smoking these clove cigarettes around the office and on the set," recalls Sheila Kehoe. "He'd throw out this comment to the crew that we would all remember him in the future every time we would smell these stinky things. He was right. Before restaurants banned smoking, I'd occasionally get a whiff of clove smoke and check to see if it might be Tom. It never was, but it made me smile."

"He's a real character. If he's not a character, then I don't know who is," says Zach Galligan. "He is one of the more unique individuals that I've had the pleasure to work with. We had a great time, and it's a colossal disappointment to me that *Nothing Lasts Forever* hasn't gotten more recognition. Whether you love it or you hate it, you've never seen anything like it."

"Another thing that's funny about Tom is that he's a director and a writer, but he's such a funny performer, too," offers Ed Helms. "He never really performs except in the real world. Going through life for him is like this fun performance piece."

"It was inspiring to me that he held on to his quirkiness and his eccentricity and his unique sense of the world," says Mike Myers.

"I think he's like a little leprechaun," says Victoria Jackson. "He has a twinkle in his eye all the time, like he's up to mischief or something."

"Tom is not childish in any way," Zach Galligan adds. "He is very much a man, but he's child-like in that he likes to play and have fun. He's mischievous, and that is one of his most endearing qualities."

"I think of Tom as kind of an imp," says Judith Belushi Pisano. "He likes things very neat and organized, and yet he's very playful."

"Tom is just this kind of happy-go-lucky, zany presence," says Lauren Tom. "It's like he doesn't even have to say anything and you feel this sort of comic energy in the air."

"I don't think I've ever met anyone as talented, as fun to work with, or just hang out with as TV Tommy," says Laila Nabulsi. "It's my dream to one day be on a SchillerVision set again."

"I just think he's the real thing," says Teri Garr. "He's totally talented, and he's too delicate for Hollywood. So he does his own thing, which is great. But he's a great artist, he really truly is."

"He just lives so well that he's always a delight to be with," says Bill Murray. "We've had a lot of good fun. We tried to stick Sergio Leone with a bill once at a restaurant in New York. That was one of Schiller's good ones. There was a table of about fourteen people and Sergio was this big, large guy. I don't know if Schiller intuited this or just decided he wanted to do it, but he decided we should try to stick Sergio Leone with this bill. So we passed the word: If people just start getting up and disappearing from the table one by one—act like they were going to the restroom or something—we'd all meet outside. But he didn't get beat with it. He got out of it—he was like the third one from the end. So we didn't catch him with the bill, but it was such a novel idea to try and catch a real movie guy and stick him with the bill. We were just a bunch of wise guys."

Zach Galligan went on to star in the highly successful *Gremlins* and its sequel, as well as films like *Waxworks*, *Cupid* and *Infested*. In 2003 he appeared on *Law & Order: Criminal Intent*.

Lauren Tom is a successful cartoon voice-over artist, best known for providing the voice of Amy Wong on *Futurama*. She has also acted in films such as *The Joy Luck Club*, *Bad Santa* and *In Good Company*.

Apollonia Van Ravenstein appeared in the Dutch film *Flodder* shortly after making *Nothing Lasts Forever*. It was her final film, and she retired from show business shortly thereafter. She married a handsome cruise ship captain with whom she travels around world.

Lorne Michaels continues his successful reign as executive producer of *Saturday Night Live*. He continues to produce movies, including the recent hit *Mean Girls*. It is unknown how long he plans to stay onboard *Saturday Night Live*, which continues to be a lucrative well of comic talent.

Howard Shore has become one of Hollywood's most sought-after film score composers. He won a total of three Academy Awards for his work on the three *Lord of the Rings* films. This makes him the first *Saturday Night Live* veteran to win the Oscar, and makes his former colleagues very proud.

Sheila Kehoe retired from costume designing for film and theatre. She currently is an interior decorator/designer in New York.

John Starke continues to work as a production designer, but has also moved to producing films such as 2004's *The Punisher*.

John Head has worked with Lorne Michaels since the 1970s, and their collaboration continues to this date.

Boaty Boatwright did not stay with MGM long after *Nothing Lasts Forever*. She is now a respected talent agent with ICM in New York, representing some of the world's biggest stars.

Laila Nabulsi worked as a production associate for several other films and later produced *Fear and Loathing in Las Vegas*, starring Johnny Depp and Benicio Del Toro.

Dan Aykroyd and Bill Murray both would love to appear in a new Tom Schiller film.

Tom Schiller lives in New York and Connecticut with his wife, author Jacque Lynn Schiller. As a young man on a train, a Swedish architect told him that he would get everything he wanted in life, only not in the way he expected. The architect was right.

Bibliography

Bart, Peter. *Fade Out: The Calamitous Final Days of MGM*. New York: William Morrows and Company, Inc., 1990.

Beatts, Anne P. and John Head, eds. *Saturday Night Live*. New York: William Morrows and Company, Inc. 1977.

Cooper, Jackie and Dick Kleiner. *Please Don't Shoot My Dog: The Autobiography of Jackie Cooper*. Penguin Group, Inc., 1981.

Hill, Doug and Jeff Weingrad. *Saturday Night: A Backstage History of Saturday Night Live*. New York: William Morrows and Company, Inc., 1986.

Jacklin Belushi, Judith. *Samurai Widow*. Carroll & Graf Publishers, 1990.

Mohr, Jay. *Gasping for Airtime: Two Years in the Trenches of Saturday Night Live*. Hyperion, 2004.

Partridge, Marianne, ed. *Rolling Stone Visits Saturday Night Live*. Dolphin Books, 1979.

Perrin, Dennis. *Mr. Mike: The Life and Work of Michael O'Donoghue*. New York: Avon Books, 1998.

Serpas, Frank III. *Saturday Net*. 2004. <http://www.io.com/~serpas/snl.html>

Shales, Tom and James Andrew Miller. *Live From New York: An Uncensored History of Saturday Night Live*. New York: Little, Brown and Company, 2002.

Woodward, Bob. *Wired: The Short Life and Fast Times of John Belushi*. Simon & Shuster, 1984.

Tom Schiller Filmography

Early Short Films 1962-1967

The Door	1962
Dos Chodos Ray	1965
Farmer's Market	1965
Supra Market	1966
Tantra Dirty	1967

Apprentice Documentary Work 1967-1972

Boys Will Be Men—Boys Club of Pasadena	1967
Vivaldi of Venice	1967
Richard Harris Special	1967
Buckminster Fuller on Spaceship Earth	1968
A Glimpse of DeKooning	1968
We Have No Art	1968
The Life and Times of Henry Miller	1969
The Henry Miller Odyssey	1969
The World of Buckminster Fuller	1970
L'Odyssey d'Henry Miller	1971
Dame Judith Anderson	1971
Anais Observed	1972

Henry Miller Asleep & Awake	1973

Schiller's Reel Saturday Night Live

The Acid Generation—Where Are They Now?	1977
Life After Death	1977
Saturday Night in London	1977

Bar Mitzvah 5000	1977
Henry Miller on Television	1977
Don't Look Back in Anger	1978
La Dolce Gilda	1978
Arrivederci Roman	1978
Sushi by the Pool	1978
Picasso, the New York Years	1979
Perchance to Dream	1979
Clones Exist Now	1979
Java Junkie	1979
Linden Palmer: Hollywood's Forgotten Director	1979
Mask of Fear	1980
Search for Akasa	1980
Art is Ficial	1981
Nothing Lasts Forever	1983
Here's Joy (The New Show)	1983
Film Boat	1984
From Here to Maternity	1986
Time Scooter (MTV)	1987
Virgin Records WEA promotional film	1987
Flapjack Floozie	1988
Baby Boom	1988

Schiller's Reel/SchillVision Saturday Night Live

Love is a Dream	1988
Broadway Story	1989
Falling in Love	1989
Dieter in Outer Space	1989
Hooked on Sushi	1990
Acting is my Life	1990
The Land Before Television	1990
The Vision of Van Gogh	1990
SchillerVision Theatre #1	1990
SchillerVision Theatre Christmas Spectacular	1991
The Story of Television: The Producer	1991

Shirley, I Love You	1991
Our Noisy Noisy World	1991
SchillerVisions: Arcocentesis	1991
SchillerVisions: Hidden Camera Commercials	1991
SchillerVisions: Exercise Machine Craze	1991
SchillerVisions: The ATM Story	1991
Million Dollar Zombie	1992
Civil Rights	1992
New York's Strangest & Most Bizarre People: Shorty, the Guy Who Can't Cross the Street	1992
Big Girl Goes to Town	1993
Dieter's Dream	1993
While the City Sweeps	1993
Criminal Encounter	1993
Will Work for Food	1993
New York's Strangest & Most Bizarre People: Tortoise Man	1993
The Violin	1994
Laura	1994
Milkman	1990
Sweet Smell of Safe Sex	1994
Steely Dan documentary	1995
Streetbeat	1991-94
Scandinavian Scene	1995
HBO Sequels You'll Never See	1998
This is Ray	1998

The *Bad Theater* Sketches

Bad Playhouse
Airdate: March 12, 1977, host Sissy Spacek
The Millkeeper by Jan Worstrad
Millkeeper Niels (John Belushi) aimlessly slaves away to keep his windmill spinning. His wife (Laraine Newman) stands beside him screaming, while Death (played by Bill Murray as Ronnie Bateman) brings in Niels' dead sister (Sissy Spacek). The play has not a single line of dialogue, because it was written before Worstrad was able to write. According to Pinth-Garnell, Worstrad's works generally deal with the existentialism of being.

Bad Cinema
Airdate: April 9, 1977, host Julian Bond
ooh-la-la! les legs! By Henri Heimeau
Pinth-Garnell is joined by author Truman Capote (John Belushi), director Lina Wertmüller (Laraine Newman), and T. Lazlo de Wizzen (a fictional film critic played by Julian Bond), who present an example of a new wave of cinema: *cinema mauvais*. The entire film consists of European film footage of people dancing in the street. Capote deems the film dazzlingly tergant—a classic of bad cinema. Wertmüller is equally critical, while De Wizzen finds himself unable to comment on the film because his expertise lies in bad 3-D insect fear films of the 1960s.

Bad Ballet
Airdate: May 14, 1977, host Shelley Duvall
Swan by Ivan Badvodinikov
A method ballet performance about an evil swankeeper named Gregor (John Belushi), the three white swans (Shelley Duvall, Laraine Newman

and Gilda Radner) and one black swan (Garrett Morris) that he mistreats with his cattle prog, and Vanya, a state poultry inspector (danced by Pinth-Garnell himself) who frees them.

Bad Opera
Airdate: October 8, 1977, host Madeline Kahn
Die Golden Klang (*The Golden Note*) by Friedrich Knabel
In this German opera, maiden Mazda (Madeline Kahn) is summoned by the gods to sing the Golden Note - but anyone who sings the Golden Note shall die. Messenger Schwarzstorm (Garrett Morris) has to deliver the note from the heavens so that she can sing it. Mazda's boyfriend Thunderstorm (John Belushi) tries to prevent Schwarzstorm from delivering the note. The piece is very difficult to sing, because the pitch of the Golden Note is so hard to reach that it sends the singer into larynx lock—meaning that she will forever hold the same note. In fact, Kahn fearfully holds the same tone throughout most of the performance, until she is brought away by paramedics.

Bad Musical
Airdate: December 10, 1977, host Mary Kay Place
Leeuwenhoek by Hans Van der Scheinen
Perhaps the best entry in the *Bad Theater* series. As Pinth-Garnell describes it, it's a triangle between microscopist Antony van Leeuwenhoek's (John Belushi) microscope, his wife (Mary Kay Place) and her Delft china, which she constantly polishes. His wife sings about wishing to be shrunk down to the size of an amoeba in order to get his attention, while Ronnie Bateman plays an ice skating enthusiast trying to woo her. The musical comes complete with a wooden shoe tap dancing performance by Gilda Radner.

Bad One-Man Theater
Airdate: March 18, 1978, host Jill Clayburgh
An Evening With… by Fred Rex, Jr.
This One-Man show is actually composed of four men and one woman who speak at the same time while they are on the stage. They separately perform excerpts from famous one-man shows, resulting in a funny but mostly chaotic stage experience. Most interesting is the cast, which Pinth-Garnell quickly reads off at the close of the show: Tom Schiller plays Nick Turner as Hal Holbrook as Mark Twain; John Belushi plays Steve Bushakis as James Whitmore as Harry S. Truman; Bill Murray plays

Ronnie Bateman as Robert Vaughn as Edgar Allan Poe, Raven in hand; Garrett Morris plays Ray Houser as Paul Robeson; and Jane Curtin plays Helen Wagner as Eleanor Roosevelt.

Bad Conceptual Art
Airdate: May 20, 1978, host Buck Henry
Pavlov Video Chicken One by Helen Trova

A 378 hour-long piece in which Helen Trova (Gilda Radner) dances like a nervous chicken on a round platform with two elevated video monitors behind her. The monitor on her left shows a close-up of Garrett Morris' wide-open left eye gazing down at Radner, while the monitor on her right is a close-up on Laraine Newman's mouth. Newman makes random remarks, such as "Hush," "Chicken dance," "Ha ha ha ha ha," "Frozen tantra," "Juices of a blind child," "Shhhh," "Maher Baba, Maher Baba," and other unrecognizable comments. Later, in his feature film *Nothing Lasts Forever*, Schiller would again poke fun at such happenings of the 1970s and 80s with Lifewalk 5000—a similarly ridiculous exhibit featuring a man walking on a treadmill and counting to a million.

Bad Red Chinese Ballet
Airdate: November 18, 1978, host Carrie Fisher
Written by Hua Tse Hua

Set on a collective farm in China in 1950, this ballet is about a Chinese border patrolwoman (played by Carrie Fisher) who continually keeps herself on her toes for the Western imperialist onslaught—sheepishly symbolized by an American baseball player (Garrett Morris) who slides onto the stage, only to be beaten by the various patrolwomen. Ronnie Bateman plays the Chinese flag bearer.

Bad Cabaret for Children
Airdate: February 29, 1979, host Kate Jackson
Written by Klaus Weiner

John Belushi is the master of ceremonies of this burlesque variety act performed in front of an audience made up entirely of children. A blind man (Garrett Morris) dances with a double amputee (Bill Murray as Ronnie Bateman) sitting on a rolling board, Laraine Newman contributes a risqué cabaret performance, and the entire cast screams "Tomorrow we go on the bus" over and over while the children try to boo them off the stage. A few years later, Schiller re-used the name Klaus Weiner for a character in his film *Nothing Lasts Forever*.

Bad Playhouse
Airdate: January 26, 1980, host Teri Garr
Mr. Potato Head by Michael O'Toonis
Lady Pinth-Garnell substitutes for her husband Leonard while he is out performing with a Swiss mime group. The unnamed piece is a dramatic musical about the Irish potato famine starring Mr. Potato Head, the pride of Ireland breed (played by Garrett Morris). Ronnie Bateman plays old Sean McGinty (also a name used frequently in Schiller's works) who wants to eat him.

Bad Conceptual Theater
Airdate: November 3, 2001, host John Goodman
The Christmas Light by Mr. Jingle Jangle.
It is said that if chimpanzees continuously type on one thousand typewriters for one thousand years, one of the chimps will have written the complete works of Shakespeare. In 1977 a theater group tried it, and twenty-four years later, *The Christmas Light* is the first piece the chimpanzees have produced. It features a family, headed by father John Goodman, sitting at the dinner table and having a meaningless argument. They slowly begin to act like monkeys. Chris Kattan is actor Ronnie Bateman Jr., who plays one of the sons in the play. This is the only *Bad Theater* sketch that was not written by Tom Schiller.

Appendix III
Don't Look Back In Anger Scripts

Like many short films and sketches, *Don't Look Back in Anger* went through numerous revisions before the final script was written. Moreover, the entire first segment of the film was cut out after it was filmed. The first script is pieced together from various drafts with hand-written notes and corrections. The second script is the complete shooting script.

These script pages are ©Schillervision. Special thanks to Laila Nabulsi.

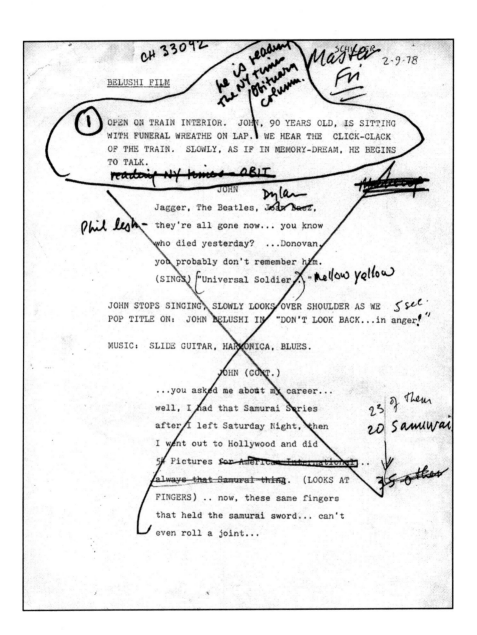

BELUSHI FILM

CH 33092 — *he is reading the NY times Obituary column.* — *Master* *Fri* *2-9-78*

① OPEN ON TRAIN INTERIOR. JOHN, 90 YEARS OLD, IS SITTING
WITH FUNERAL WREATHE ON LAP. WE HEAR THE CLICK-CLACK
OF THE TRAIN. SLOWLY, AS IF IN MEMORY-DREAM, HE BEGINS
TO TALK.

reading NY times - OBIT

JOHN

Dylan

Jagger, The Beatles, Joan Baez,

Phil lesh — they're all gone now... you know

who died yesterday? ...Donovan,

you probably don't remember him.

(SINGS) "Universal Soldier" "mellow yellow"

JOHN STOPS SINGING, SLOWLY LOOKS OVER SHOULDER AS WE *5 sec.*
POP TITLE ON: JOHN BELUSHI IN "DON'T LOOK BACK...in anger!"

MUSIC: SLIDE GUITAR, HARMONICA, BLUES.

JOHN (CONT.)

...you asked me about my career...

well, I had that Samurai Series

after I left Saturday Night, then   *23 of them*

I went out to Hollywood and did   *20 Samurai*

5 Pictures for American International..

always that Samurai thing. (LOOKS AT   *35 other*

FINGERS) .. now, these same fingers

that held the samurai sword... can't

even roll a joint...

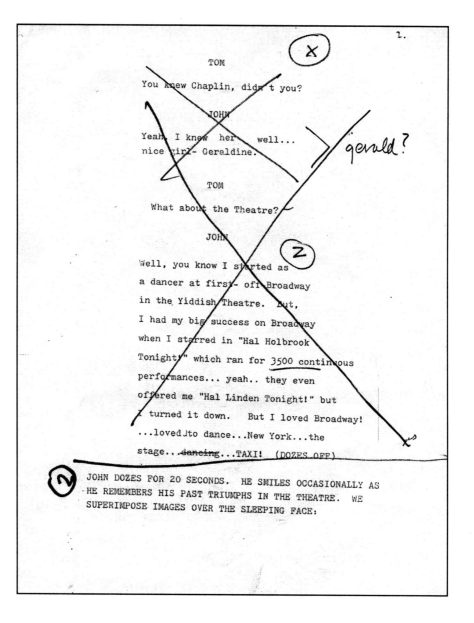

TOM

You knew Chaplin, didn't you?

JOHN

Yeah, I knew her, well...
nice girl- Geraldine.

gerald?

TOM

What about the Theatre?

JOHN

Well, you know I started as
a dancer at first- off Broadway
in the Yiddish Theatre. But,
I had my big success on Broadway
when I starred in "Hal Holbrook
Tonight!" which ran for 3500 continuous
performances... yeah.. they even
offered me "Hal Linden Tonight!" but
I turned it down.   But I loved Broadway!
...loved to dance...New York...the
stage...dancing...TAXI! (DOZES OFF)

JOHN DOZES FOR 20 SECONDS. HE SMILES OCCASIONALLY AS
HE REMEMBERS HIS PAST TRIUMPHS IN THE THEATRE. WE
SUPERIMPOSE IMAGES OVER THE SLEEPING FACE:

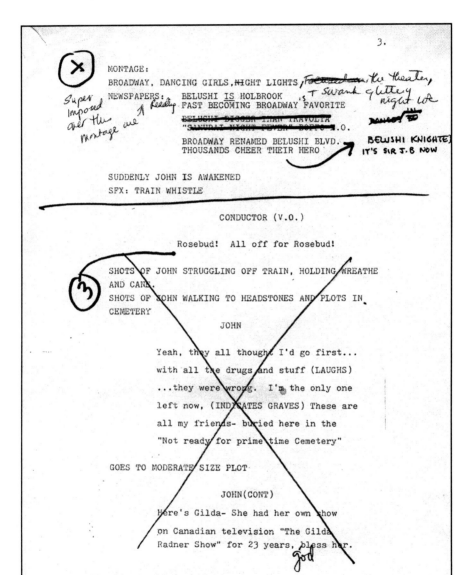

3.

⊗ MONTAGE:
Super imposed over the Montage are BROADWAY, DANCING GIRLS, NIGHT LIGHTS, ~~Focused~~ *in the theater,*
NEWSPAPERS: *A Reading* BELUSHI IS HOLBROOK *'s* T *swank glittery*
FAST BECOMING BROADWAY FAVORITE *night spot*
~~BELUSHI BIGGER THAN TRAVOLTA~~
~~"SAMURAI NIGHT FEVER" BOFFO~~ B.O.   ~~BANGO~~

BROADWAY RENAMED BELUSHI BLVD.   BELUSHI KNIGHTED
THOUSANDS CHEER THEIR HERO   IT'S SIR J.B NOW

SUDDENLY JOHN IS AWAKENED
SFX: TRAIN WHISTLE

                    CONDUCTOR (V.O.)

          Rosebud! All off for Rosebud!

③ SHOTS OF JOHN STRUGGLING OFF TRAIN, HOLDING WREATHE
AND CANE.
SHOTS OF JOHN WALKING TO HEADSTONES AND PLOTS IN
CEMETERY
                    JOHN

          Yeah, they all thought I'd go first...

          with all the drugs and stuff (LAUGHS)

          ...they were wrong. I'm the only one

          left now, (INDICATES GRAVES) These are

          all my friends- buried here in the

          "Not ready for prime time Cemetery"

GOES TO MODERATE SIZE PLOT

                    JOHN(CONT)

          Here's Gilda- She had her own show

          on Canadian television "The Gilda

          Radner Show" for 23 years, bless her.
                              God

2.

NEW PLOT SMALL TOMB.   ~~JOHN THROWS DOWN FLOWER AS.~~

                    JOHN
          Here's Laraine Newman's plot:
          ~~some~~ some say she murdered
          her D.J. husband- then she
          had a pecan farm in the valley.
          Poor thing was this big when she died.

NEW PLOT: LARGER

                    JOHN
          Jane married a stockbroker, had 2
          children, ~~3 grandchildren~~- lived
          Upstate- died of complications during
          cosmetic surgery.

NEW PLOT, SMALLER

                    JOHN
          Garrett taught black theater
          for many years and died of an
          overdose of heroin.

~~NEW PLOT. WITH AMERICAN FLAG (LIKE A SOLDIER'S GRAVE)~~

          NEW PLOT.

3.

JOHN

Bill lived the longest... 38 years.

but he died happy... ~~in the saddle,~~

~~if you know what I mean.~~ ~~He~~

~~was also happy because he had jus~~t

he had just

grown his mustache back. Probably

still growing.

HUGE TOMB, LAVISH, GARISH, LOTS OF ARTIFICIAL FLOWERS

JOHN

Chevy died right after his first

film "Foul Play" with Goldie

Hawn.... ~~even after re-marrying~~

daily

~~she still sends flowers~~ to his

~~tomb from Beverly Hill~~s.

NEW PLOT: MORE OF A MEMORIAL- LIKE INSET PLAQUE

JOHN

I guess Danny loved his Harley too

clocked him at

much. They ~~say he got up to~~ 175

an hour- (WEEPING)- then it was just

I had to identify the body- I could tell it was Danny

a blur. (POINTS) What's left of him   *'cause of*

The webbed

is here.   *toes.*

He had them you know

INTO CAMERA

JOHN

Let me tell you something.

(MORE)

4.

                    JOHN

It's very rare- in <u>this</u> lifetime

at least, that you get to work with

people you love and care about...

<u>these people</u> were the <u>greatest</u>

<u>bunch of people I knew</u> and I miss

every one of them.

I guess I'd have to say- the money,

the fame, everything that came after

that, the Saturday Night Show was

probably the most meaningful, important

transcending experience of my life.

I sometimes wonder. Why am I still

alive- why? All my friends are gone!

CLOSE UP
                    JOHN

    I'll tell you why--- because I'm

    a dancer!!!!

MUSIC: ROUMANIA ROUMANIA
DANCE OUT OF GRAVEYARD, OVER TOMBS, *LONG PULL*
FADE OUT.   *BACK SHOT*
    John dances on graves.   *REVEALING HUGE CEMETERY*

Tom Schiller
February 1978

JOHN BELUSHI IN

DON'T LOOK BACK... IN ANGER.

OPEN ON TRAIN INTERIOR. JOHN, 90 YEARS OLD, IS SITTING
WITH FUNERAL WREATH ON LAP. HE IS READING THE NEW YORK
TIMES OBITUARY COLUMN. WE HEAR THE CLICK-CLACK OF THE
TRAIN. SLOWLY, AS IF IN MEMORY-DREAM, HE BEGINS TO TALK.

                   JOHN

       Jagger, The Beatles, Dylan, Phil Lesh,

       they're all gone now...you know who died

       yesterday? Donovan. You probably don't

       remember him. (SINGS) "They call me

       Mellow Yellow..."

JOHN DOES A SLOW LOOK OVER HIS SHOULDER AS WE FLASH ON TITLE:

       JOHN BELUSHI IN:
       DON'T LOOK BACK... in anger!

MUSIC: BLUES

             JOHN (CONT)

       I had that Samurai series after I left

       Saturday Night. Then I went out to Hollywood

       and did 54 pictures- 23 of them were Samurai

       pictures- (LOOKS AT FINGERS)...now, these same

       fingers that held the samurai sword, can't even

       roll a joint.

             TOM

       You knew Chaplin, didn't you?

                    JOHN

Yeah, I knew Chaplin well... Geraldine Chaplin.

                    TOM

That's Television and Film... what about

the Theatre?

                    JOHN

The Theatre! Well, you know I was a dancer

for many years - that's how I've kept so

young I guess... but what really catapulted

me to success were the five thousand performances

of "Hal Holbrook Tonight". Yeah they even offered

me "Hal Linden Tonight" but I said no. But I

loved Broadway... New York... the Stage...TAXI!!

JOHN DOZES FOR 20 SECONDS. HE SMILES OCCASIONALLY AS HE
REMEMBERS HIS PAST TRIUMPHS IN THE THEATRE. WE SUPERIMPOSE
IMAGES.
MONTAGE:
BROADWAY, DANCING GIRLS, NIGHT LIGHTS, THE THEATRE, AND SWANK
GLITTERY NIGHT LIFE.
SUPERIMPOSED OVER THIS MONTAGE ARE NEWSPAPERS READING:

        BELUSHI IS HOLBROOK
        FAST BECOMING BROADWAY'S FAVORITE

        BROADWAY RENAMED BELUSHI BLVD.
        THOUSANDS CHEER THEIR HERO

        BELUSHI KNIGHTED
        IT'S SIR JOHN BELUSHI NOW

SUDDENLY JOHN IS AWAKENED.

SFX: TRAIN WHISTLE

                    CONDUCTOR (V.O.)

           ROSEBUD! All off for ROSEBUD!

JOHN EXITS TRAIN HOLDING WREATH AND CANE.

SHOTS OF JOHN WALKING TOWARDS GRAVESITE.

                   JOHN

       Yeah, they all thought I'd go first...

       I was the " live fast, die young, and

       leave a good-looking corpse" type...

       they were wrong. I'm the only one left

       now. (INDICATES GRAVES) These are all

       my friends here, buried in the "Not

       Ready for Prime Time Cemetery." Let's have

       a look.

MODERATE SIZE GRAVE.

                   JOHN

       Here's Gilda - she had her own show on

       Canadian television - "The Gilda Radner

       Show" for many years.But I still get to see

       her in the re-runs. Cute as a button... God

       bless her.

page 4

NEW PLOT.

>   JOHN
>
> Here's Laraine Newman's plot. Some say
>
> she murdered her D.J. husband - then she had
>
> a pecan farm in the valley. Poor thing was
>
> this big when she died.

NEW PLOT.

>   JOHN
>
> Jane married a stockbroker, had two children,
>
> lived Upstate, and died of complications
>
> during cosmetic surgery.

NEW PLOT.

>   JOHN
>
> Garrett taught black theater for many
>
> years and died of an overdose of heroin.

NEW PLOT

>   JOHN
>
> Bill lived the longest... 38 years. But
>
> he died happy cause he had just grown his
>
> mustache back. Probably still growing.

NEW PLOT

>   JOHN
>
> Chevy died right after his first film
>
> "Foul Play" with Goldie Hawn.

page 5

NEW PLOT.

JOHN

I guess Danny loved his Harley too much.

They clocked him at 175 an hour (WEEPING)

Then it was just a blur-- I had to identify

the body. I could tell it was Danny cause

of the webbed toes. He had them, you know.

INTO CAMERA

JOHN

Let me tell you something. It's very

rare, in this lifetime at least, that

you get to work with people you love

and care about... these people were

the greatest bunch of people I knew

and we were all friends. I guess I'd

have to say - the money, the fame,

everything that came after that, the

Saturday Night Show was the best

experience of my life. I sometimes wonder...

Why am I still alive? Why me? All my friends

are gone.

CLOSE UP

JOHN

I'll tell you why --- because I'm a dancer!!!!

MUSIC: ROUMANIA ROUMANIA
JOHN DANCES ON GRAVES.
LONG PULL BACK SHOT REVEALING HUGE CEMETERY.

Tom Schiller's Broadway Video Newsletter

9 LINE

truth   honesty

the official house organ of the 9th Floor   VOL 1   NO. 2   FEB 10 198

— OUR DREAM —

A-5
REGAL 10-CUP AUTO-DRIP COFFEE MAKER

ARTIST'S CONCEPTION OF NINTH FLOOR LUXURY DREAM REMODELING: WITH COFFEE AMENITY BAR INCLUDED.

Herald-Dispatch Huntington, W.VA.
Sammy and Lorne to sing

Scientists say the chances that Lorne Michaels and Sammy Davis,Jr. singing at the same time somewhere in the world, together, are high. Michaels, known to hum or whistle Canadian ditties during showering, or while being driven to work in his 250,000 dollar cadillac limousine was unavailable for comment.

9 LINE MOVIE PICK

with CHEVY CHASE

"6 SWEDISH PUMP JOCKEYS"

Long lines form at one gas station. Not because of a gas shortage but a surplus of sex as 6 beautiful Swedish girls man the pumps
colour, 35 mm   Running Time: 85 minutes

PEOPLE ON THE MOVE

Matt Newman - "Working with Zweibel is like working in the study hall of a great rabbi. I admire him immensely. Trouble is he won't touch money. I always end up buying lunch."

9 LINE congratulates Al & Frannie Franken on the birth of their baby girl. Schiller donates lung to Lenox Hill Hospital in honor of event. Says "Even though breathing is mo difficult now, I wanted to share my happiness with the Frankens".

**9 LINE DREAM GIRL
SONIA BEVELMAN**

Leslie Begelman -- Profile in Courag
"Working for Schiller isn't easy. He makes me clean the typewriter keys after each page of the script and keeps talking about karma, God and the moon."

\#

Elia Katz wins 9 Line Oscar Wilde look-alike contest. Says next script will be Haiku.

\#

Mum's the word from Herb Sargent.

HORST VEIT WORLD SALES

Hong Kong to Mifed
Joey Kong
William Kong
Edwin Kong
Jimmy Shaw
Vee King Shaw

9 LINE

THEFT LUCRATIVE

Theft of juices and soda from
kitchen on 10 brings much needed
revenue towards refurbishment
of offices on 9.

"LO TECH"

WE LIKE LO-TECH

-relaxed dress codes
-boss not breathing down neck
-bohemian atmosphere spurs
 creativity

VARIETY

PICTURES   5

Nine talks to TOM S.

9 - How's your film coming?
TS- I wasn't aware I was to be
    doing one. I'm still
    waiting to see Lorne.
9 - Are you doing any redecorating
    in your office?
TS- I'm talking wall-coverings
    with Rick Traum.
9 - Who are your heroes?
TS- Proust, Traum, Abel Gance.
9 - What do you think about the
    10th floor?
TS- I hope to God we'll all be
    friends.

L.A. To N.Y.
Allison Assante
Kenn Brodziak
David Keh
Nancy Kelly

Tom Schiller greets Lorne Michaels on a rare visit to 9th floor
As beverages were served, unity and solidarity were stressed.

FACES OF 9 GREET YOU

VOLUME ONE NUMBER TWO

THE OFFICIAL JOURNAL OF THE TENTH FLOOR

Editors' Prayer

Dear Lord

Watch Over Us And All Our Friends

On The Tenth Floor

May Broadway Video Prosper

May The Broadway Pictures Succeed

May Lorne and All Employees

Find Happiness and Peace.

Amen.

Goodbye KATHY!

Last Thursday employees from Broadway Video and Pictures gathered to wish Kathy Pintauro (SNL '75-80) a fond farewell. "I'll miss Broadway Video a lot," said Kathy. It's no secret that Kathy is pregnant and expecting in March.

The party included coffee, two kinds of cake and brightly colored balloons. Among the guests attending was John Belushi (SNL '75-79) who gave Broadway Video employees Cristina McGinness and Cherie Fortis hugs. "It was like being held by a big teddy bear" said Cristina. "I'd like to be hugged again," added Cheri, who then took Cristina's hands and they danced a little jig to further express their delight.

Everyone had a good time and returned promptly to their desks within the hour to get back to the business of keeping Above Average the best company in the world. We'll all miss "Minky" and wish her the best!

"10" apologizes for the delay in this week's issue. Like everyone else, we were waiting for the arrival of the Franken baby--so "10" held the presses with two headlines ready to go. It seems that Franny takes deadlines about as seriously as Al. (Just a gentle ribbing from the editors of "10.")

the Grad bag...

Janine Dreyer (SNL '76-'80) can be heard singing on the soundtrack of an upcoming documentary... CAUGHT! At Friday's screening of Metropolis: Susan Forrestal, looking lovely as usual. We salute her as this week's "10 Girl." Look sharp, gals--next week it could be YOU. (PS-all girls here are perfect tens)... Producer Lorne Michaels (SNL '75-'80) addressed students at Yale University last week, much to the horror of Jim Downey (Harvard '70-74). Mention New Haven and he turns crimson!

NEWS FOLLOW-UP!

With February arriving this week, it's nice to see most people cooperating and changing the pages of their calendars.

People are reminded that, when not reading the days of the week, they may observe the Broadway Video address and phone number conveniently printed under the attractive logo.

February, it should be noted, has 28 days in the month this year.

Lorne Michaels and Benny Video seen here clowning for the camera. They met earlier this week to discuss Benny Video merchandise already in production.

AT"TEN"TION!

FROM OUR MAILBAG

Dear Editors:

Great first ish!! Only one complaint: How about a large-type editon for those of us with failing vision. Keep up the good work!

M.N.
9th Floor

P.S. I bet you don't print this.

Dear Editor:

Loved your first issue - hope you have many more. One question, though, if I want to write a letter to the editor, where do I address it? Thanks.

Tom Schiller
avid reader

P.S. how about "10" binders for all the issues?

Good idea, Tom. And thanks for your letter. It was a..."10" ! -Ed.

My Cherie

a word from cherie fortis

Hats off to Nord! The new offices are looking beautiful!

"TOP 10" INTERVIEW

Just when you thought it was safe to get out on the tenth floor, that Animal House zany John Belushi (SNL '75-'79) dropped by to turn the place upside-down. We cornered the Bear Man for an interview that will cure your blues, brother!

10: Mr. Belushi--

JB: John.

10: So John, what brings you to Broadway Video?

JB: When I'm in New York, I come to the tenth floor first. I like to hang out and smoke a joint with Nils.

(Ed. note: Nils Nichols, featured in Top 10 Interview, Vol. 1 No. 1)

10: What's your favorite food?

JB: Cantalope and cottage cheese.

10: Will you do "But noooo" for us?

JB: Oh come on, guys.

10: Really, will you do it?

JB: No.

SPECIAL "BABY" ISSUE

"10"

VOLUME ONE NUMBER THREE

THE OFFICIAL JOURNAL OF THE TENTH FLOOR

FRANKEN FATHERS FEMALE; FRANNIE FEELING FINE!

Al and Frannie Franken became the proud parents of a baby girl on Sunday, February 8, at 8:40 a.m.

Nils Nichols, on hearing the news of the arrival on Tuesday, said he thought it was "great."

"MY OWN STORY" BY AL FRANKEN

As Told To "10"

Puffing a Santa Ynez cigar, Al Franken visited the offices of "10" and told us how he took part in the delivery of his daughter.

"It was a great experience but it was a little hairy—not the baby, but the experience," Al said chuckling.

"I remember when the editors of "10" used to razz me for being in the office when Frannie was about to have the baby. I would tell them not to worry, and how labor takes up to 15...even 24 hours. I thought Frannie and I would have lots of time for the...delivery. I was on top of the world..."

Al stops to think a moment.

"Little did I know Frannie's labor would be only two hours and forty minutes."

Al starts talking fast and sweating.

(Continued on page two)

The baby was delivered at Lenox Hill Hospital in New York City. She weighs seven pounds, three ounces, and is 23 inches tall, making it "the tallest baby in the nursery," according to her father, Al.

The baby has been named Thomasin Davis Franken, in honor of Tom Davis (SNL '75-80), currently an employee of Broadway Pictures.

Tom Davis and Al Franken are long time friends and business partners. Their comedy act, "The Franken and Davis Show," has been performed in front of numerous church groups, colleges, and on national television.

One of their routines, "World War III" has been performed hundreds of thousands of times.

Phoebe and Joe Franken, Al's parents, and his brother Owen, were at the hospital on the day of the delivery. Frannie's mother Frances will be arriving next Monday.

Frannie and Thomasin leave the hospital this morning.

"10" ASKS READERS— YOU BE THE JUDGE!

Thomasin Davis Franken was named for Thomas James Davis. She was delivered by Dr. James Thomas.

Frannie Franken was born on October 8. Her daughter, Thomasin, was born on February 8, many years later.

Editorials

"10" SOUNDS OFF!

IN PRAISE OF FAMILY

Frannie and Al now have two families: their own, thanks to the addition of Thomasin last Sunday, and a bigger one here at 1619 Broadway.

As soon as Thomasin is old enough, we hope Al and Frannie will bring her around for all of us to share. Truly, a child is a great gift, and can also be very helpful at everything from licking envelopes to rearranging cassette tapes on a shelf.

With Mommy affiliated with Broadway Video, and Daddy over at Broadway Pictures, it will be hard for Thomasin to decide which department to work for first.

But one thing is certain-- we know that Thomasin will truly give her regards to Broadway (Video and Pictures!)

WE DOUBT IT

Al has a slight cold, so when he visits his daughter in the nursery, he must wear a surgical mask, covering most of his face. Perhaps Thomasin thinks her Daddy is...The Lone Ranger?!?

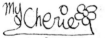

My Cherie

a word from cherie fortis

Lincoln's Birthday!
Valentine's Day!
Washington's Birthday!

In the midst of seasonal fun, it is important to remember that crime never takes a holiday. Lock doors when leaving!

CORRECTION

The editors' prayer in last week's issue of "10" should have read:

Dear Lord
Watch Over Us and All Our Friends
On The <u>Ninth</u> and Tenth Floor

"10" regrets the error.

"MY OWN STORY"

(Continued from page one)

"The baby was a breech. Instead of coming out "head" first, it was "a--" first. I'm sorry to say it like that, but it's true. May I have a glass of water?"

Al takes sip of water provided by "10"

"Then, in the middle of the delivery, the doctor recognized me from television and started asking me about my work. I was really annoyed."

"10" knows Al was lying.

"But when I saw my beautiful new daughter, I was flabbergasted. It was a very moving moment."

For a complete description of Al's television work, see top story.

"ROOM FOR ONE MORE"

Appendix V
Complete Nothing Lasts Forever Program

February - March 1983

To The Audience -

It gives me great pleasure to welcome you
to the very first screenings of "NOTHING LASTS FOREVER."
The film has been created for the maximum
enjoyment of you: the audience.
I made the film in 1952 in Culver City but,
because the original negatives were lost, it was
never released. I managed to find employment as
a waiter over the ensuing years until the negatives
were mysteriously uncovered in Irving Thalberg's
basement. The picture was put together and now will
be released, hopefully, by M-G-M as soon as they
figure out what to do with it.
I would like to thank all the people who helped
make this picture possible.
Now, relax, let go and I hope you enjoy the show.

TOM SCHILLER

Main Title Billing
"NOTHING LASTS FOREVER"

Metro-Goldwyn-Mayer
Lion Head Trademark

A Broadway Pictures Production

Metro-Goldwyn-Mayer
Presents
NOTHING LASTS FOREVER

Starring
ZACH GALLIGAN

With

APOLLONIA   LAUREN
   van   TOM
RAVENSTEIN

And

DAN AYKROYD
   IMOGENE COCA
      ANITA ELLIS
         EDDIE FISHER
            SAM JAFFE
               BILL MURRAY
                  PAUL ROGERS
                     MORT SAHL

Music by
HOWARD SHORE

```
              "Luna Hula"
                 and
          "Nothing Lasts Forever"
             words and music by TOM SCHILLER
                                and HOWARD SHORE

          Music Arrangements by
          CHERYL HARDWICK
```
```
          Co-Producer
          JOHN HEAD

          Associate Producer
          JOHN STARKE

          Production Associate
          LAILA NABULSI
```
```
          Production Manager
          JOHN H. STARKE

          First Assistant Director
          FREDRIC BERNER

          Second Assistant Director
          MARK McGANN
```
```
          Sound Recording...............AL MIAN
          Make-Up.................BARBARA KELLY
          Hair Stylist.............VERNE CARUSO
          Scenic Chargeman.........JAMES SORICE
          Property Master...JOE CARACCIOLO, Jr.

          MPAA Emblem              I.A.T.S.E.
          #26856                    Insignia
```
```
          Edited by
          KATHLEEN DOUGHERTY
          MARGOT FRANCIS
```
```
          Art Director      Costumes
          WOODS MACKINTOSH  SHEILA KEHOE
```

Director of Photography
FRED SCHULER

Written by
TOM SCHILLER

Produced by
LORNE MICHAELS

Directed by
TOM SCHILLER

The Players

ADAM BECKETT	ZACH GALLIGAN
MARA HOFMEIER	APOLLONIA VAN RAVENSTEIN
ELOY	LAUREN TOM
FATHER KNICKERBOCKER	SAM JAFFE
HUGO	PAUL ROGERS
TED BREUGHEL	BILL MURRAY
DAISY SCHACKMAN	IMOGENE COCA
BUCK HELLER	DAN AYKROYD
UNCLE MORT	MORT SAHL
AUNT ANITA	ANITA ELLIS
EDDIE FISHER	HIMSELF

Supporting Players

SWEDISH ARCHITECT	JAN TRISKA
HELEN FLAGELLA	ROSEMARY DE ANGELIS
LU	CLARICE TAYLOR
MAURICE BLAGET/CONDUCTOR	JOHN GARSON
HOTELIER	BERT WOOD
MR. BOYLE	MICHAEL KIMAK
LUNARTINI HUSBAND	KING DONOVAN
LUNARTINI WIFE	DORTHA DUCKWORTH
ALPHACRUISER STEWARD	AVON LONG
FREIDA SHIMKUS	ANDREA COLES
LUNAR TRAM GUIDE	KIYA ANN JOYCE
MR. BROWN	TIGER HAYNES
DR. BRONNER	HIMSELF

```
CARNEGIE HALL OLD TIMER  . . . . . . . .EDWIN COOPER
STAGE MANAGER . . . . . . . . . . . . . . . .WALT GORNEY
HILLBILLY  . . . . . . . . . . . . . . . . . . .RAYNOR SCHEINE
AUDIENCE STUNTS  . . . . . . . . . . . . . .HARRY MADSEN
                                SANDY RICHMAN
TRAIN MOTHER . . . . . . . . . . . . . . . . .IDA BERNADINI
CHILD. . . . . . . . . . . . . . . . . . . . .MARIA PICCININNI
BUSINESSMAN  . . . . . . . . . . . . . . . .MILTON SEAMAN
JOYCE . . . . . . . . . . . . . . . . . . . . . . .LEORA DANA
CENTRAL PARK BUM  . . . . . . . .BRUCE MILLHOLLAND
TOULOUSE LAUTREC . . . . . . . . . . . . . . . .ERIC AVARI
ART TEST MODEL  . . . . . . . . . . .JOANNE GARAHAN
ESPRESSO WAITER  . . . . . . . . . .PETER CHRISTENSEN
GERMAN ON TREADMILL  . . . . . . . .MARC ALDERMAN
LUNARCRUISERS . . . . . . . . . . . . . .CALVERT DeFOREST
                                EVELYN METRO
                          ALFRED DE LA FUENTE
                                 POLLY LOGAN
                           DRUMMOND ERSKINE
                                 JOAN ARLISS
                                SONIA ZOMINA
SKYLOUNGE PIANIST  . . . . . . . . . . .MOULTRIE PATTEN
LUNAR MAIDENS  . . . . . . . . . . . . . . . .CHINA CHEN
                                  SUSIE CHIN
                               LUCIA HWONG
                                   FAYE MAR
                               JOANNA PANG
                              ATSUMI SAKATO
                               INGRID WANG
LUNAR SHOPPING OBSERVERS. .ANDREAS KATSULAS
                           FREDERICK COFFIN
CARRIAGE DRIVER  . . . . . . . . . . .LAWRENCE TIERNEY
```

CASTING
LOIS PLANCO

SET DECORATOR	JUSTIN SCOPPA
ASSISTANT ART DIRECTOR	PAUL EADS
SCRIPT SUPERVISOR	LYNN LEWIS LOVETT
CASTING ASSOCIATE	GLENN DANIELS
EXTRA CASTING	BRUCE DEVAN
MEN'S WARDROBE	LEE AUSTIN
WOMEN'S WARDROBE	PATRICIA EIBEN
CAMERA OPERATOR	CRAIG DiBONA
FIRST ASSISTANT CAMERA	GABOR KOVER
SECOND ASSISTANT CAMERA	BRUCE MacCALLUM
BOOM OPERATOR	JEFFREY HAAS
PLAYBACK/RECORD	PETER MIAN
GAFFER	BILLY WARD
CONSTRUCTION CARPENTER	RONALD PETAGNA
CONSTRUCTION GRIP	JAMES GARTLAND
STANDBY SCENIC	COSMO SORICE
KEY GRIP	NORMAN BUCK
BEST BOY	JAMES WALSH
DOLLY GRIP	RONALD MAZZOLA
SET DRESSERS	MORRIS WEINMAN
	DAVID WEINMAN
	WILLIAM DURNIN, JR.
	DANIEL GROSSO
	KEVIN McCARTHY
PROPS	JOHN McDONNELL
	MICHAEL CARACCIOLO
ELECTRICIANS	JAMES MALONE
	GEORGE POTTER
	THOMAS FORD
SUPERVISING SOUND EDITOR	MAURICE SCHELL
SOUND EDITORS	LOU CERBORINO
	DANIEL L. LIEBERSTEIN
MUSIC EDITOR	TODD KASOW
RE-RECORDING MIXER	TOM FLEISCHMAN
MUSIC RECORDING/MIXING	JIM BOYER

ASSISTANT FILM EDITORS	JON NEUBURGER
	SPENCER GROSS
EDITORIAL CONSULTANTS	MUFFY MEYER
	ELLEN HOVDE
STOCK FOOTAGE RESEARCH	JILL FRANK
	NILS NICHOLS
ASSISTANT TO TOM SCHILLER	DIANNE DREYER
ORCHESTRATIONS	HOMER DENNISON
CONDUCTOR	JAMES YANNATOS
ADDITIONAL ORCHESTRATIONS	TOM PIERSON
	ANDREW STEIN
MUSIC CONTRACTOR	LEW DELGATTO

"POLONAISE" OPUS 53 IN A FLAT
BY FREDERIC CHOPIN
PERFORMED BY JOSEF LHEVINNE, AMPICO 69833B

"WINTER WIND" OPUS 25, NO. 11 ETUDE IN A MINOR
BY FREDERIC CHOPIN
PERFORMED BY AURORE LA CROIX, AMPICO 57594H

"IT'S ONLY A PAPER MOON"
MUSIC BY BILLY ROSE
LYRICS BY E.Y. HARBURG AND HAROLD ARLEN

"OH! MY PA-PA"
MUSIC BY JEFFREY PARSONS
LYRICS BY JOHN TURNER AND PAUL BUNKHARD

"LUNA HULA"
CHOREOGRAPHED BY LUCIA HWONG

"NOTHING LASTS FOREVER"
VOCAL PERFORMANCE BY MARA BECKERMAN

VOCAL CHARACTERIZATIONS BY
PAUL FREES

PRODUCTION OFFICE COORDINATOR	GAIL GEIBEL
LOCATION MANAGER	DAVID STARKE
LOCATION ASSISTANT	IRIS MARCH
ASSISTANT TO THE PRODUCERS	CHERIE FORTIS
ASSISTANT TO LORNE MICHAELS	CRISTINA McGINNISS
LOCATION AUDITOR	JOAN McQUADE
ASSISTANT AUDITOR	NELLIE NUGIEL

PRODUCTION ASSISTANTS	KEN ORNSTEIN
	JOE WINOGRADOFF
	COLLEEN ATWOOD
	SANDY CLOSE
	BARRY NICHOLS
	DEBORAH REISSMAN
	NANCY GRANT YALTKAYA
STILLS	ANDREW SCHWARTZ
FILM PUBLICIST	TED ALBERT

TITLES DESIGNED BY
R/GREENBERG ASSOCIATES, INC.

Executive in Charge of Production
BOATY BOATWRIGHT

OPTICAL EFFECTS
COMPUTER OPTICALS

ADDITIONAL GRAPHICS
KEN KNEITEL

PROCESSING BY TECHNICOLOR® NEW YORK

PRINTS IN METROCOLOR®

"NOTHING Lasts FOREVER"
FROM

MGM/UA
ENTERTAINMENT CO.

Metro-*Goldwyn*-Mayer
presents

"NOTHING *Lasts* FOREVER"

A

BROADWAY PICTURES

Production

Bill Murray as Ted Breughel.

End Notes

1. That year, Miller made up the festival jury alongside such prominent personalities as filmmaker Marc Allégret (the director of such films as *Plucking the Daisy*, though now more notable as the mentor of director Roger Vadim and the discoverer of Brigitte Bardot) and author Georges Simenon (the murder mystery novelist of over four hundred books, including the *Maigret* series). The other big films that year were Fellini's *La Dolce Vita* (the Golden Palm winner), Michelangelo Antonioni's *L'Avventura* and Ingmar Bergman's *The Virgin Spring*. With such competition, Kon Ichikawa's *Kagi* film adaptation was an unusual choice.

2. Because a variety show called *Saturday Night Live with Howard Cosell* premiered on ABC a few weeks earlier, the show was initially called *NBC's Saturday Night*. It later changed to just *Saturday Night*, until in 1977, after Cosell's show was long cancelled, it became *Saturday Night Live*. Cosell's variety hour included The Prime Time Players, a repertory of sketch comics including Bill Murray. As a response, Lorne Michaels' cast was named The Not Ready for Prime Time Players.

3. The exceptions were head-writers Chase and O'Donoghue, who weren't supposed to become cast members initially.

4. Coe did not last long at *Saturday Night*. The other cast members proved to be capable and believable enough in playing older characters, so Coe's name was removed from the opening credits after the first three episodes. He was completely dropped later in the season, having made only a few appearances.

5. Walter Williams' Mr. Bill has his own official web site at http://www.mrbill.com.

6. During the same episode, with host Kirk Douglas, Schiller also wrote a sketch for Bill Murray's character Nick the Lounge Singer. It is the only such sketch that was not written by Murray, Dan Aykroyd, Tom Davis and Paul Shaffer. In each sketch, Nick has a different last name, depending on where he is performing. For example, in previous sketches, Nick Summers played at a resort, Nick Winters sang at a ski-lodge, and Nick Wings performed in a First Class airplane lounge. In this entry, Nick Collins is brought in as a last-minute replacement performer at a bar-mitzvah. Schiller also appeared in the sketch as the master of ceremonies who introduces Collins.

7. Elmes had already served as director of photography on David Lynch's *Eraserhead* and would go on to work with the illustrious director on *Blue Velvet* and *Wild At Heart*. More recently, Elmes shot a trio of Ang Lee films: *The Ice Storm*, *Ride With the Devil* and *Hulk*.

8. Hackett was a one-time model and New York stage actress who shortly after appearing in *Mask of Fear* would go on to be nominated for a Best Supporting Actress Academy Award for her work in Neil Simon's *Only When I Laugh*. Throughout much of *Mask of Fear*, Hackett is asleep when she's on camera. Ironically, Hackett loved to sleep and after she died of cancer in 1983, her tombstone read "Go Away—I'm Asleep." Garner was a veteran television actor and a regular on his brother James' long-running show *The Rockford Files* as well as its numerous television movie follow-ups.

9. The Honker character also made a cameo appearance several years later in *Ghostbusters*, although that scene was deleted so as not to confuse the viewers by having Murray playing two different characters.

10. Years later, Bill Murray even held on to Schiller's player piano while he moved out of New York City. Murray offered to buy the piano and agreed to sell it back when Schiller wanted it back. Player pianos cannot simply be put into storage. They have to be taken care of, so Murray kept the piano until one day Schiller wanted to buy it back. "I was really torn because I was happy that he bought it back, but I really loved that piano," Murray recalls. "Player piano rolls are fantastic because it's not just one person playing the piano. There's like six hands playing the piano, so it played this really complex stuff. It was great fun to have. You'd have a party and you just keep putting these rolls on."

11. Starke's list of credits as a Production Manager includes 1982's *The World According to Garp* and 2003's *Bad Boys II*. His producer credits include 1979's *Winter Kills* and 2004's *The Punisher*.

12. Schiller wrote "snip snap snorum, hej kakalorum" in his script, but it is more commonly written as "snip snap snorum, high cockalorum." The rhyme has no meaning or English translation.

13. Ellis was a popular singer but today is best known for providing Rita Hayworth's singing voice in *Gilda*.

14. Sahl is an influential Lenny Bruce-era comedian, whom Woody Allen has cited as his main inspiration.

15. After Belushi passed away, Aykroyd made *Ghostbusters* and *Spies Like Us* with Bill Murray and Chevy Chase, respectively. Aykroyd's other script, *Never Say Mountie*, wasn't made.

16. Oddly, *Job Switching* was not written by Bob Schiller. Tom Schiller's father did not join the show until a few years after that episode aired.

17. 'Belt' is a name that Schiller has used in several short films, just like Victor De Cordova, Mary Toonis and Irving Pivnick. Schiller came up with those names when he was younger, and they are listed or appear in many of his works.

18. The 20-minute film was in part composed of props and footage that were put together for two different feature film projects that were cancelled when the war broke out. The rocket launch from *Weltraumschiff 1 startet* later became associated with the 1950s animated film and series *The Space Explorers*, in which portions of the film were tinted blue and the spaceship was renamed 'Polaris.'

19. Hibbert was Sweeney's real-life husband at the time, and later played the memorable part of the Gimp in *Pulp Fiction*.

Index

271

About the Author

Michael Streeter was born and raised in The Netherlands and moved to the United States in 1995 at age fourteen. A film history expert, he has seen more than three thousand films and holds a B.A. in Film from Webster University. *Nothing Lost Forever* is his first book. His website is www.mstreeter.com.

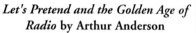

Printed in the United States
112985LV00004B/286-291/A